Transience Captured

The Life and Art *of* Kenneth Draper

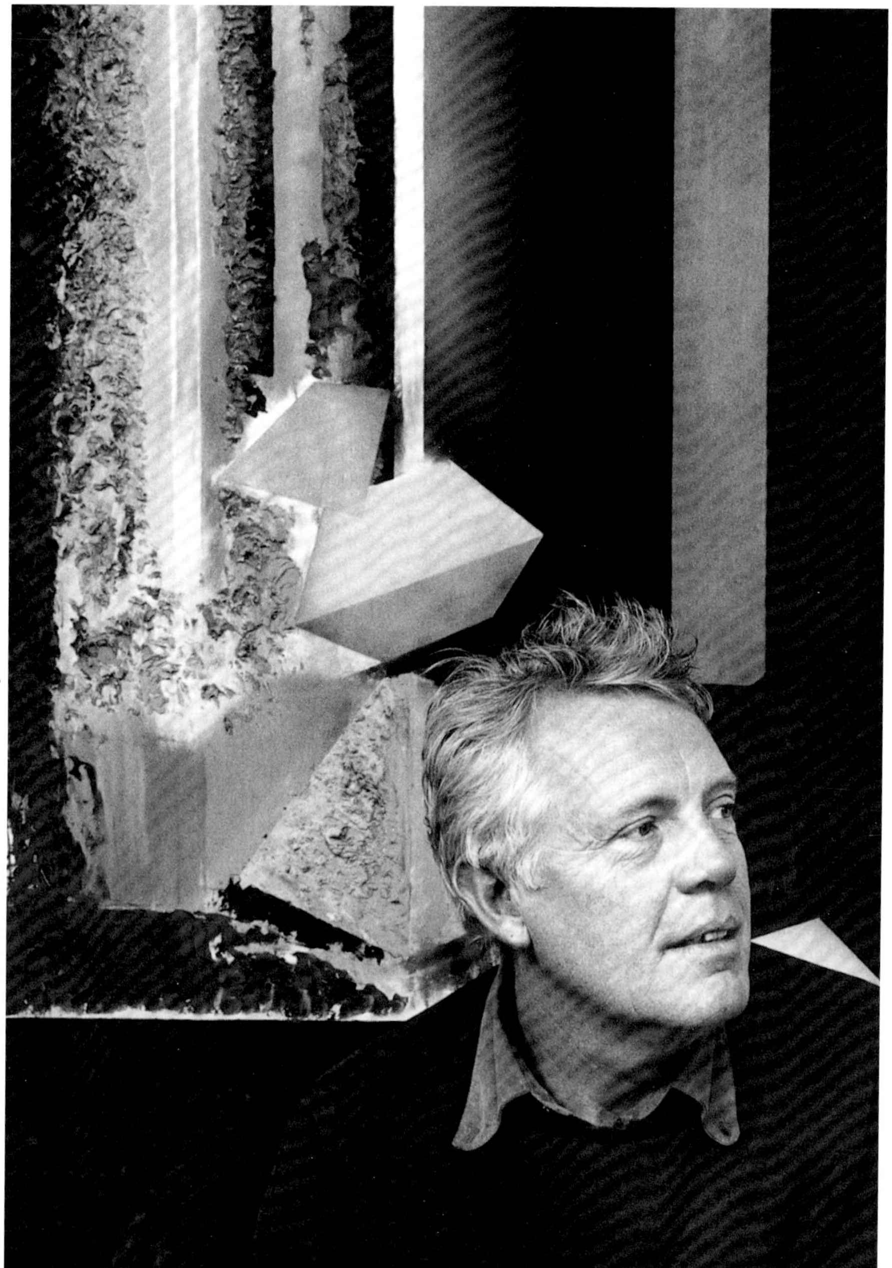

Transience Captured

THE LIFE AND ART *of* KENNETH DRAPER

Roger Berthoud

HART GALLERY
London & Nottingham

Front Cover: **Interior 1993**
Pastel on Paper
20 × 18 inches

Back Cover: **Fall 1985**
30 × 25 × 12 inches

ISBN: 0 9520759 6 2 Hard back
0 9520759 7 0 Soft back

Previous Publications:
David Blackburn and the Visionary Landscape Tradition
Sasha Grishin

Man & Measure: The Paintings of Tom Wood
Duncan Robinson

Designed and printed by Jones & Palmer Ltd. (0121) 236 9007

Acknowledgements

My first debt is to Kenneth Draper's dealers, John and Kit Hart, for kindly suggesting that I should write this text. My second is to Ken himself and his partner Jean Macalpine — for answering all my questions so openly, and for the warmth of their hospitality in Menorca. My thanks also, for their time and patience, to Ken's fellow artists and contemporaries Nigel Hall and John Carter; to his former art teacher Jean Arblaster; and to his friends and collectors John Ball and Tom West. I am also indebted to my neighbour, the critic Keith Patrick, for wise advice and the loan of several valuable catalogues.

Contents

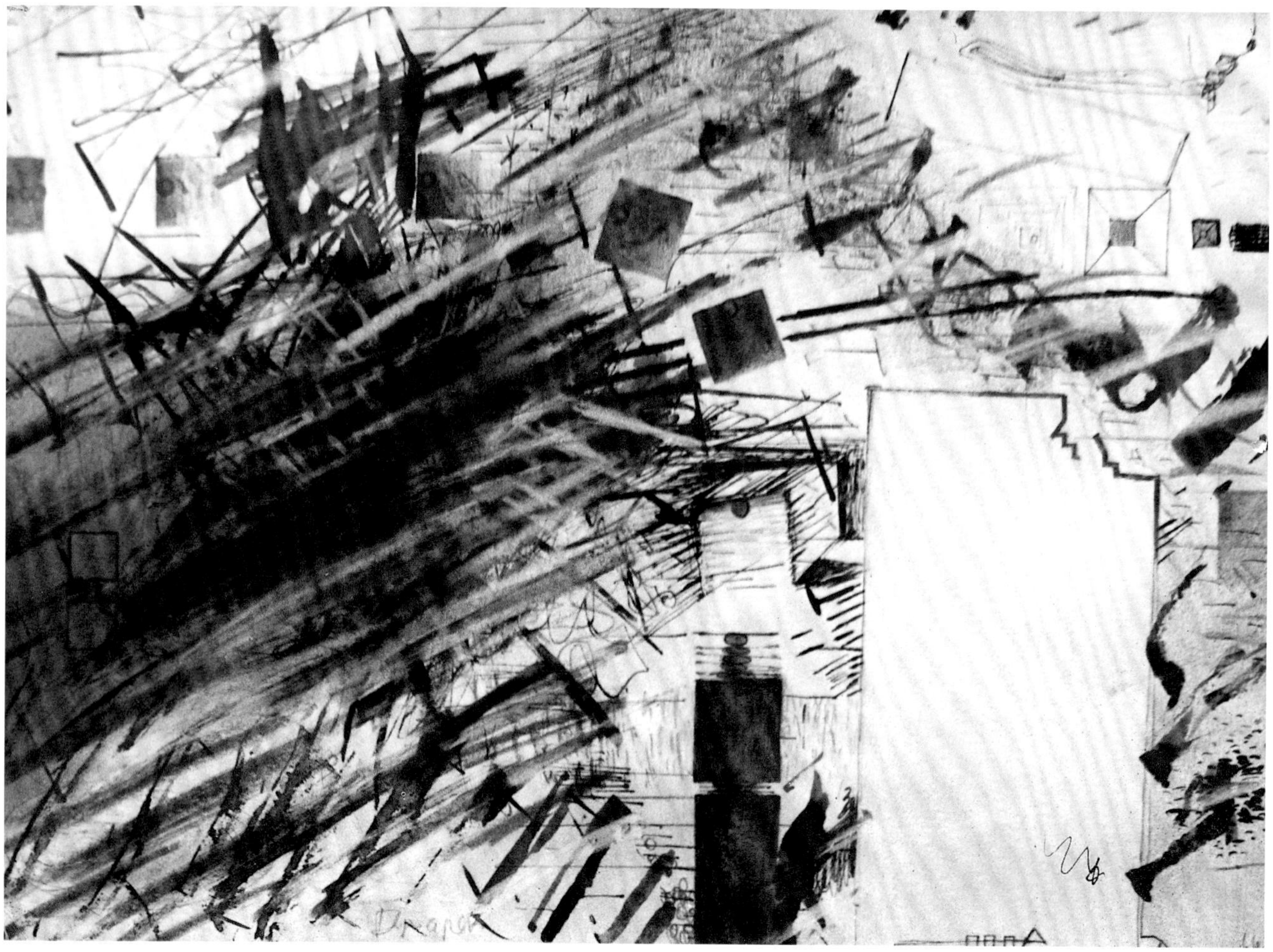

Composition 1964
Pastel on Paper
10 × 12 inches (25.5 × 30 cm)

Transience Captured

The Life & Art of Kenneth Draper

by Roger Berthoud

The shaping of a vision

Just a few hundred yards from Ken Draper's home on the island of Menorca there stands a hill covered with shrubs, giant cacti and wild olive trees. This hill, like so many on the island, is composed of limestone, and into its honey-coloured flank a series of square entrances has been cut. They are part of an ancient, disused quarry called Robadones, whose proportions and subtle tones take the breath away. It is like a cathedral, except that the columns left by those past hewers of stone are vaster in girth than the pillars of even the most grandiose place of worship. Light streams in from the openings, which are fringed by cacti and shrubs that seem to be peering in. The walls of this great edifice — for such it seems — still bear the scrape-like markings left by the tools used, in pre-mechanised times, to extract the stone. Where light strikes the surface, the honey hues turn almost white. Deeper in, damp has created subtle shades of green, and a sombre pale grey prevails.

This quarry is typical of the world that Draper has made his own. Its interior and the vegetation that caps it have inspired a number of the pastels that have latterly been his main concern. Yet Menorca has many similar treasures, as we shall discover; and to their inspiration Draper adds half a century of widely travelled experience. From the Yorkshire and Derbyshire of his childhood through India, Pakistan, Uganda, down the Nile and through the deserts and canyons of western USA and the gorges of Provence, he has drawn and enriched his sense of colour and form. **Plates 23 & 38**

Whether he is working as painter or sculptor, this artist celebrates the natural world, and especially those parts of it on which man has left memorable marks. Although aware of the prevailing concepts and fashions within the international world of art, Draper has serenely trod his own path, well clear of an art world "in whose overlit shallows thin voices are heard proclaiming their own emptiness to be a 'new development'", as the Australian-born writer Robert Hughes has put it.[1] Indeed, the British art historian Frances Spalding believes that Draper's very lack of associations has helped him to earn "a fixed and lasting place in British art".[2]

His strikingly coloured and encrusted sculptures, with their teasing *trompe-l'œil* explorations of space, are unique in conception and execution, as close to paintings in some respects as to sculpture. Many of the same techniques are used in his mixed media paintings on wood, from which sculptural forms often seem to float towards the spectator. The pastels, whether executed in the landscape itself or in the studio from pencil sketches, capture his response to nature in all its rich variety. Ranging from overtly descriptive views of a waterfall or hillside to near-abstract distillations inspired by sea, rocks, mist or sunsets, they stand in the great tradition of English landscape painting, and particularly of Turner: sometimes brilliantly coloured and passionately intense, sometimes tenderly catching a hillside veiled in mist, sometimes — by contrast — almost Klee-like and playful in their balancing of forms.

Structure, mood and light are conveyed with many-layered subtlety. Here, light seems to shine through where a layer has been scraped away to reveal what is hidden beneath. There, a seductively rich zone of textural effects tugs the eye away from the picture's centre. These pastels are not so much visionary as lyrical: hymns to the richness of the world. Yet a kind of tension holds mere seductiveness at bay and keeps them vital, mysterious and slow to yield up their full richness. Few who see them fail to respond.

The Draper story begins in 1944 in what is spiritually if not geographically the Yorkshire mining village of Killamarsh: Sheffield is the nearest large city, but Killamarsh itself lies just over the border in Derbyshire. His father, Albert Draper, lived there all his 79 years, going to work in the local mine when he was 11 years old, and remaining at the coal-face until he retired — still remarkably fit — at the age of 65. He was, Draper recalled, a very tough and wise man, and he had a marked talent for drawing:

> I've still got a book of beautiful drawings he did at school when he was 11. He was always designing things, not that any of his designs were ever used: different pithead gear, how to stop the cages crashing together, that sort of thing. He had an incredibly inventive mind. As a miner he was obsessive. He would talk about the work he had done that day, about being underground in a tunnel three foot high all day, with water in it — and he was a big man. He was buried twice in cave-ins, and when he was 35 he was told he should never go down the mine again. But he said there was nothing else, got himself better, and went back down.[3]

Draper's mother, born Dorothy Lamb, came from a prosperous family of butchers in Gainsborough, Lincolnshire. Although she was five years younger and from a much more comfortable background, she fell in love with the big, rough miner immediately on meeting him through a cousin who lived in Killamarsh. She was a great story-teller with a wild sense of humour who loved to be the centre of attention. The whole family was musically talented. Ken's mother was a very good pianist. His father played the cornet well enough to compete in brass band competitions all over the North. His eldest brother, Ernest,who became a headmaster, played and taught the organ, while the middle sibling John was another accomplished pianist. "Our Ken", as his mother called him, started to learn cornet and piano as a child, but art soon took over. He became conscious of his talent for drawing at the age of seven:

> It was one of those crazy little things. We were doing Roman Britain at school, and we had to draw a Roman chariot and horses from an illustration. The teacher passed around a cardboard cut-out, which you had to draw around and then fill in. I said 'I don't need the cut-out', drew the chariot and thought: 'Yeah, I'm good!' I've still got the drawing.

Soon afterwards, when he was eight, disaster struck. His back started to arch — children called him old hunchback — and his parents were told that he had a suspected TB spine. For some eight months he was kept in bed at the Rivelin Valley Hospital on the outskirts of Sheffield, strapped down on his back, head rigidly held in a harness with boards on either side and weights hanging over the back of the bed to keep him absolutely still.

> During the day they would wheel us out onto a kind of verandah with mock-Corinthian cornices. So my entire reality for eight months was a ceiling or the sky, and I became an expert on the play of light, with a strong sense of peripheral vision. There was a flagpole on top of this building. I remember watching it every day in the summer, the way the clouds passed over it. I don't remember it as having been a nightmare at the time, but I still have nightmares about it, that I'm strapped in this harness. One of the most extraordinary things was learning to walk again. It's something you don't remember as a child. The whole thing seemed totally impossible. I think that's had a lot of effect on my work, much of which is concerned with a sense of balance, especially the early pieces of sculpture.

Although he had had three hours' tuition a day in hospital, he was inevitably far behind his contemporaries when he emerged aged nine and a half. Further cossetting was required, since any knock was thought likely to cause a relapse. At first he had to study at home, returning full-time to school only some six months before the 11-plus, Reading his exam questions was hard enough, let alone answering them, he recalled. So off he went to Killamarsh's secondary modern school, starting at the bottom of the B stream, but topping the class in nearly every subject in the A stream by the time he left at the age of 15: he was determined not just to catch up but to be the best.

It's impossible to tell whether Draper would have become an artist had he been spared those traumatic and enfeebling eight months on his back. The talent was always there. But all the attention he received, on top of being the youngest of three children, gave him a strong sense of being different, even special. And because he was excused sport, physical training, swimming and the like, he had the time to develop his gift — and the perfect art teacher was to hand. Her name was Jean Arblaster, she was fresh from Goldsmiths' College School of Art in London, aged only 23, slightly eccentric, swift to spot his talent, and soon became his heroine. Draper can never forget her telling him: "You can do this, you can go to art school", and he has remained in touch with her ever since. She in turn remembers his powers of concentration, his "creative honesty", as she calls it, the accuracy of his eye when drawing and his feel for tonal values.[4]

His first drawings were of the extraordinary landscape that surrounded him, with its eerily beautiful pithead gear and massive cones of waste slag. Up these climbed little trucks that constantly added to the pyramids:

> All that earth had been underground, and I remember always being fascinated by that weird, kaleidoscopic displacement: it's a theme that has run through my work. Dad told me one of the seams was about half a mile under where we lived, and that was about three miles from where the mine was. He took me down the mine once when I was about 14. It was a reality I thought I knew, because he had talked about it so much. It was very much as I imagined it, though probably darker and dirtier.

Chesterfield College of Art, to which he now proceeded, turned out to be a happy experience. The aim was to pass the old Intermediate exam, and the equivalent of five O-levels was required to qualify to teach in schools. He worked hard, attending the local Technical College in the evenings, and scraped through. The art school suited him well:

> It was very small, maybe 15 to 20 students, and very much drawing-based: most of the time one was pencil-drawing out in the landscape or cities, life and still-life drawing, very academic. And a wonderful Polish sculptor, Ludwig Kuzniarz, introduced me to sculpture, which I had never made before, and to the work of Moore and other sculptors. Even at that stage I was equally interested in both painting and sculpture. I made a very realistic wood-carving for the final exam — sculpture was an option.

At the end of the course he inspected various art colleges in London, the capital to which he had long dreamed of coming, and plumped for

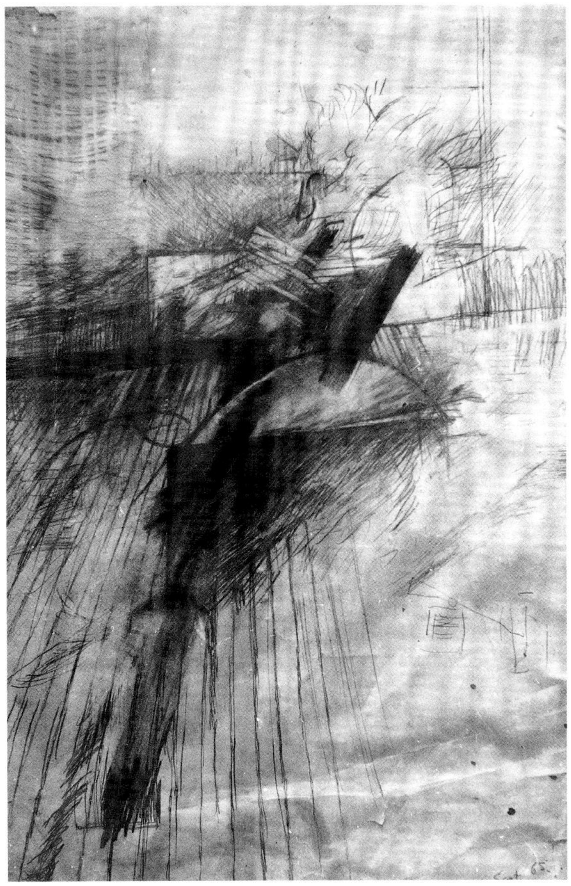

Figure in a Room 1965
Pencil on paper
30 × 18 inches (76 × 46 cm)

Kingston College of Art: he liked the idea of being a bit out on the edge, rather than in the centre of town at St Martin's. There was an innocence about the tall, lanky, enthusiastic North Country lad in those days that has not entirely vanished:

> Three of us went down from Chesterfield to Kingston, and we were the first northern students for a long time. They made us very aware of our northernness, though in a very nice way. When people asked me where I was from I would say Killamarsh, which of course no one had heard of. For the first time I realised I had an accent, which was a real surprise to me — though I knew there were some funny people who spoke posh where we spoke properly!

Even at his interview he was not sure whether he wanted to go into the sculpture or painting department. He came down in favour of painting, because he would then be able to spend one day a week in the sculpture department,whereas the painting department would be closed to him if he did sculpture.There were other gains. The old National Diploma in Design (NDD), sometimes called the Nothing Doing Diploma[5] and since 1946 the national and centrally examined higher qualification in practical art, was still in force. Its narrow prescriptions had a deadening effect on Kingston's sculpture department; the painting department seemed to be open to more possibilities, though life painting and figure composition were obligatory. As for the NDD, it was soon to be phased out under the recommendations of the first Coldstream report and superseded by the more liberally conceived and flexible degree-standard Diploma in Art and Design (Dip AD).

Following Coldstream, art colleges acquired degree-giving quasi-university status, along with considerably improved facilities and more students. All this undoubtedly contributed to a proliferation of sculptural talent over the next two decades. The benefits were already felt in Draper's second year at Kingston, 1963/4, when Prunella Clough, Bryan Kneale and Alf Dunn all came to teach part- time, transforming the atmosphere.

Kneale had started as a painter before becoming a sculptor, while Dunn, another Yorkshireman, was both a print-maker and sculptor. So both understood his enthusiasm for three as well as two-dimensional work:

> I had been doing a lot of things on my own at home, making constructions in glass cases, with balsa wood and tissue paper: they didn't seem to be anything to do with college work. Suddenly it all changed. Bryan Kneale said: 'Bring them in', and he and Alf Dunn were very encouraging.

Conscious of the sacrifices his father had made to send him to college, staying down the pit to earn more money, Draper worked very hard. The life-drawing classes could be irritating: every 20 minutes or so there would be a break. He would carry on drawing, placing the figure within the environment of the room rather than, as prescribed, simply producing an isolated figure on a white piece of paper. It was then that he evolved the concept of a transient image or figure, coming or going within a static context, which would preoccupy him for several years. He was also trying at this stage to render space itself as something that lived and moved in its own right, having no less importance than the objects within it. Many drawings of rooms and some paintings resulted, portrayed from different angles and generally with a human presence.

Then suddenly the end of the two-year NDD course loomed and with it the old, conventional exams. So it was back to straight painting and figure drawing. In the event, he and his fellow students all seemed to scramble successfully through. The college's teaching staff had evidently been impressed by Draper's interest in sculpture and by his constructions. They decided to give him an unofficial, postgraduate year to make sculptures and enable him to apply to the sculpture department of the Royal College of Art in Kensington Gore.

He now had ample opportunity to explore three-dimensionally his preoccupation with rooms and transient presences. It all went back, he believes, to his recollections of his spell in hospital. This had given him an acute awareness of the contrast between his confinement and the space, sky and clouds outside. Being obliged to keep his head rigid had also, as mentioned earlier, preternaturally sharpened his peripheral vision. Learning to walk again at the age of nine, with its accompanying sense of the precariousness of balance in movement, had in turn given him a heightened sense of his body as a highly complex mechanism and arrangement of devices to achieve movement.

A good deal of that sense of complexity was to mark Draper's sculpture over the next few years. One of the first works to emerge from Kingston was called *Evolve 64*. It stood on the floor and consisted of two glass cases, representing rooms, set within an outer frame, representing a safe environment. Eventually the two cases were suspended from a central pivot in the larger frame, and could be pushed around by hand so that they revolved and reflected each other. The other substantial piece, called *Lindear*, was later acquired by the curator and critic Bryan Robertson, thus becoming the first sculpture Draper had sold. *Lindear* too was an exploration of claustrophobic interior spaces. Starting as a shallow wall box, it seemed altogether too sombre. To inject some optimism, Draper added a complex series of projections that thrust forward towards the viewer but could best be seen from the side. A balancing rod with balls gave a sense of that transient presence. Made of wood, aluminium and card and painted mainly dark green, it represented an important step in his sculptural exploration of space.

Plate 2

In his third year at Kingston, Draper also gained some hands-on experience by helping Bryan Kneale assemble his metal sculptures for an exhibition at the Redfern Gallery. He did the same the following year when Kneale was preparing for a show held in February 1966 at the Whitechapel Gallery. It was then that he first met Bryan Robertson, the Whitechapel's director.

To gain entrance to the Royal College of Art's sculpture department, students had to produce evidence of competence at life modelling. Draper discovered this only shortly before the deadline for submitting his portfolio. In Kingston's sculpture department he slapped together some sort of figure in a couple of days. Even in the cleverly angled photographs he had taken it looked to him pretty terrible. The interviewing board consisted of Bernard Meadows, the RCA's professor of sculpture, flanked by Ralph Brown, Elisabeth Frink, Bob Clatworthy — and Bryan Kneale, the only non-figurative sculptor among them and Draper's consistent supporter. While Ken was talking about his abstract constructions, Ralph Brown jumped up and pulled out one of the photographs of the clay model. "Now, Draper," he said, "can you tell me about the relationship of this figure to the rest of your work?" Draper replied: "There isn't any relationship, none at all." Brown asked why he had done it: for the exam, Draper replied. Asked what he thought of it, he said: "It's terrible, absolutely awful!" In the silence that followed, Draper was convinced he had failed. Then suddenly they all burst out laughing. Asked whether he realised he would have to do life modelling for the first six weeks of every term in the first year, he made suitably enthusiastic noises about how interesting that would be.

Even before he was accepted, there had been two substantial boosts for his self-confidence. Since the 1920s, the Redfern Gallery in Cork Street had been one of the relatively few galleries in the London's West End to promote "modern" art: Henry Moore and Barbara Hepworth had made their public debuts there in a mixed show in 1924. Bryan Kneale had shown both his paintings and sculpture there since 1954, and had introduced Draper to its most active director, the engaging Harry Tatlock Miller. After seeing Draper's work, Miller wrote him a letter offering him a one-man show the following year, when he would be 21 — potentially making him the youngest artist the gallery had ever shown. He was somewhat taken aback when Draper telephoned him and said: "Well, I'll think about it." There was a good reason for this uncharacteristic reaction: Draper knew that Bernard Meadows would not allow students in his department to have connections with commercial dealers while at the RCA. "Can we do it in three years' time?", he asked Miller after explaining the dilemma. "Dear boy," said Harry, "We'll do it any time you're ready."

The second boost came in 1965, when to his surprise he won the prestigious Young Contemporaries Prize for two sculptures: the year previously he had submitted seven large paintings, and not one had even been accepted for the big exhibition. Neither of the prize-winning sculptures has survived, but one was a very large, free-standing piece made of painted wood and aluminium which Draper likens to an exploded painting.

There was another big development in his life that summer. In August 1965, he married a teacher in Kingston's fashion department, Heather Liévin Beste, who was a few years older than him and with whom he had been living for 18 months in Putney. Although they were together only five years, Draper remains indebted to her not just for bringing up their son Adam, who was born in December 1966, but for her strength and steadying influence in those important years. They remain good friends.

The Royal College, to which he at last went in October 1965, was still trailing clouds of glory from the beginning of that vibrant decade. It was principally the intake of painting students in 1959, including David Hockney, Derek Boshier, Allen Jones, R.B. Kitaj and Peter Phillips, along with such earlier students-turned-teachers as Peter Blake, Dick Smith and Joe Tilson, that had identified the RCA in the public mind with all that was liveliest and most inventive in art and design. That talented cohort — Allen Jones apart, since he was thrown out at the end of his first year — had left in 1962, when the Pop Art movement reached its peak. Bernard Meadows had taken over the sculpture department in 1960. His prime aim was to encourage individuality, a far more difficult requirement than it might seem, as he recalled:

> All artists have this problem. It's easier to sit back and reflect what has already been done, and conform. It's not easy to be yourself, it's one of the most difficult things. You have to learn that it's a very lonely business, you're on your own. You can't blame anybody else.[6]

Meadows proved to be a strict though fair disciplinarian, and was particularly quick to stamp on anything that looked derivative. The chief competition, of which all his students were very much aware, came from St Martin's School of Art near Covent Garden. In 1959 its presiding genius, the sculptor Anthony Caro, had gone to America, communed with the high priest of abstract expressionism, the critic Clement Greenberg, met the sculptor David Smith, and returned to produce a dazzling succession of abstract, welded, bolted and painted steel sculptures that effectively changed the course of contemporary sculpture.

All Caro's new work stood not on a plinth but on the ground. Back at St Martin's, he and his fellow teachers and their students set about questioning the whole basis of sculpture, with William Tucker emerging as the chief theoretician. Drawing upon Heidegger and existential philosophy, this dedicated group sought to create a world, or non-world, of strange presences decontextualised and stripped of familiar associations even if they incorporated banal objects.[7] Prominent among them were Phillip King, Tim Scott, David Annesley, Michael Bolus and Tucker himself. Caro's own work retained an elegant lyricism that marked it out from the more cerebral products of many of his colleagues and students. Their work was shown in quantity in the second of Bryan Robertson's New Generation exhibitions, at the Whitechapel in 1965.

But even as these sculptors were making their mark, a reaction was taking place at St Martin's: students such as Barry Flanagan, Richard Long, Bruce McLean and Gilbert and George rebelled against the production of objects and what seemed like the doctrinaire approach of their seniors. Whether the work of these younger artists involved bags of sand, a minimal adjustment to a landscape in the course of a walk, or performance, it was essentially impermanent. The idea and its presentation were more important than the thing.

All this made its impact on Draper:

> Not only Caro, but the whole St Martin's school, King, Tucker and so on, were such a powerful force for a particular kind of sculpture that I think the gang of us at the College felt — though it wasn't exactly said at the time — that we had to find another way. At the same time we were very aware of the possibilities in sculpture which Caro had thrown up.

Among those at the RCA with him were John Panting and Nigel Hall, who became his close friends, Carl Plackman, John Maine, Richard Wentworth and Martin Naylor. It is a measure of their ability, and of Meadows' success in bringing out their individuality, that all went on to make their names in very different ways. Sadly, Panting was to die in 1974 in a motorcycle accident.

Draper made only four sculptures while he was at the Royal College: all very large and complex structures which he also spent a great deal of time painting and repainting. The first, called *Arena*, took him the best part of a year and a half. It stood around 14 feet high and was made of wood, but looked more like steel:

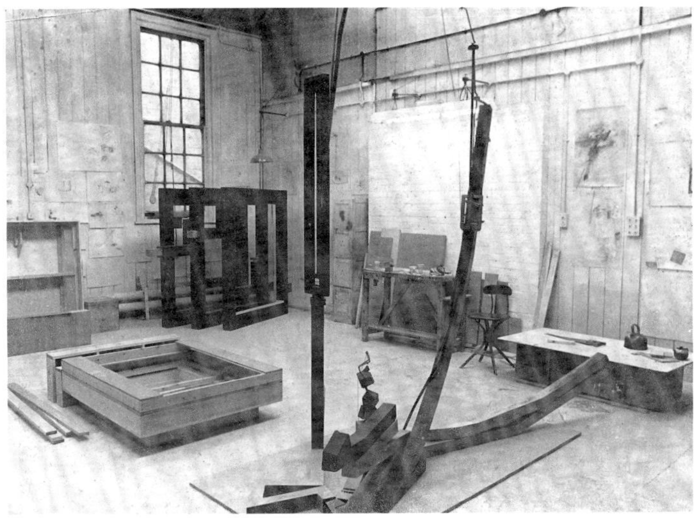

RCA Studio with *Arena* (foreground) *Three Frames* (background)

> It ran along the ground and turned back on itself, then went up and up: the whole idea was that it was a set of events — abstract cause and effect. In one part there might be a square section, then a piece would wind around almost like ivy . . . I always thought of it in relation to walking again. It was like a haptic sensation, which means feeling something within your own body, an energy.

Arena was first shown at the Redfern's summer exhibition in 1968. The second piece, *Three Frames*, was a mere six feet high. Its main components were three wooden frames, interrelated in such a way as to give a sense that something was moving between them. In making this, Draper first become aware of the spectator and the possibility of leaving clues at the front of the sculpture that would create a false expectation of what lay around the other side — and thus a sense of surprise and mystery based on memory. Draper believes that his Royal College creations were the most purely sculptural of his career. Although he might spend two months painting one of them, they were conceived essentially as objects. Later he would be concerned to reduce what could, if not very prettily, be called the "objectness" of his sculptures and give them something of the illusory quality of paintings.

There was a nightmare element in Draper's last few pre-exam months at the RCA. Although he had been completely happy with his wife Heather, he was at this stage swept off his feet when he met an exotically beautiful Indian girl from the painting department. Her name was Nadiya Jinnah, and her family would before long be thrown out of Uganda by the infamous Idi Amin, along with all other Asians. Ken hoped that this affair would pass. But it did not, and with a heavy heart he left Heather and their three-year-old boy not long after finishing at the RCA, seemingly in the grips of a force stronger than himself.

[1] Robert Hughes, *The Shock of the New* (Thames & Hudson 1980) p. 376.

[2] *Contemporary Art* magazine, Vol. 1 No 3. spring 1993 p. 29.

[3] unless otherwise specified, all quotations are from five interviews recorded by the author in London and Menorca in 1995/6.

[4] letter from Jean Arblaster to RB dated 26 April 1996.

[5] quoted from David Halliwell's "Little Malcolm and his Struggle against the Eunuchs" in Christopher Frayling's *The Royal College of Art: 150 years of Art and Design* (Barrie & Jenkins 1987), p. 173.

[6] interview with Bernard Meadows, London, 11 January 1996.

[7] *The Sixties Art Scene in London* by David Mellor (Phaidon 1993), p. 94, catalogue of a major exhibition at the Barbican 11 March – 13 June 1993.

Events and encounters

It is a rare graduate from art college who does not have to do some teaching to earn a living. True, the Hockney generation had become commercially successful even while at the Royal College of Art, and painting students would increasingly seek to make a mark as early as their valedictory exhibition. But even with the prospect of a one-man show at the Redfern the following year, Draper — still a very slow worker — needed the modest income that even two days of teaching a week would provide. He found it, in this year of student unrest, at Hornsey College of Art in north London.

Earlier that year Hornsey had experienced the most serious breakdown in staff–student relations of any London art college. The students objected that the college was run by an inaccessible élite composed of the Principal and some senior staff. They also complained that it lacked a coherent academic plan and any social and recreational amenities — all this while having probably the worst accommodation of any major art college in England. The result was first a lengthy student sit-in, which many of the staff before long joined, followed in May 1968 by a seizure of the college's premises by the student body.[1] Eventually a series of reforms was introduced, and there was an intake of fresh part-time teaching staff. Draper was part of this. Although his commitments there involved only two days' teaching a week, he enjoyed his four-year association with Hornsey enormously. Hubert "Nibs" Dalwood, who became a close friend until his death in 1976, was in charge of sculpture, Mike Tyzack of painting. The painters Norman Stevens and Harry Thubron were also there, as were Draper's Royal College friends Nigel Hall and Martin Naylor. All departments worked together in a single vast space, which made for a full and free exchange of ideas between teachers and students alike.

Being not much older than many of the latter, Ken formed closer relationships with them than in subsequent teaching spells, when the age gap had widened. Students quite often came to the studio he had rented in Borough Market, south of London Bridge. Teaching helped him to clarify his ideas, he found: talking to a student one day and working in his studio the next, he would suddenly realise that the student's problem was his too, or how much more clearly he could have explained something.

At last, in 1969, he had that long-promised one-man debut at The Redfern Gallery. From that seminal third year at Kingston, only *Lindear*, borrowed from Bryan Robertson, was included; and *Three Frames* from the RCA years. The remaining five sculptures were new, and were complemented by 20 of his effervescent and often illusionistically three-dimensional pencil studies. Draper was touched when his former teacher at Kingston, Prunella Clough — very much a painter's painter — became the first purchaser, buying a small drawing. The Arts Council, an influential public patron, bought two large sculptures, and one went to the enlightened Leicestershire Education Authority.

Later that year Draper accompanied Nadiya and her parents to India and Pakistan, an experience that was to have a lasting impact on his work. Nadiya's father had gone to Uganda from Bombay, a city whose extremes both alarmed and fascinated Draper: not just of wealth and poverty, but of East and West, the florid Victorian Gothic architecture of the city centre contrasting strongly with both the poverty of those living in the streets and the warmth of music parties and other activities on the beach.

To the north-east of Bombay, not far from Aurangabad in Maharashtra state, they visited the astonishing cave temples of Ellora and Ajanta. At Ellora there are 33 caves, 12 of Buddhist origins, four Jain and the rest Hindu, set in an escarpment of reddish volcanic stone and dating mainly from the seventh and eighth centuries. The entire complex is in effect a single great sequence of sculptures, many minutely detailed, carved from the living rock and recognised as the greatest site of Hindu art in central India — and one of the great monuments of the world. Most remarkable of all is the Kailasantha temple, whose precincts include a vast courtyard 276 ft long by 154 ft wide, and a 96 ft high central tower, life-sized elephants, larger-than-life lions, flying gods and much else besides. Parts of the courtyard stand in brilliant sunlight from the Deccan plateau, other parts are enveloped in deep blue shadows cast by the surrounding mountains. The effect, according to one scholarly observer, is so exalting as to render the observer positively feverish.[2]

What Ellora is to Hindu art, the Ajanta complex is to Buddhist sculpture and, above all, wall painting, of which it provides the only known surviving examples dating from the first century BC to the seventh century AD. These caves are set in a wild and desolate region, carved into the side of a horshoe-shaped hillside. Here are courtyards surrounded by the cells of monks, and great halls lined with carved columns, all hewn from solid rock. Some of the carvings show a remarkable psychological penetration and are very moving.

From these aesthetically pole-axing experiences they proceeded to New and Old Delhi and thence to what, for all its familiarity as an image, remains one of the great sights of the world: the Taj Mahal at Agra.

Again, Draper loved the contrast. From the small town of Agra, with its cows, oxen, bells and scruffy markets, they stepped through the gates of the Taj Mahal into a cool, astonishing space, across which stands that majestically symmetrical monument to a leader's love. Outside, ramshackle everyday life prevailed. Inside, all was purity, and the spirit ruled. The highlight in Pakistan, at least in terms of visual impact, was the excavated city of Mohenjodaro. Located in northern Sind, Mohenjodaro was part of the remarkably sophisticated Indus Valley (sometimes called Harappan) urban civilisation that flourished roughly between 2500 and 1800 BC. The city's striking red-brick remains reveal the brilliantly engineered water supply and sewerage system that enabled its citizens to enjoy fresh water, baths and toilets at a time when Europeans were living in primitive villages.

From there they headed north to Lahore, the handsomest city in Pakistan with its broad avenues and pink-stoned forts and mosques; then on to Rawalpindi, near the new capital of Islamabad in the lower foothills of the Himalayas, a scenically beautiful region full of the remains (at Taxila, for example) of northern India's Buddhist era. Flying back to Karachi in a tiny plane gave Draper his first experience of a kaleidoscope of landscape seen from a low altitude.

Not surprisingly, this first trip out of Europe had a big impact on the 25-year old from Killamarsh. Of his many impressions, three in particular were to stay with him and seep into his work. The first was the way, in India especially, in which the architecture seemed to grow out of the ground: landscape and temples appeared to echo each other, to form part of an organic whole, with colour an integral part of the form. The second was the way in which extremes of light and shadow virtually dematerialised solid objects, an effect he would seek to use in his sculptures. The third was a new sense of space and openness, which he was to explore in the huge overhead wall-pieces that he started making the following year. Of one of these, *Horizons 1971*, he has said:

> The fact that a spectator is required to see it from below came from an experience in flying in a light aircraft low across the deserts of Pakistan, and imagining a landscape with vertical thrusts seen from underneath, as if the land were a layer of movements. I wanted also to convey a sense of successive horizons and distant planes in a vast landscape, and ironically I could only attempt this in sculpture by making a structure to be seen from below.[3]

Some of these impressions were reinforced in April/May 1971 by his first visit to the USA, courtesy of the Mark Rothko Memorial Award. His seven-week trip, the outlines of which were organised for him by the award's secretariat, took in New York, Boston, Washington, Philadelphia, Chicago, San Francisco and Los Angeles, at an ideal time of year. The prospect could scarcely have been more exciting:

> I'll never forget that first view of Manhattan, which thrills me even now: driving up from the airport, seeing that graveyard with its crosses and monuments, and behind it the skyscrapers of New York in a kind of montage. Then getting into Manhattan, the sheer beauty of its scale. Although I was exhausted, I walked around that night until 3 a.m. I was staggered by the energy of the place, the colour, lights, sounds and people.

Here he was at the heart of a vibrant culture whose painters had over the past quarter century toppled Paris from its long-held position as the focal point of contemporary art. From the donors of his bursary he already had numerous introductions. As a bonus, his friend Bryan Robertson was at hand to welcome and guide him. Robertson had recently started a five-year appointment directing the State University of New York Museum in Purchase, not far from New York city. In his dazzling 16 years as director of the Whitechapel Art Gallery in London's East End he had arguably done more than anyone else to clinch the reputations of leading British artists and deepen British knowledge of contemporary American painting: Pollock, Rothko and Tobey were among those whose retrospectives he had organised, and across the USA he was formidably well connected.

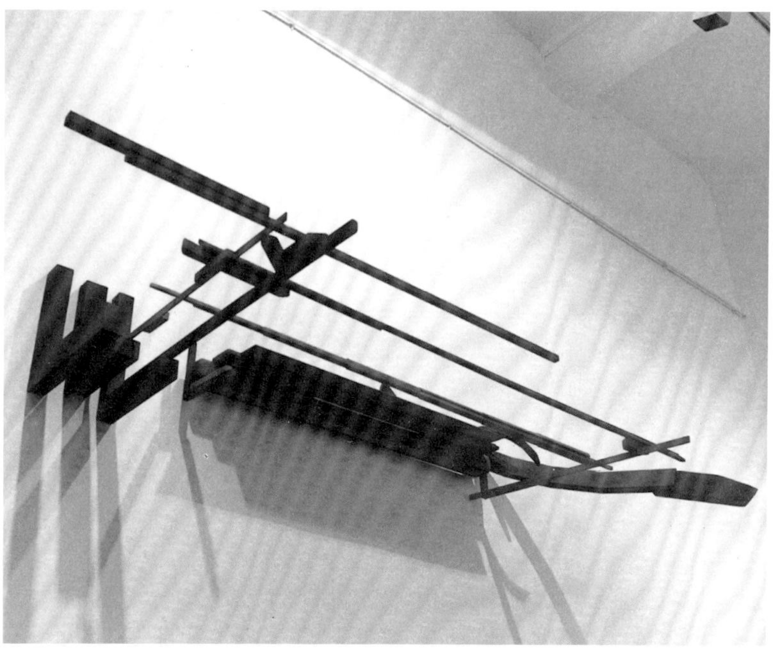

Horizons 1971
Wood, Steel, Oil Paint
18 × 108 × 54 inches (46 × 274 × 137 cm)

Draper was already a fervent admirer of Rothko, Pollock and Jasper Johns. Now that he was actually in America, he found his appreciation and understanding of other, less familiar American artists taking on a new dimension. Franz Kline, for example, stood revealed in all his power and beauty. In New York, Draper met Jasper Johns, Helen Frankenthaler and Pollock's widow, Lee Krasner Pollock. Richard Diebenkorn, to whom he was introduced in California, proved to be remarkably generous. On their first encounter, Diebenkorn fetched out much of his own work to show Ken. Then he asked what sort of work his young visitor did, invited him to return that evening, and went through Draper's photographs: a young artist's dream come true. Diebenkorn's *Ocean Park* series has been described by Robert Hughes as "surely one of the most distinguished meditations on landscape in painting since Monet's waterlilies".[4] A decade later they were to make a strong impact on another Yorkshire artist from the same London stable, David Blackburn, when he was in the USA.[5]

In Los Angeles, Draper met two locally well-known Californian artists, Don Potts and Ken Price: if some of their work had seemed a little trite in reproduction back home, it looked very different in a Californian context. The colour supplement world of that era had given Draper the illusion that artists in London were more or less instantly aware of what was going on in the States. He now realised that there was no substitute for first-hand experience.

The sense of revelation was not confined to American art. The great museums in virtually every city he visited had much stronger holdings of European art from the Impressionists onwards than any British museum. Whether he was in the Metropolitan, Guggenheim or Whitney museums or the Museum of Modern Art in New York, the Art Institute of Chicago, the Philadelphia Museum of Art, the Museum of Fine Arts in Boston, to mention only a few, he was dazzled by what he saw; and there was no let-up when he was shown great private collections. It reached a point where he felt that another five great Picassos or Monets would give him some sort of visual hernia. At the same time he was partying most evenings, visiting many studios, and sleeping too little. It was a relief when at last he persuaded someone to take him into California's desert interior. The general response had been: "But there's nothing there!", to which he would reply: "That's why I want to go!" They got up around 4 a.m. one day and drove into the desert called Joshua Trees, named after its extraordinary cactus trees but also notable for its gigantic rounded and yellowish rocks, which reminded Draper somewhat of Brimham Rocks in Yorkshire. It was not just a respite from that overload of great art and American hospitality, but provided an interesting comparison with what he had seen on the Indian subcontinent. For someone always weighing up space and colour, two deserts are that much more interesting than one, since comparisons can be made. Returning to New York, Draper had the impression of being back in Europe, so different did it seem to California.

In the longer term, those packed, exciting weeks in the USA greatly enriched the mulch of knowledge and visual experience from which his mature work would grow. Their immediate effect, he believes, was to change his sense of scale and increase the power and intensity of his work. His absence abroad also increased the mild panic he felt about his impending first involvement in a major survey of contemporary British sculpture. Called simply British Sculptors, it was scheduled at the Royal Academy in Piccadilly for January 1972, just nine months after his return: a big boost but a daunting challenge.

For the room which he had been allotted all to himself he made three very big overhanging wallpieces. **Plate 5**
One of these was 30 ft long and projected 16 ft from the wall. Because it would be placed much higher at the RA than was possible in his studio, he made a little trolley with wheels, on which he could sit and move up and down, to see it from a lower perspective — a spectacle the author is sorry to have missed. Some of its parts being too big for his studio, he never saw it complete until he installed it at the RA. There it was intended to float above the spectator, defying gravity and giving a sense of space and wide horizons. From far enough back it looked almost flat. As the spectator moved up to it, it expanded and opened out, giving it the illusory quality for which he strove (Draper prefers the word "illusive", an alternative if unusual form of "illusory"). His friend Nigel Hall thought these overhead pieces were

"terrific. Ken was doing wonderful work at that time, and we had in common this interest in overhead space, the rather oppressive qualities of overhang."[6]

An unfortunate effect of that "illusiveness" was to make his sculpture peculiarly resistant to photography, a real handicap. A photograph can only freeze one of a whole spectrum of possible views, giving no sense of its depth, nor of which bits are where in space, which flat and which three-dimensional. Nonetheless, the rising young sculptor was photographed for the *Observer* colour magazine up a ladder installing his giant piece.

Sculpture, as opposed to painting, was where the action was in the 70s. Thanks in part to the St Martin's revolution, sculpture had burst into a plethora of new, fragmented domains. These included land and environmental art, body art, performance art, kinetic art, conceptual art, installations, and arte povera, which celebrated the detritus of civilisation. Although minimalism had reached its peak in the 60s, its influence lingered on. Its leaders were the Americans Sol le Witt, Don Judd and Carl André, the acquisition of whose *Equivalent VIII* (the notorious "Bricks") by the Tate Gallery in 1976 ushered in an era of derisive tabloid newspaper comment on contemporary art.

Common to most of these movements, and central to conceptualism, was the artist's desire to make the spectator think rather than merely feel. Just about any material or medium could be and was used, often with considerable wit: never have the evocative powers of humble objects been so thoroughly exploited. In some respects it was an exciting period, in others dispiriting, not least because much of even the gallery-going public was left behind by what often seemed like self-conscious cleverness.

Marcel Duchamp had much to answer for: as long ago as 1917 he had displayed an inverted porcelain urinal and called it *Fountain*, thus pioneering the concept of the "ready-made", an everyday object that becomes a sculpture because the artist has selected it — yet depends on a gallery context to be recognised as an object of art. Draper was more intrigued by what Duchamp had written than by what he had produced. His awareness of current trends was further sharpened in 1976, when he began teaching at Goldsmiths' College, one of the main crucibles of conceptualism in Britain.

His own work was far from ignoring the spirit of the times. The large early pieces were in their own way about events and encounters within each individual structure, and owed something to minimalism's preoccupation with boxes and modular frames, and also to Caro's exploration of space. He had also sought to go beyond the notion of sculpture as a straightforward object: hence those neat if sometimes complex plots to surprise the spectator and deceive the eye as it moved towards, around or under his pieces. But, in retrospect at least, Draper thinks of the 70s as the dark ages: literally so in one respect, since there was little serious interest in colour, to him an indispensable element.

Around 1975 his own work went through a significant sea change. He attributes it to a reaction against his first big commission. The latter resulted from an Arts Council competition for a sculpture for the John Dalton Building at Manchester Polytechnic. It was to be a huge piece, measuring 30 ft in both height and length, and 7 ft wide. The component parts were made over 12 months of 1973 and 1974 in his Borough studio and assembled on-site. He was not particularly pleased with the result, and therefore not too dismayed to be told unofficially three or four years later that it had been done away with after being badly vandalised.

Tired of spending so much time even on small sections of large pieces, Draper decided in 1975 to concentrate and distil his work and make much smaller pieces. Among these were a series of diminutive,
Plate 6 heavily impastoed, slightly box-like wallpieces around six inches long, minimal only in scale, since they

were landscape-based and derived much of their power from their encrusted surface and glowing colours. Draper thought of them as little bombs, so concentrated were they. Previously he had worked mainly in wood, to which he then added a skin of generally sombre paint. Now, by contrast, he mixed raw colour pigment into materials — usually resin or plaster — which he then bonded to wood or steel surfaces. As in his memory of India, the colour became part of the form, rather than being merely superimposed on it.

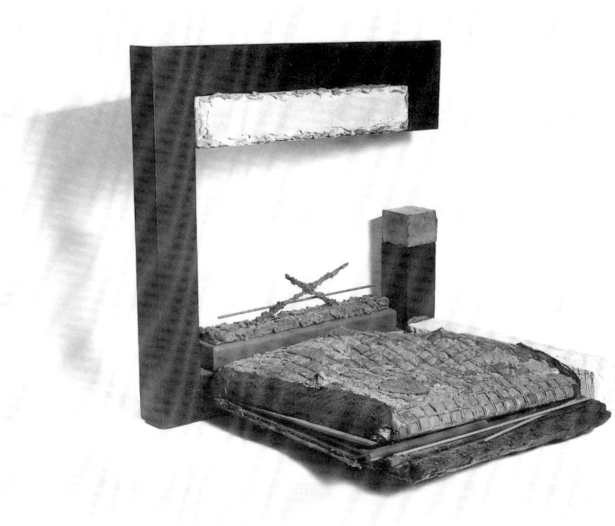

Ajanta Shadows 1977
Wood, Steel, Resin
16 × 16½ × 16 inches (41 × 42 × 41 cm)

A case in point was *Ajanta Shadows 1977*, in which a formalised cloud is held by a frame above an undulating landscape lit by a sunset in a symphony of dark brown, pink, violet and dark blue. Another was *Eclipsed Labyrinths 1978*. This looks a bit like an abstract painting that has burst forward from its frame. The central panel is thickly loaded with rich colours — sombre reds, black, brown, a strong ochre, green splashes — while above hangs a half disc representing one of the swift sunrises that had amazed Draper in India. **Plate 27**

These and the little box pieces were included in his second show at the Redfern Gallery, in 1978. There would be a few more of the old, essentially linear works, including a commission for Bradford University called *Oriental Gateway* that drew on Indian experiences and again took almost a year to complete before its installation in October 1980. But Draper was now set firmly along the landscape-oriented path that he has since trodden in a variety of modes.

Associated with these developments came another important change. Until the mid-70s he had — aside from notes of landscapes seen on his travels — used his pencil drawings to explore sculptural ideas set in a deep space. Many of these were far too complex to be executed, and fizzing with an energy reminiscent of Roberto Matta's paintings. Now that he was making smaller sculptures that could be made and changed relatively quickly, he found himself wanting to explore in drawings ideas thrown up in thinking about these sculptures.

Since colour now played so integral a role in the sculptures, the drawings too should logically be in colour. From early days he had enjoyed using pastels, whether the chalk or oil varieties, and to this swift and vivid medium he now turned. Despite the growing importance of landscape in his sculptures, these early pastels were still in the main geometric, exploring cones, cubes, ellipses and the like. But gradually they became less and less explorations of sculptural ideas, more and more self-contained drawings in their own right and tending in the direction of landscape. A sense of form and depth was now created by the density of coloured "marks" as well as by the use of line. For Draper, colour represented energy as well as the potential emotional charge it gave the viewer. Increasingly, colour became the link between his sculpture and his drawing. **Plate 7**

Meanwhile, Draper's domestic life had also been undergoing various changes. In 1972 he and Nadiya had suddenly decided to get married in her native Uganda. They paid a second and decidedly dangerous visit to Kampala a few months later that year to rescue what they could of her family's valuables and papers: her parents had been on a visit to London when Idi Amin ordered all Asians to quit the country. In 1976, they had moved from their studio and flat in Borough Market to a rented flat in the Barbican development on the edge of the City and a studio in Kingsland Road, not far away near the Old Street roundabout. But London was becoming oppressive, and Draper was doing too much teaching: two days a week at Bristol Polytechnic (formerly the Royal West of England Academy); one day a week at Goldsmiths'; and odd days at Camberwell School of Arts and Crafts. A predominantly rural decade was at hand. Bristol was axed from the teaching schedule, and in 1978 they rented an old farmhouse in East Bilney, near East Dereham in Norfolk.

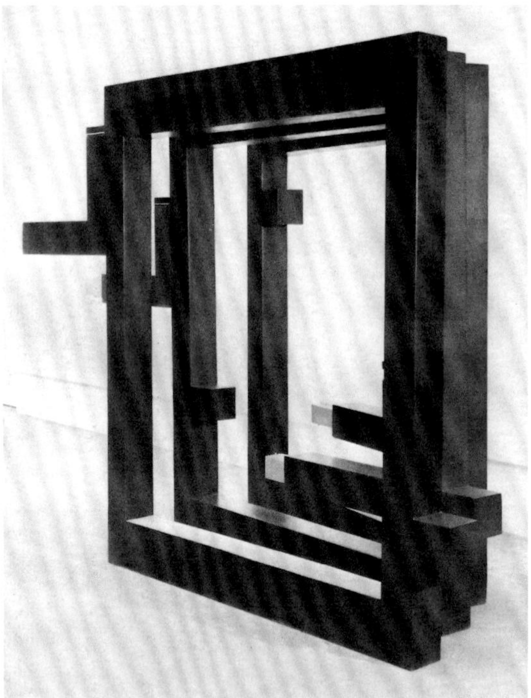

Three Frames 1966–67
Wood, Aluminium, Emulsion Paint
69 × 108 × 36 inches (175 × 274 × 91 cm)

Nadiya, whose own work was becoming increasingly abstract and formal, was none too happy there, especially when Ken was away teaching. A possibility arose for him of a teaching post in the USA, to which she longed to go and where she had a cousin. When Draper decided to stay in England, it seemed sensible for her to give New York a trial year. Their relationship had been very close but often stormy. In the event, she loved New York and stayed. Despite the distance they have remained the best of friends, keep very much in contact across the Atlantic, and see each other periodically.

Her place in Ken's life was taken by Jean Macalpine, a student in the print department at Bristol. She subsequently decided that landscape photography was her *métier*, and has pursued it with great success. Their relationship was soon tested by a spell living in a caravan in Garboldisham, Suffolk: perhaps rashly, Draper had with three other artists, Michael Kenny, John Ashworth and John Loker, and an architect, Gary Ward, bought a large coach house and stable block there in 1979. But before they could move in and use the studio, it had to be converted. Jean, a free spirit with a remarkably positive outlook, was equal to the test, and they have been together ever since, their careers as complementary as their temperaments.

Working in Norfolk with teaching sorties to London, Draper spent the first half of the 80s developing his sculpture and consolidating his reputation as a genuinely original practitioner in that medium. Among his exhibitions were a one-man show in 1981 at the Warwick Arts Trust in Pimlico, London; two shows with the German-born painter Paul Feiler in southern Germany in the same year; and representation in two important exhibitions: British Sculpture in the Twentieth Century at the Whitechapel Gallery in 1981 and The Sculpture Show at the Hayward and Serpentine galleries in London in 1983. The show at the Whitechapel, then under the direction of Nicholas Serota, was in two parts, with 1951 as the watershed between them. In a catalogue essay covering Draper and his Royal College contemporaries, Fenella Crichton saw his *Three Frames 1967* as one of the first intimations of the RCA students' reaction against the St Martin's ethos. For Crichton, the "secretive aura" of his small, densely coloured wall pieces was "a natural development from the subtlety of his earlier large-scale pieces". As for the big Bradford commission, *Oriental Gateway 1980*, for all its "playful and human quality", it represented a "serious response to the extremism and illogical aspects of Indian architecture and landscape".[7]

The Sculpture Show two years later embraced 50 artists chosen by three selectors: the sculptors Paul de Monchaux and Kate Blacker and the ubiquitous Ms Crichton. Draper was, however, not in her team but de Monchaux's, along with his friends and contemporaries Nigel Hall, John Maine and Carl Plackman. This large and important exhibition was something of a landmark in its display of the richness and diversity of talent in contemporary British sculpture. As Crichton said in her catalogue essay: "There is a greater range of objects and activities that are called sculpture today than has ever been the case in the past." While lamenting that modern art's growing complexity had made it the province of a select few, she believed that this new sculpture "has begun to address a wider audience: its inspiration is both more universal and more human, and some of it refers freely to the art of other cultures, and uses archetypal forms, symbolic imagery, dreams and other intensely subjective material."[8]

It was another way of saying that sculpture was returning to the basic sources of the fine arts, albeit in highly contemporary forms. Certainly sculptors as various as Stephen Cox, Alison Wilding, Tony Cragg, Anish Kapoor, David Mach and David Nash drew on a very wide spectrum of inspiration and materials. In the course of his notes on de Monchaux's artists, the art historian Nicholas Wadley wrote:

> Kenneth Draper's latest work is more pictorial than it has ever been and quite uninhibited in its explicit references to visual experiences . . . Since 1978, when he moved to Norfolk, the basis in landscape of his work has, if anything, become clearer. The sorts of visual paradox that he observes are the dematerialisation of form by light on the one hand and the appearance of concreteness in such insubstantial phenomena as layers of morning mist, for instance, on the other. These extremes are paralleled by his own ambition to assimilate into sculpture certain properties of painting.

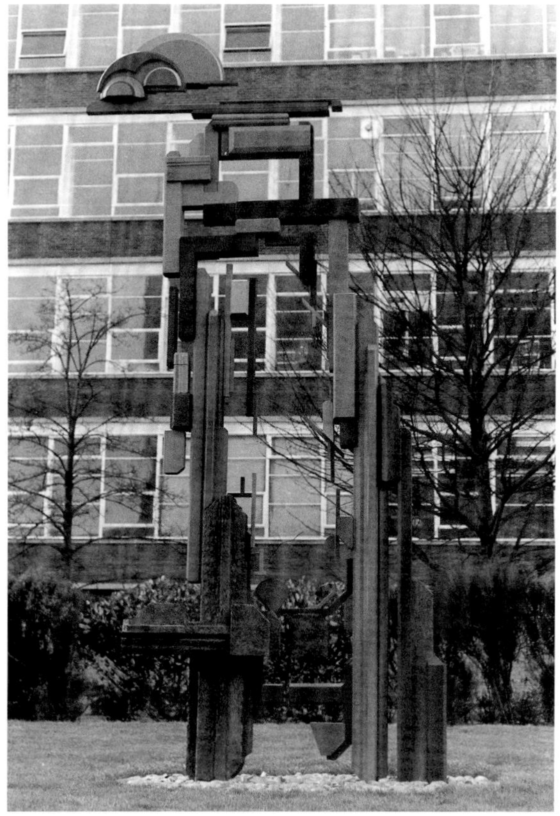

Oriental Gateway 1977–80
Wood, Steel, Resin, Oil Paint
16 × 8 × 2 feet (488 × 244 × 61 cm)
Bradford University

Among the visual experiences, Wadley cited Draper's visit to the Ellora cave temples, which inspired a wall-piece in the show called, simply, *Ellora 1981*: one of four sculptures shown, along with two large works on paper. On Draper's recommendation, Nigel Hall too had been to Ellora, and several of his exhibits, with titles like *Cave No. 10 (Echoing)* and *Horizontal Excavation*, both from 1983, reflected his response. **Plate 9**

For all the range of sculptural talent displayed in this show, a come-back for painting — even for figurative painting — was already under way. Among established figures who struck out against the aridity of conceptualism were the painters R.B. Kitaj and David Hockney. In 1976 Kitaj had promoted figure drawing and painting in a show called The Human Clay, which he assembled at the Hayward Gallery in London for the Arts Council. Hockney joined him in publicly arguing the importance of life classes in art schools, a cause for which Henry Moore, too, had long fought.

Through the 80s, Francis Bacon's reputation soared to new heights; underestimated figurative painters such as Lucian Freud, Frank Auerbach, Leon Kossoff, loosely labelled School of London by Kitaj, enjoyed a new esteem both at home and abroad; younger painters like John Bellany and Ken Kiff emerged from the relative obscurity in which they had been toiling; and over at the Whitechapel, Serota had been introducing such German neo-expressionists as Georg Baselitz and Anselm Kiefer to the British public. They featured strongly in the influential Royal Academy show in 1981, The New Spirit in Painting. In Scotland the outlines of a new school were descried in the work of such narrative yet symbol-laden artists as Steven Campbell and Adrian Wizsniewski. Meanwhile, as Western economies and Japan boomed, art market values soared alarmingly.

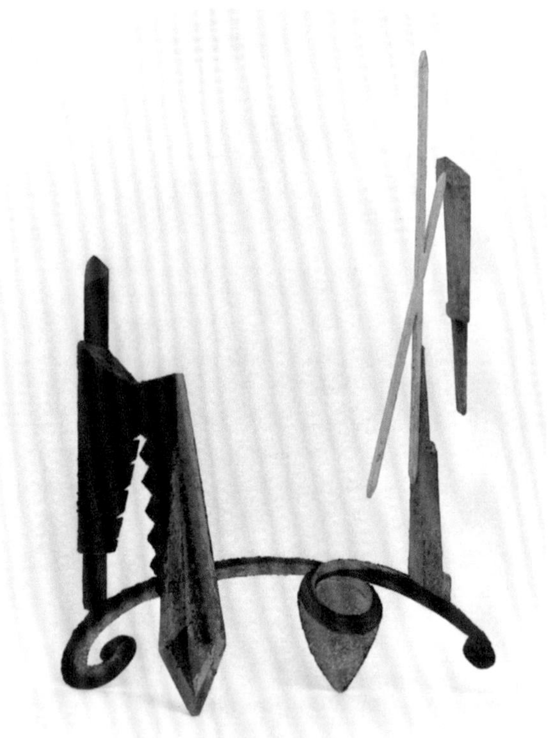

Autumn Tide 1981
Wood, Steel, Resin, Colour Pigment
30 × 25 × 7 inches (76 × 63 × 18 cm)

It was in this overheated if more positive era that Draper went, in October 1985, to work in New York for a few months. It is a testament to his continuing friendship with Nadiya that he not only worked and stayed in her spacious studio but took his son with him: at 18, Adam was taking a year "out" before starting a law degree at the University of East Anglia in Norwich.

Draper had been in New York in early 1984 for six weeks, and had found a good deal of interest in his work. A young sculptor called John Albers (no relation to Josef), with whom he became friendly, introduced him to the Friedus Ordover Gallery, who offered to include some of his pieces in forthcoming group shows. Albers was making strange, surrealist painted wall constructions that interested Draper, and introduced him to many other people.

Encouraged by the level of interest in his work, Ken was seriously thinking of moving to America. But after some months in which he spent more time in New York than in England, he found himself missing the understatement, the subtlety, the restraint of Europe. The longer he spent in the States, the more European he felt. That feeling was reinforced by a short holiday he and Jean had taken in Menorca just before he left for New York in October 1985. It was an experience that would change their lives — and Draper's work.

[1] Report of the Select Committee on Education and Science 1969, quoted in Art Education: Documents and Policies, pp. 114–120.

[2] Sherman E Lee in his *A History of Far Eastern Art* (Prentice Hall & Harry N Abrams Inc. 1994), pp 227–235 *(Ellora)* and pp.122–128 *(Ajanta)*.

[3] KD interviewed by Bryan Robertson in catalogue of one-man show at the Warwick Arts Trust, London SW1, April/May 1981.
4iop. cit. p. 159.

[5] *David Blackburn and the Visionary Landscape Tradition*, by Sasha Grishin (Hart Gallery 1994) p. 28.

[6] interview with the author, London, 8 March 1996.

[7] *British Sculpture in the Twentieth Century*, edited by Sandy Nairne and Nick Serota, Whitechapel Art Gallery 1981, pp. 224 and 232, illustrations pp. 226 and 233.

[8] catalogue of The Sculpture Show, Arts Council 1983, p. 50.

Between reality and illusion

To many of his current collectors and admirers, Ken Draper is first and foremost a painter. He says himself that all his work has been done from a painter's point of view, and that all his heroes (early Giacometti apart, perhaps) have been painters: they include Rembrandt, Turner, Picasso, Matisse, Klee, Rothko, Johns, Sutherland and Lanyon. Yet up to the mid-1980s he was known, as we have seen, exclusively as a sculptor, albeit one whose work was becoming increasingly painterly and whose skills as a draughtsman had always been recognised. It is true that since the mid-70s his drawings had increasingly been done in pastels and had become things-in-themselves rather than ideas, however impracticable, for sculptures. But they still absorbed a relatively small part of his energies, and they were not yet overtly based on specific landscapes — let alone executed outside, in front of the subject.

That first visit to Menorca in September 1985, prior to his longish sojourn in New York, marked a turning point. His response to the primeval nature of this small island prepared the way for the ensuing switch of emphasis towards landscape-based painting and drawing.

As so often in life, it was pure chance that took him and Jean there. A schoolfriend of hers had a small property in Es Castell, a village within walking distance of the capital, Mahon (Mao in Catalan). This friend had long urged Ken and Jean to visit her there or use the flat. Now she was about to sell it. At the same time, Draper was advised by his doctor to take a holiday. He was suffering from stress: creating something from what is within can be very demanding.

It is hard not to fall for Menorca, given reasonable luck with the weather. Although the island is less than 30 miles long, it contains an extraordinary variety of terrain, from gently rolling pastureland to beetling coastal cliffs: Cornwall often springs to mind. Exposed trees are bent over by the ferocious tramuntana wind that periodically rampages through. Menorca's most striking features are its huge, mainly disused limestone quarries; its T-shaped megalithic monuments called taulas and conical stone constructions called talayots, all around 3,000 years old; its ubiquitous and beautifully made dry-stone walls; and its gorges and crests of limestone and whorled red sandstone. Despite these attractions, to which rich fauna and flora and beautiful beaches must be added, the island is relatively undeveloped, which is how most of the 60,000 Menorcans seemingly hope it will remain.

For Ken and Jean, it was a case of love at first acquaintance. They were particularly taken with the first few quarries they discovered. Most of these are, unlike the one described at the beginning of this book, open to the skies. One or two of the oldest are quite shallow, and seem more like archaeological excavations than quarries. Wild olive, fig and almond trees have taken them over, often growing out of the rock face, sometimes splitting great hunks of limestone in their desperate bid to reach soil and moisture.

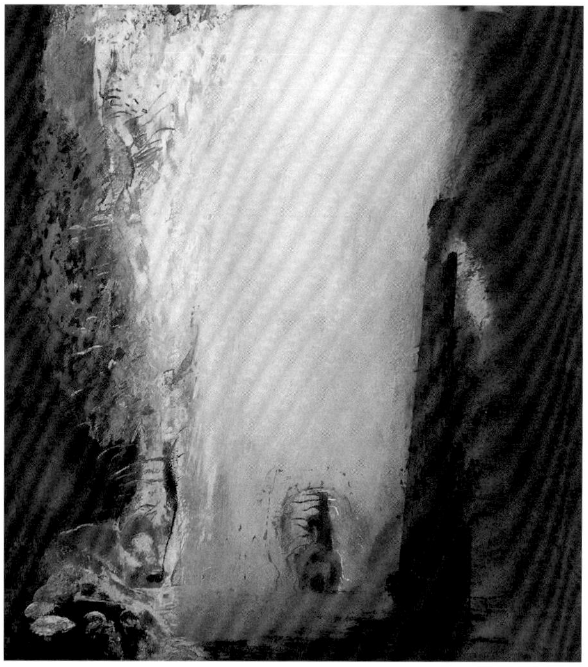

Quarried Light 1995
Pastel on Paper
20 × 18 inches (49 × 44 cm)

The more recent ones, cut by machine rather than by hand, have not yet weathered and remain a buttery white, except for the occasional long, reddish stain where soil-tinted rainwater has drained down. Their hugely deep walls remain deeply scored at regular intervals by the cutting and extracting machinery, sometimes vertically, sometimes horizontally, sometimes both. The contrasts between the white of these walls, the blue of the sky and the green of the pine trees that fringe their rim are stunning and have inspired a number of Draper's pastels and Jean's photographs.

Both remained haunted by Menorca in the following months, he in New York, she in Norfolk. When he returned to England the following March, they decided they had to buy Jean's friend's place, irrational though it seemed at the time. The first time Draper really worked in Menorca was when they went back that July and August. Inspired by the richness of the subject matter, he took out a set of pastels and worked directly from nature for the first time in at least 20 years. Generally, from now on, he attempted when working alfresco to capture his subject in a single day. Mainly it is a question of light. This is likely to be quite different the following day: either he catches the effect in a day, or he starts again. On studio-based works on paper he will often take much longer, though sometimes the paper can take no more and becomes a physical write-off. Inside or outside, the method is the same. Oil pastels are laid upon chalk pastels, and vice versa, with much spraying of fixative after each application. Frequently he will scrape off a layer or two with a finger nail or palette knife, to create those unique effects of light shining through. As he explains:

> Using pastel, rather than paint or watercolour, is like using the earth itself: it is pigment in its purest form. I can build up or take away, impel or dislocate the 'earth', with the maximum of continuity or flow and no need to wait for paint to dry.

Some of the resulting images were relatively literal, and he was at first quite shy about showing them to friends and collectors. Others, though clearly landscape-based, were more abstracted and ambiguous. From the start his aim was to capture the spirit and energies of a particular place, and to strike a delicate balance between the spiritual and the physical: he likens the process to a musician interpreting a score, bringing into play sight, perception, vision, imagination, feeling and emotion.

In the great Romantic tradition, he finds he responds most to primeval landscapes, coarse, rugged, weather-battered, eroded:

> A rock or tree, worn on one side and bent over by prevailing winds, a valley cut by ice, a river inlet, a cove by the sea, rocks worn by the force of the water, land dried and cracked by hot sun, mud banks and silt left by receding seas or rivers, and mines and quarries, with their magical revelation of man's presence.

Plate 42 While breaking new ground with these pastels, Draper continued to make sculpture through the late 80s, using mainly rolled galvanised steel. This became even more clearly related to landscape via the pigment-coloured resin paste that he bonded to its surface: he would often think of the colour before the form. For Draper, colour is energy, and it is this energy that links his sculpture and his pastels. But his sculptural output was to fall — temporarily at least — in the 1990s: ironically, more or less from the moment he was elected a Royal Academician in 1990 on the basis of his reputation as a sculptor. Since then he has made only two or three pieces. When he had a show in the Friends' Room at the RA in 1993, it was of his paintings and pastels rather than his sculptures.

An unexpected effect of his alfresco Menorcan drawing expeditions was to trigger a return to the landscapes of his childhood in Yorkshire. Between 1988 and 1990, for example, he and Jean made around four trips to Teesdale alone, renting various cottages. During a visit in 1990 to Grassington in Yorkshire he started doing small paintings on plywood panels, using the same mixture of oil paint and **Plate 14** resin coloured with pigment that he applied to his sculptures. The resin dries very rapidly and hard, and can be chiselled, sanded or cut in ways impossible with oil paints. The pigment he also applied directly to the plywood. Draper tries to endow these paintings with a powerful sense of being objects (heavy frames reinforce that impression), and sees them as a link between the pastels and the sculpture. But they have formed only a small proportion of his output.

Where subject matter was concerned his preference, attributable to his childhood experiences, was for landscapes bearing the mark of man:

> Although I had never put people in my paintings since 1963 or 1964, I have always thought I wanted a kind of humanity in my work. Quarries, mines, dry-stone walls: they are not made for any aesthetic reasons, but they give off a kind of energy and a trace of man that make them more extraordinary than something built to look extraordinary.

The lead-mining outcrops in Teesdale called the Hushings were a case in point: **Plate 11**

> They would dam the water at the top, and when it had built up high, they would pull away the chocks and it would rush down the mountain at great speed and cut into the land. The miners would then dig the lead out of the earth that had been dramatically dislodged by the rushing water. The dam would then be rebuilt and the process repeated. Gradually, over the years, they had cut these incredible scars into the hills. All you see, now that they're completely overgrown, are those strange, dry riverbeds cutting down from the hillsides.

At St Austell in Cornwall he found another mining operation whose effects appealed to him. There the **Plate 17** hills were hosed before the clay was extracted, the water collecting in little reservoirs rendered turquoise by chemical acidity and interspersed with cones of waste. But nature in all its untamed glory also inspired him, and he trod literally in the footsteps of Turner to capture the waterfalls of the North, and especially of Teesdale, trying to locate himself precisely where Turner himself had sat. With the great man metaphorically peering over his shoulder, it was a daunting experience. Waterfalls — High Force in Teesdale was a favourite subject — embody one of the great ambiguities that he sought to convey in his **Plate 43** work:

> You've got all this incredible power, and sometimes a very sharp line of water. Yet you know as you look at it that it's disappearing. The bit you're looking at has now moved to here, and another bit is there. It's made up of millions of tiny drops of water which become this power force.

For all the importance that Menorca began to assume in their lives, they initially spent only about three months a year in their small flat there and continued to be based at the big studio in Norfolk. They also retained the Barbican flat where Jean had her dark room. Then in 1989 they fell for another small, wind and sea-battered, much quarried island: Portland, strictly speaking a peninsula thanks to the causeway that joins it to mainland Dorset. They had first observed its strange and slightly sinister bulk when staying at Chilcombe in Dorset with John and Caryl Hubbard: John is an American-born painter, Caryl a former picture dealer who became chairman of the Contemporary Art Society and had been a Rothko Foundation member.

Portland, as Ken knew from teaching at Camberwell, was where many art students went on carving expeditions, and on Chesil Beach there was a beautiful gallery run by Margaret Somerville, who had taught art history at Camberwell. She not only put on shows but invited artists for a residency in a flat above the gallery. Soon Ken and Jean called in on the way back from Cornwall, loved what they saw of Portland and agreed to do a show and three-week residency soon afterwards. So happy were they during those weeks that Draper said to Margaret Somerville: "If I can get a studio, we're going to stay here for a while." Next day she walked in and said: "I've got you a studio." It offered only about a quarter of the space available in Garboldisham, but it was in an old farm building among wood and metal workshops — a real working community, yet just a minute from the beach. They soon decided to rent a small cottage a short walk away in Fortuneswell.

Fortuneswell, with its steep streets, lichen-covered roof slates on higgledy-piggledy houses, screaming seagulls and dramatic sea views, in many respects resembles St Ives in Cornwall. But walking along the edge of the cliffs you could be on a miniature, more monochrome version of Menorca. Portland's unique feature is Chesil Beach, which runs around and along the Portland end of the vast and magnificent Lyme Bay. Starting on the Dorset coast near Abbotsbury, ten miles away from Portland, the beach is unusual not least in having the sea on one side and a narrow stretch of water called the Fleet on the other: before the present bridge was built, this natural causeway was the only link between the mainland and the island. Steeply raked on both sides and sometimes reaching a height of 40 ft in parts, it seems to rear up. When the sea is even moderately rough, the sound of its billions of pebbles being ground together fills the air.

Turn almost any corner on the island and there is the sea with all its endlessly changing dramas. From the Portland cottage in this realm of light Ken and Jean could watch 20 ft high waves coming in from 15 miles out, and extraordinary sunsets that thrilled Draper:

> I've seen incredible sunsets in India and Africa, but never like the ones over Lyme Bay. The sun always sets on the water. We'd just sit there in the kitchen marvelling. The sea would be different every day: sometimes a white-out with a red sun, sometimes every colour you can think of.

For Draper, sunsets symbolise the miracle of regeneration: the death of a day, with the promise of rebirth in tomorrow's dawn. Nothing really dies; everything is transformed.

During the residency Paul Feiler, the painter with whom he had shared those two shows in Germany in 1981, suggested he might find William Desmond, of the Austin Desmond Gallery in Bloomsbury, receptive to his work. Ken reckoned he might be offered participation in a mixed show. In the event, Desmond offered to take him on as a gallery artist. Since around 1982 Draper had quite enjoyed doing his own dealing and the contacts it gave him with collectors and museums. In financial terms there was an obvious benefit, in that he kept the full proceeds rather than surrendering a substantial percentage to the dealer. On the negative side there was a great deal of hassle, much tiresome paperwork and, most seriously, a big reduction in the time available for creative work. He got on well with Desmond, a larger than life if sometimes emotional and difficult Irishman, and agreed to sign up with him. They attended the 1989 Chicago art fair together, and agreed that Draper should have a one-man show in the Austin Desmond Gallery in March 1991.

The day before it was due to open, Desmond took his own life, seemingly weighed down by financial and other personal worries. The art world was shocked, Draper the more so for having stayed at the dealer's home near Exeter and got to know his wife and children. The opening of his exhibition was delayed for a week. It was a sad and stressful time for all concerned, and seems to have triggered the heart problem (atrial fibrillation) which Ken first experienced the day after he dismantled the show and drove back to Portland. Happily, his heart responded to treatment in Weymouth Hospital and has since been under control.

Having had little previous contact with the gallery's other partner, John Austin, Draper subsequently decided to resume his independence. Between 1991 and 1994, most of his time was spent on Portland. Jean having moved her dark-room to the cottage there, for the first time they enjoyed a relatively settled, semi-rural life. Ken's son Adam helped make this possible. Having finished law school and started work as a solicitor in the West End, he had acquired a spacious, beautifully converted warehouse flat in EC2. His willingness to keep and show Ken's work there played a key part in enabling his father to spend so little time in the capital. Only in 1994, having come to know, like and trust his fellow Yorkshireman John Hart and his wife Katherine, did he join their London stable.

The Harts were recent recruits to the art world from medicine and marine biology respectively, but all the more energetic and open-eyed for that. Starting with a small gallery attached to their home in Linby, near Nottingham, they soon acquired premises in Upper Street in Islington, north London, where they show ceramics as well as paintings, drawings and sculpture.

It was a measure of the mark being made by Draper's landscape-based drawings (as pastels are technically classified) and paintings that his work should have been included for an exhibition in New York in May 1992 entitled The Poetic Trace: Aspects of British Abstraction since 1945. It was held at the Adelson Galleries on 77th Street, and the other artists were Gillian Ayres, Prunella Clough, Alan Davie, Terry Frost, Patrick Heron, Roger Hilton, Ivon Hitchens, Howard Hodgkin, John Hoyland, Peter Lanyon, Ben Nicholson, William Scott and William Tillyer: a strong selection tipped in the direction of the St Ives school, with Draper and Tillyer representing a younger generation. In the course of a typically mellifluous introductory essay, the London critic Mel Gooding observed: "Draper's 'landscapes' are perfect examples of the British tendency to distill an abstract mood from earth and water and the weather that envelopes them. They are also pictures of a moment, an experience refracted through reverie, invested with an emotion remembered and recorded in the very substance of the work."

A year later, Frances Spalding neatly summed up that preoccupation with transience when, in an appreciative assessment in the magazine *Contemporary Art*, she said: "His static images reconcile a sense of flux with a search for fixity." In the last two decades, she observed, the artists who appeared to have survived best were dogged individualists, "or those who, like Ken Draper, share only a tangential relationship with the issues of the days . . . Draper's refusal to follow any minimalist or didactic extreme has allowed him more freedom to develop than his contemporaries. It has also left unhindered his responsiveness to place."[1]

That faculty was much in evidence during a two-week cruise down the Nile in autumn 1992. The journey was conceived primarily as a sightseeing holiday, and Draper was far from sure whether any work would result. In the event, he was forcefully struck on the journey not just by the ancient temples but by the horizontality of the landscape:

> It was weird. There was this wonderful strip of green for three or four hundred yards on either side of the river, then the dunes and the desert: the huge, extraordinary Nile, with an extraordinary flat, linear civilisation knitted **Plate 47**

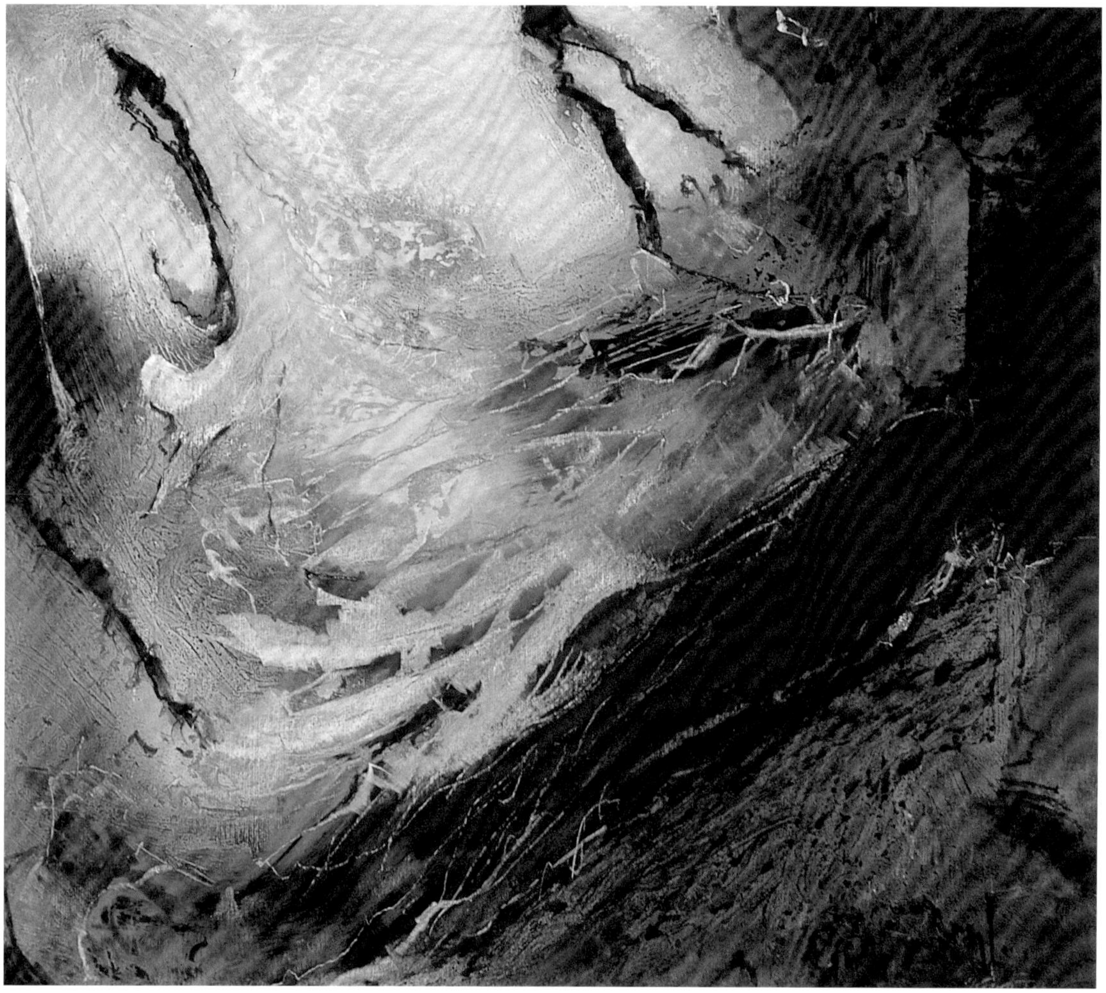

Canyon Void, Arizona 1994
Pastel on Paper
14 × 16 inches (35 × 41 cm)

> to its banks. I'd always tried to avoid a format that has anything to do with a horizon or a horizontal that says 'landscape'. Yet this was so powerful that it kept coming into the drawings, which got darker as the Nile got darker and darker.

The sombre refulgence of these pastels, with often a dominant black shot through with red and yellow, was influenced by one of the high points of the trip: a *son et lumière* show at a temple on an island near Aswan. Ken felt a powerful sense of what it had been like to be there 5,000 years earlier, observing to Jean: "This feels more like reality than the reality!" **Plate 46**

Because they were moving so quickly from place to place, he reverted to his old practice of making pencil drawings. He used these notes as a starting point for pastels and paintings when he returned home to Portland, suffusing what emerged with the remembered emotions of the trip. It seemed to work well, and he has adopted the same form of pencil notation on subsequent travels.

Two of these sorties proved particularly fruitful. One was to Arizona and New Mexico in 1993, the other to Provence the following year. When they arrived in November, the deep West was in the grips of exceptionally cold weather. Thanks to last-minute cancellations following a heavy snowfall, they were able to secure a room late in the evening in a hotel that overlooked the Grand Canyon. As Draper recalls:

> Next morning I opened the door expecting to see this great hole in the universe — and it looked like Yorkshire. There was a grey mist over everything, and apparently it had been like that for two days. We went out later and suddenly there was a hole. Gradually it started to clear, layer by layer, and then the sun broke through. It was the most electrifying experience: a whole area would open up and a cloud would come vertically up into the sky. It was like watching God painting. Everything I've ever believed and thought about seemed to be taking place before my eyes.

Later they went to Monument Valley, a scenic antithesis: where the Grand Canyon goes down, the gigantic purple rocks that give Monument Valley its name rise dramatically from a flat desert. There were more excitements: the Painted Desert and Petrified Forest; the Bell Rock at Sedona; and, in New Mexico, the Echo Canyon and Bandelier Canyon, which produced some work of searing intensity. **Plates 44 & 45**

On the second high-yield trip they stayed with the Harts at their holiday home in the Luberon, and Draper was greatly struck by the Gorge of Verdon (the only European canyon on the North American scale), by the red and yellow ochre quarries of Roussillon and Rustel and the mystic aura of Carluc Abbey, all of which — despite appalling weather — proved inspirational. **Plates 50, 51 & 52**

That was in October 1994, when they were on their way to settle finally in Menorca. The move would not have been possible without a trustworthy and energetic dealer to generate and handle sales in England and the USA, where the Harts have a relationship with the Peter Bartlow Gallery in Chicago. An artist cannot live in a place like Menorca and be his own dealer.

Paradoxically, once settled there he found himself working for months from pencil sketches made in France. This did not mean that his experiences in Menorca played no part in what emerged. An artist's imagination is not compartmentalised. Rather it is incremental. To be immersed in any landscape is to add it permanently to a store of impressions. Every picture draws on the sum total of memories. That is one reason why Draper believes in replenishing his stock with frequent trips abroad.

And yet how painful the process of conscious or unconscious selection from that treasury can be. The artist is not operating in a void. The history of Western art presses on him — or should do: Draper likes to quote Goethe's saying that "he who cannot draw on three thousand years is living hand to mouth".

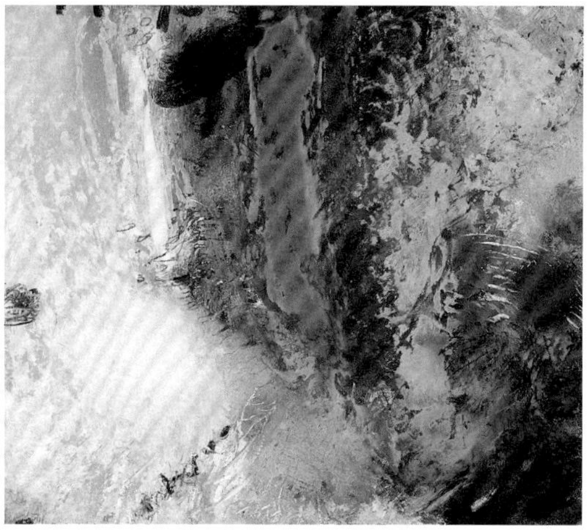

Rustrel, Noon, Provence 1995
Pastel on Paper
14 × 16 inches (35 × 41 cm)

Furthermore, he (or she) will generally want to communicate with a fair proportion of those who will see the work. It must be neither too esoteric nor too facile in its appeal, if it is to endure:

> People say 'It must be so wonderful to be an artist.' But every time you look at a blank sheet of paper, you think: is it possible not only to start again on that little white universe, but can you push it further — not only in your own terms, but to make your pals worried by what you're doing! You want other people to respond to the push you're making. At a private view of two or three years' work, half of you wants everyone to say: 'Wonderful. Marvellous. Incredible!' But if that happens, the other half of you says you haven't been challenging enough. They can grasp it too easily.

When working, Draper likes to be in a state he describes as edginess. If he is too conscious of what is happening on the paper, he risks losing the original trigger of inspiration; as he puts it, "If you don't know what you're doing, you're lost. If you know too much, you've had it!" What emerges on paper should have its own edginess too, capturing the sense of transience that is one of his constant goals. Hence the attraction of those deep quarries, with their extremes of light and shade and their reminders of the attraction/repulsion he felt for the mines that constantly threatened his father's life and limbs.

Draper endeavours to hint at what he is striving for in the titles of his pictures. These can, he believes, help promote communication between artist and viewer, acting a bit like a personal introduction. An evocative title can prompt people to look for an undercurrent they might not otherwise notice, something hidden, something ambiguous. The ones he chooses often allude to the intermediate states that he seeks to convey. Typical examples include: *Light through Dark, Dark into Light, On Reflection, Transient Light, Shadowed Edge, Secret Place,* and *Eclipse*; as Tom West, one of his collectors, observed affectionately: "There's an eclipse at least once a year for Ken."

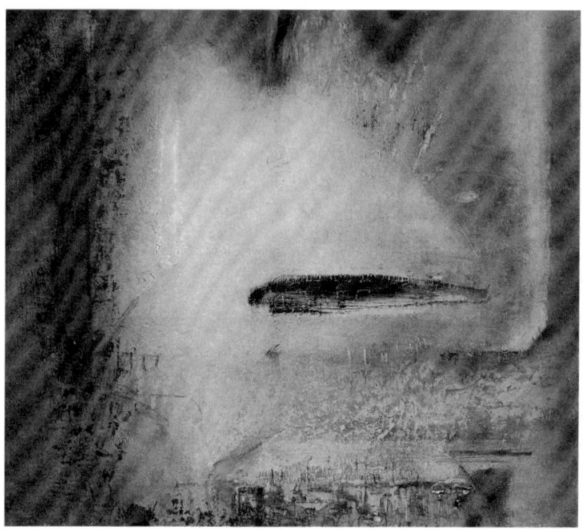

In Solitude, Carluc, Provence 1995
Pastel on Paper
18 × 20 inches (44 × 49 cm)

Of the dozen or so of Draper's keenest admirers, the one who has had most influence on his life is John Ball, a biologist, who lives in London and is also a major collector of the work of Keith Vaughan. Ball first met Draper, by chance, at the Redfern Gallery in 1984: he was asking a director of the gallery what Draper, whose sculptures he had liked, was doing these days when the man himself bounded down the stairs. Ball and his friend Gordon Hargreaves later went to see Ken first at the Barbican flat and then in Norfolk, and bought a couple of sculptures. A friendship developed. Ken and Jean stayed with Ball in his flat in Keswick on one trip to the Lake District. It was Ball who first interested the dealer William Desmond in Draper's work, and who later introduced Ken to the Harts. Over and above buying a substantial number of Ken's sculptures and pastels he has thus played a significant supportive role in Draper's career. The contribution of such people to Britain's cultural life is under-appreciated.[2]

This appreciation of Draper's life and work opened with a glimpse of an ancient quarry in Menorca that has inspired a number of his pastels. An episode in a nearly-new one at the other end of the island, which had also been inspirational, provides a suitable conclusion.

The recently abandoned quarry, near the old capital of Ciutadella, was unique not least in its inaccessibility: a giant, dazzling white vertical tomb cut into a field, its floor a hundred or so feet down attainable only by iron rungs up one side. On a fine day it held only dazzling, reflected light orchestrated on its saw-scarred vertical walls by slow-moving shadows. Into this eerily pure white space Draper would sometimes spend a whole day peering, attempting to capture its magic on the paper in front of him. Now, towards the end of my seven-day visit to Menorca, he was looking forward to showing it to me. Imagine his horror when, leaning over the stone wall surrounding it, we saw a scene of desecration. Into each of the two corners opposite us rubble had been tipped: to the left, quarry rubble composed of damaged limestone blocks and a vast quantity of white dust; to the right, builders' rubble in which rough boulders and discarded wood bulked large. Even while we looked despondently down, the silence was shattered as a truck tipped a huge load onto the builders' pile. As the falling rocks hammered flat panels of unwanted wood, the sound of the crashing and rumbling was genuinely shocking. Inexorably the heavier rocks descended to the bottom, some appearing to settle, only to break the emerging silence as gravity tugged them lower with a fresh rumble.

Something almost perfect had been destroyed. Yet even from this scene of vandalism, a kind of beauty was beginning to emerge in Ken's mind. Studying the twin piles, the one white, the other brown, he saw they formed near-perfect cones. They were light and darkness, antithetical yet already merging at the bottom. They took his mind back to those cones of slag that had loomed so large on the physical and mental landscape of his childhood. With all their latent energy and violence they confirmed Draper's conviction that nothing really dies, everything is reborn. Soon, he reflected, that wonderful, meditative chamber of light would disappear altogether. The field would return to its original state, and cattle would graze like clouds atop his memory of space. The Fall would finally be redeemed.

It need hardly be said that two days later, when he had fully digested the visual and aural dramas of that afternoon, he set to work to capture those cones and the impact they had had on him. After much travail, a pastel of great subtlety and beauty resulted: he called it, understatedly, *Aftermath*. From an apparent setback Draper had wrung a symbolic victory. **Plate 58**

This episode could be seen as a microcosm of his life as a whole, a life that has transformed the handicap of those childhood months of head-clamped suffering into a propelling force. Draper's energy and enthusiasm remain contagious, his personality larger and more generous than life. He is unusual among artists in speaking with warmth about his fellow practitioners, among whom he has many friends. His openness, combined with his gifts as a raconteur and a wide range of enthusiasms, make him exceptionally good company, though those who dislike being hugged should stay well away. His generosity of spirit, his energy and his love of life are reflected in his work. Amid so much art that is glib, meretricious and spiritually empty, Draper is producing work that ravishes the eye and nourishes the soul. I hope this book will help a wider audience to share the joy that his many admirers have already found in it.

1 *Contemporary Art*, spring 1993, Vol. 1 No. 3 p. 29.

2 interview with John Ball, London 15 February 1996.

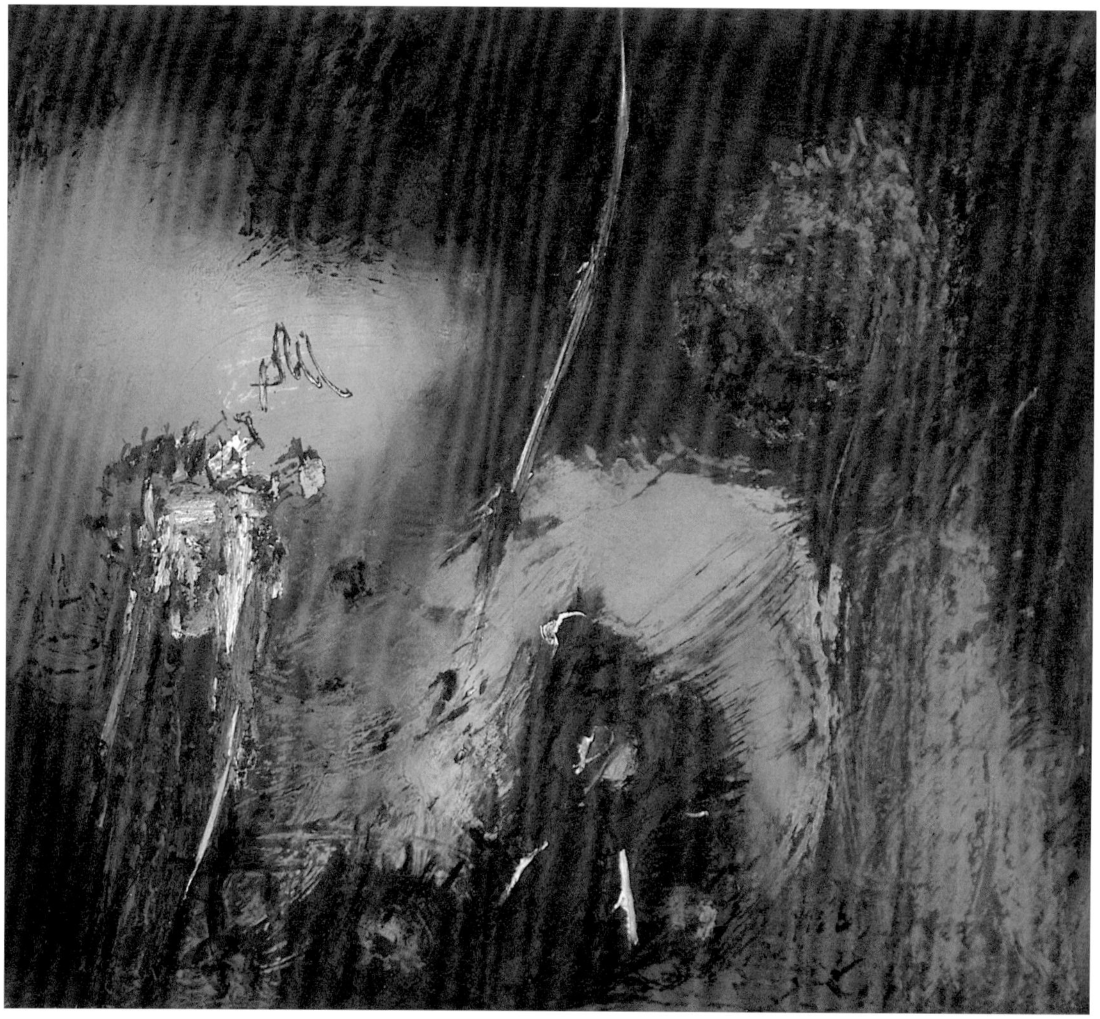

Survival 1995
Pastel on Paper
18 × 20 inches (44 × 49 cm)

Vergänglichkeit festgehalten

KENNETH DRAPER — Leben und Werk

von Roger Berthoud

Nur einige hundert Meter von Ken Drapers Haus auf Menorca gibt es einen Hügel, bedeckt mit riesigen Kakteen, Sträuchern und Olivenbäumen. Dieser Hügel, wie so viele auf der Insel, besteht aus Kalkstein, und in eine seiner honigfarbenen Seiten ist eine Reihe von viereckigen Eingängen gehauen. Sie sind Teil eines altertümlichen, nicht mehr genutzten Steinbruchs, dessen Ausmaße und subtile Farbtöne atemberaubend sind. Es sieht aus wie ein Dom, nur daß die Säulen, welche von jenen Steinbrechern hinterlassen worden waren, weitaus größer sind, als es die Kapitelle selbst der großartigsten Andachtsstätte jemals sein könnten. Licht flutet von den Öffnungen herein, welche gesäumt sind von Kakteen und Sträuchern, die den Eindruck machen, als wollten sie einen verstohlenen Blick ins Innere werfen. Die Mauern dieses wunderbaren Gebäudes — so scheint es — bergen immer noch die eingeritzten Markierungen, die die Werkzeuge der Arbeiter in Zeiten vor der Mechanisierung hinterlassen haben. Dort, wo das Licht die Oberfläche berührt, verwandeln sich die honigfarbenen Töne beinahe in Weiß. Weiter drinnen hat die Feuchtigkeit sehr verschiedenartige Grüntöne geschaffen, und ein düsteres, fahles Grau setzt sich allmählich durch.

Dieser Steinbruch ist typisch für die Welt, die Draper zu seiner eigenen gemacht hat. Sein Inneres und die Vegetation, die dieses Innere bedeckt, haben Draper zu einer Reihe von Pastellzeichnungen inspiriert, welche in letzter Zeit sein Anliegen sind. Menorca hat jedoch noch mehr Schätze zu bieten, wie wir noch sehen werden, und zu deren Inspiration fügt Draper ein halbes Jahrhundert an Erfahrungen, gesammelt auf zahlreichen Reisen, hinzu. Vom Yorkshire und Derbyshire seiner Kindheit über Indien, Pakistan und Uganda, den Nil flußabwärts, und durch die Wüsten und Canyons im Westen der USA, bis hin zu den Schluchten der Provence, stets hat er unablässig gezeichnet und seinen Sinn für Farbe und Form vervollkommnet. Gleich, ob er als Maler oder Bildhauer arbeitet, dieser Künstler feiert die Natur, besonders die Teile davon, wo der Mensch unauslöschliche Spuren hinterlassen hat. Obwohl er sich der vorherrschenden Modekonzepte innerhalb der britischen Kunstwelt durchaus bewußt ist, hat sich Draper sehr gelassen seinen Weg gebahnt. Tatsächlich glaubt der britische Kunsthistoriker Frances Spalding, daß Drapers Mangel an Assoziationen ihm geholfen hat, sich einen festen und dauerhaften Platz innerhalb der Kunst Großbritanniens zu verdienen.

Seine Skulpturen, großzügig mit eindrucksvollen, auffallenden Farben überzogen, mit ihrer verlockenden *trompe-l'oeil*-Exploration des Raumes, sind einzigartig in ihrer Planung und Ausführung, Bildern ebenso nahe wie Skulpturen selbst. Viele derselben Techniken werden verwendet in Drapers "mixed media"-Gemälden auf Holz, von welchen aus oftmals skulpturähnliche Formen zum Betrachter hinzuschweben scheinen. Die Pastellzeichnungen, gleich, ob sie in der Natur selbst ausgeführt wurden oder im Atelier nach Bleistiftskizzen, fangen diese Reaktionen auf die Natur in all ihrer ganzen Vielfalt ein. Von eindeutigen und anschaulichen Ansichten eines Wasserfalls oder eines Berghanges bis hin zu fast abstrakten Werken, inspiriert vom Meer, Nebel, Felsen oder Sonnenuntergängen, sind Drapers Bilder der großen Tradition englischer Landschaftsmalerei verbunden, besonders Turner: manchmal brilliant coloriert und leidenschaftlich intensiv, manchmal zärtlich einen im Dunst verschleierten Berghang einfangend, manchmal — im Gegensatz dazu — fast wie bei Klee spielerisch das Gleichgewicht ihrer Formen findend.

Struktur, Stimmung und Licht werden mit vielschichtiger Feinheit und Raffinesse ausgedrückt. Hier scheint das Licht hindurchzuscheinen, wo vorher eine Schicht entfernt wurde, um zu enthüllen, was darunter verborgen war. Da lenkt eine verführerisch reichhaltige Zone struktureller Effekte das Auge vom Zentrum des Bildes ab. Diese Pastellzeichnungen sind nicht so sehr visionär als vielmehr lyrisch: Hymnen an die Vielfältigkeit der Welt. Es gibt nur wenige, die vom Zauber dieser Bilder nicht eingefangen werden.

KENNETH DRAPER wurde als jüngster von drei Söhnen 1944 im Bergwerkdorf Killamarsh nahe Sheffield in Yorkshire geboren. Sein Vater, Albert Draper, arbeitete von 11-65 Jahren im örtlichen Bergwerk und hatte ein bemerkenswertes zeichnerisches Talent. Seine Mutter, eine geborene Dorothy Lamb, entstammte der wohlhabenden Familie eines Metzgers in Gainsborough in Lincolnshire. Die ganze Familie hatte musikalisches Talent. "Unser Ken", wie seine Mutter ihn nannte, lernte als Kind, Klavier und Kornett zu spielen, aber bald gewann die Kunst die Oberhand. Im Alter von sieben Jahren wurde er sich seines zeichnerischen Talents bewußt, als er eine freihändige Kopie einer römischen Pferdekutsche anfertigte.

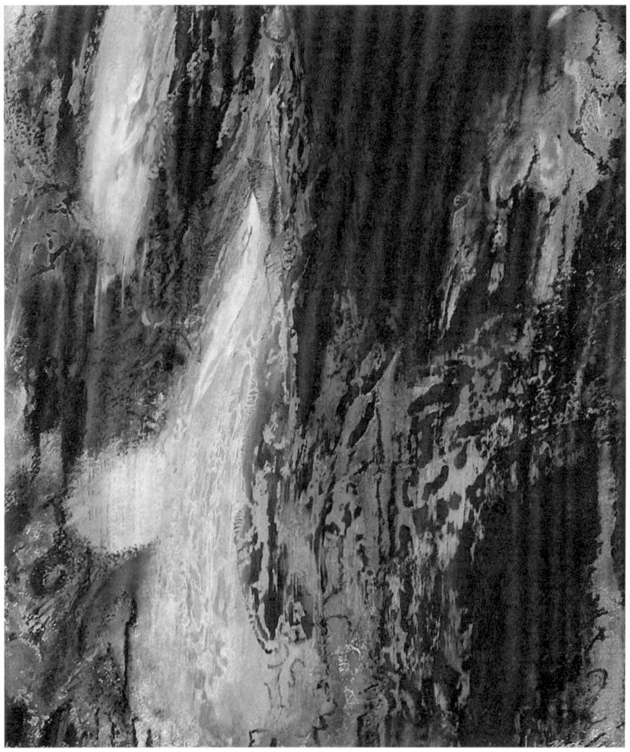

High Place/Falaise de Buoux 1995
Pastel on Paper
16 × 14 inches (41 × 35 cm)

Bald danach, als er acht Jahre alt war, wurden seine Eltern davon unterrichtet, daß bei Kenneth der Verdacht auf eine schwere Erkrankung des Rückgrates vorlag. Ungefähr acht Monate mußte er im Rivelin Valley Hospital in einem Außenbezirk von Sheffield zubringen, festgeschnallt auf dem Rücken liegend, den Kopf mit Gurten ruhiggestellt, mit Brettern an beiden Seiten und Gewichten hinter dem Kopf herabhängend, um ihn absolut ruhigzustellen. Als er entlassen wurde, mußte er wieder laufen lernen, eine Erfahrung, die ihm die Frage des Gleichgewichts zu einem lebenslangen Anliegen in seiner Kunst werden ließ.

Es ist unmöglich zu sagen, ob Draper auch Künstler geworden wäre, wenn ihm die traumatische Erfahrung dieser kräftezehrenden acht Monate erspart geblieben wäre. Sein Talent war von Anfang an da. Aber all die Aufmerksamkeit, die ihm zuteil wurde, besonders in der Schule von seinem Kunstlehrer Jean Arblaster, gab ihm ein starkes Gespür dafür, anders, ja sogar etwas Besonderes zu sein.

Seine ersten Zeichnungen zeigten die außergewöhnliche Landschaft, die ihn daheim umgab, mit ihrer schaurigen, unheimlichen Schönheit der Grubenausrüstungen und der riesigen Schlackekegel. Kleine Lastwagen erklommen sie, was die seltsamen Pyramiden immer noch höher werden ließ. Draper war fasziniert von diesen merkwürdigen Verschiebungen.

Chesterfield College of Art, wohin Kenneth nach Beendigung der Schule ging, war ziemlich klein und paßte ihm gut in seine Pläne. Nach drei Jahren harter Arbeit dort, in denen er sowohl Malerei als auch Bildhauerei studierte, ging er nach London, wo er ebenfalls drei Jahre am Kingston College of Art verbrachte. Dort studierte er zunächst Malerei, dann Bildhauerei, gefolgt von drei weiteren Jahren am Royal College of Art.

Es war auch am Kingston College, wo er sein Konzept von der Vergänglichkeit einer Vorstellung oder Figur entwickelte, ein Kommen und Gehen innerhalb einer statischen Umgebung, und dieses Konzept beschäftigte ihn über mehrere Jahre. Damals versuchte er auch, den Raum als etwas darzustellen, das sich im Rahmen seiner eigenen Gesetze bewegt und lebt, und das nicht weniger Bedeutung hat als die Objekte darin. Viele Zeichnungen von Räumen und einige Gemälde waren das Resultat, dargestellt aus verschiedenen Perspektiven, und im allgemeinen in Anwesenheit eines Menschen. Im letzten dieser drei Jahre in Kingston schuf er einige bedeutende Skulpturen.

Am Royal College, wo er im Oktober 1965 zu studieren begann, schuf er nur vier Werke, alles sehr große und komplexe Stukturen, an welchen er auch eine Menge Zeit mit Malen und Übermalen verbrachte. Für das erste Werk, "Arena", brauchte er fast eineinhalb Jahre.

Das zweite Werk, "Drei Rahmen", vermittelte ein Gefühl, als ob sich etwas zwischen den hölzernen Rahmen bewegte. Als er dieses Werk schuf, wurde sich Draper erstmalig des Betrachters bewußt und der Möglichkeit, auf der Vorderseite einer Skulptur Anhaltspunkte zu hinterlassen, die ein falsches Erwartungsbild von dem erschaffen würden, was auf der anderen Seite verborgen ist — und auf diese Weise ein Gefühl von Überraschung und Geheimnis zu kreieren, das auf Erinnerung basiert.

Nachdem er das College abgeschlossen hatte, nahm er für einen Tag in der Woche eine Teilzeitarbeit als Lehrer am Hornsey College of Art im Norden von London an. Da er selbst nicht viel älter als die meisten Studenten war, bildeten sich enge Beziehungen mit ihnen heraus, enger als in späteren Zeiten der Lehrertätigkeit, als der Altersunterschied bedeutend größer war. Ziemlich oft kamen Studenten zu ihm ins Studio, das er in Borough Market, südlich der London Bridge, gemietet hatte.

Die Lehrertätigkeit half ihm, sich über seine Ideen klarzuwerden und er fand heraus, wenn er sich mit seinen Studenten unterheilt, das deren Probleme auch die seinen waren.

Im folgenden Jahr, 1969, hatte er sein Debut in der Redfern Gallery im Londoner Westend, wo der Arts Council, ein einflußreicher und bekannter Patron zwei große Skulpturen kaufte. Im selben Jahr reiste er nach Indien und Pakistan, was eine nachhaltige Wirkung auf seine Arbeit haben sollte. Im Nordosten von Bombay, nicht weit entfernt von Aurangabad im Staate Maharashtra, besuchte er die außergewöhnlichen Höhlentempel von Ellora und Ajanta, welche einen Höhepunkt hinduistischer Bildhauerkunst und Wandmalerei darstellen. Nachdem er das Taj Mahal in Agra gesehen hatte, ging er weiter nach Pakistan, wo die Ausgrabungen der Reste der Stadt Mohenjodaro den Höhepunkt seiner Reise darstellten. Diese altertümliche Stadt war einst Teil der bemerkenswert hochentwickelten Indus–Tal–Zivilisation, welche ihre Blütezeit ungefähr zwischen 2500 und 1800 v.u.Z. hatte. Als Draper in einem winzigen Flugzeug über Pakistan flog, sah er das erste Mal eine Landschaft wie durch ein Kaleidoskop aus einer geringen Höhe.

Unter den nachhaltigsten Eindrücken von dieser Reise war zweifelsohne die Art und Weise, wie–besonders in Indien–die Architektur gleichsam aus dem Boden herauszuwachsen schien: Landschaft und Tempel schienen ineinander widerzuhallen, schienen Teile eines organischen Ganzen zu sein, wobei die Farbe einen integrativen Teil der Form darstellte. Ein anderer sehr starker Eindruck war der, wie extremes Licht und extremer Schatten feste Objekte gleichsam dematerialisierten, ein Effekt, den er bei seinen Skulpturen anzuwenden versuchte. Er gewann außerdem ein neues Gespür für Raum und Offenheit, welches er in den großen Wandbildern verwenden sollte, die er im folgenden Jahr zu erschaffen begann.

Einige dieser Impressionen wurden noch verstärkt, als Draper im April/Mai 1971 zum ersten Mal die USA bereiste. Sein siebenwöchiger Aufenthalt führte ihn nach New York, Boston, Washington, Philadelphia, Chicago, San Francisco und Los Angeles, und das zu einer idealen Jahreszeit.

Hier war er inmitten einer lebendigen Kultur, deren Maler es über die vergangenen Jahre geschafft hatten, Paris von seiner führenden Position als Zentrum der zeitgenössischen Kunst zu verdrängen. Draper war schon damals ein leidenschaftlicher Bewunderer von Rothko, Pollock und Jasper Johns. Als er nun tatsächlich in Amerika war, nahm seine Bewunderung auch für andere, weniger bekannte Künstler eine neue Dimension an. In New York traf er Jasper Johns, Helen Frankenthaler und Pollocks Witwe, Lee Krasner Pollock, und in Kalifornien traf er unter anderen Richard Diebenkorn.

Dieser Sinn für Enthüllung war nicht auf amerikanische Kunst beschränkt. Die großen Museen praktisch jeder Stadt, die er besuchte, hatten viel größere Bestände an europäischer Kunst, angefangen bei den Impressionisten, als jedes britische Museum.

Diese mit Ereignissen angefüllten, aufregenden Wochen in den USA bereicherten sein Wissen und seine visuellen Erfahrungen enorm, woraus ein Wachstum und eine Reifung seiner Arbeit resultierte. Der unmittelbare Effekt, so glaubte Draper, sollte sein Empfinden für Maßstäbe verändern und die Kraft und Intensität seiner Arbeit erhöhen.

Einen Beweis für diese Entwicklung gab es anhand einer großen überhängenden Wandskulptur, welche er für eine Ausstellung zeitgenössischer Bildhauerei an der Royal Academy in Picadilly für Januar 1972 schuf, wo er einen eigenen Ausstellungsraum bekam. Das größte dieser Kunstwerke sollte über dem Betrachter schweben, sich über die Gesetze der Schwerkraft hinwegsetzend, und sollte ein Gespür für Raum und weite Horizonte vermitteln. Wenn man weit genung entfernt stand, wirkte es fast flach. Bewegte man sich aber darauf zu, dehnte es sich aus, öffnete sich und lieferte auf diese Weise die beabsichtigte Illusion.

Die großen frühen Werke erzählen auf ihre eigene Art über Ereignisse und Begegnungen innerhalb jeder individuellen Struktur. Sie sind in gewisser Weise zurückzuführen auf die Beschäftigung des Minimalismus mit Kastenformen und Rahmen in Modulbauweise und auch auf Anthony Caros Untersuchungen des Raumes. Draper beabsichtigte, weit über die Vorstellung der Skulptur als direktes, geradliniges Objekt hinauszugehen: weg mit den klaren und übersichtlichen, wenn auch manchmal komplexen Darstellungen, um den Betrachter zu überraschen und das Auge zu täuschen, wenn es dem Kunstwerk näher kommt, dahinter–oder darunterschaut.

Um 1975 durchlief Drapers eigene Arbeit eine bedeutender Veränderung. Er hatte genug davon, so viel Zeit für einen großen Auftrag für Manchester Polytechnik aufzuwenden, und so entschied er 1975, sich in seiner Arbeit auf das Wesentliche zu konzentrieren und bedeutend kleinere Werke zu schaffen. Unter diesen befand sich eine Serie winziger, annähernd kastenförmiger Wandskulpturen, etwa 15cm lang, mit dick aufgetragener Farbe. Sie waren klein aber nur in ihren Ausmaßen, da sie auf wirklichen Landschaften basierten und einen großen Teil ihrer Kraft ihrer ungewöhnlichen Oberfläche und ihren leuchtenden Farben zu verdanken haben. Sie waren so konzentriert, daß Draper sie mit kleinen Bomben verglich.

Vorher hatte er hauptsächlich mit Holz gearbeitet, auf welches er dann eine Schicht dunkle, düstere Farbe aufbrachte. Nun–im Kontrast dazu–mischte er reine, unverdünnte Farbpigmente in verschiedene Materialien, im allgemeinen Harz oder Gips, welche er dann auf das Holz oder eine Stahloberfläche auftrug. Wie auch in seinen Erinnerungen an Indien, wurde hier die Farbe vielmehr zu einem Teil der Form als lediglich als eine zusätzliche Schicht aufgetragen zu werden. Diese Stücke und die kleinen kastenförmigen waren 1978 Teil seiner zweiten Ausstellung in der Redfern Gallery. Außerdem waren da einige der älteren, hauptsächlich linearen Arbeiten zu sehen, eingeschlossen ein Auftrag für die Universität in Bradford, der auf Erfahrungen in Indien aufbaute und wiederum fast ein Jahr in Anspruch nahm, bevor es im Oktober 1980 installiert wurde. Aber Draper war nun von seinem landschaftsorientierten Weg, den er seitdem auf verschiedene Arten begangen hat, nicht mehr abzubringen.

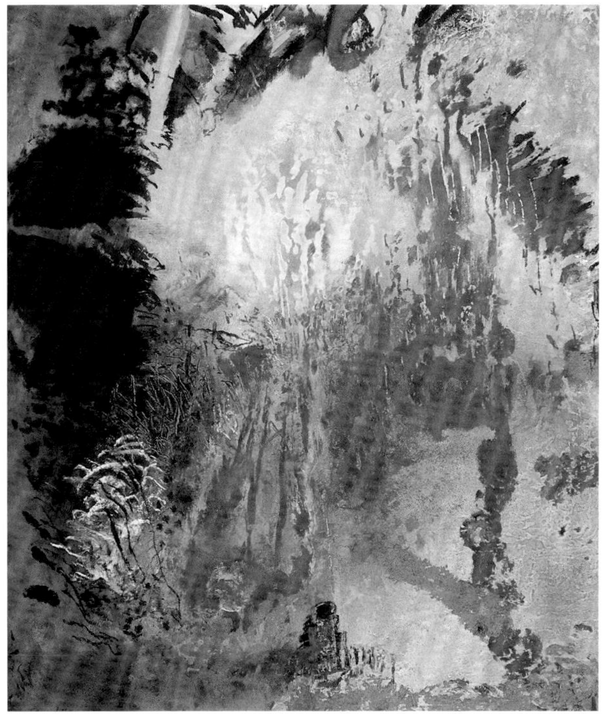

High Cave/Noon 1995
Pastel on Paper
20 × 18 inches (49 × 44 cm)

Diese Entwicklungen brachten noch eine andere Veränderung mit sich. Bis in die Mitte der 80er Jahre hinein hatte Draper, abgesehen von einigen Landschaftsskizzen, die er auf seinen Reisen angefertigt hatte, seine Bleistiftzeichnungen benutzt, um bildhauerische Ideen in einem tiefen Raum zu untersuchen. Jetzt, da er kleinere Skulpturen schuf, die er relativ schnell herstellen und verändern konnte, wollte er in seinen Zeichnungen Ideen untersuchen, die durch das Nachdenken über seine Skulpturen hervorgebracht wurden.

Seit die Farbe eine solch integrative Rolle in seinen Arbeiten spielte, mußten seine Zeichnungen nun logischerweise auch farbig werden. Seit früher Kindheit hatte er gern Pastellfarben verwendet, gleich ob Kreide oder Öl, und nun wendete er sich diesem flinken, lebendigen Medium zu. Allmählich verloren seine Zeichnungen die Aufgabe, bildhauerische Ideen zu erforschen, sie wurden mehr und mehr zu eingenständigen Werken mit eigenen Gesetzen, welche sich in Richtung Landschaftsmalerei bewegten. Ein Sinn für Form und Tiefe wurde nun kreiert durch die Dichte der farbigen Striche und durch die Verwendung von Linien. Für Draper repräsentierte die Farbe ebenso Energie als auch die potentielle emotionale Stimulierung, die sie auf den Betrachter überträgt. Allmählich wurde sie zum Verbindungsglied zwischen seinen Skulpturen und seinen Zeichnungen.

Draper arbeitete nun in Norfolk, wo er sich in einem alten Pferdestall ein großes Studio eingerichtet hatte. Er verbrachte die erste Hälfte der 80er Jahre damit, seine bildhauerischen Fähigkeiten weiterzuentwickeln und seinen Ruf als ernsthaften Praktiker dieses Mediums zu festigen.

Während er heutzutage für die Mehrheit seiner Bewunderer vor allem ein Maler ist, war er bis zur Mitte der 80er Jahre ausschließlich als Bildhauer bekannt, wenn auch als einer, dessen Arbeiten mehr und mehr "malerisch" wurden und dessen Fähigkeiten als Zeichner stets anerkannt waren. Noch immer aber nahmen seine Zeichnungen einen relativ kleinen Teil seiner Arbeitszeit ein, und sie basierten auch noch nicht eindeutig auf bestimmten Landschaften-geschweige denn solchen, die im Freien, direkt vor dem Objekt sitzend, ausgeführt wurden.

Ein Besuch bei einem Freund in Menorca im September 1985, gemeinsam mit seinem neuen Partner, dem Fotografen Jean Macalpine, markierte einen Wendepunkt. Seine Reaktion auf die urzeitliche Natur dieser kleinen Insel ebnete den Weg für den nachfolgenden Schwerpunktwechsel hin zu Landschaftsmalerei und -zeichnungen.

Es ist schwer, sich nicht in Menorca zu verlieben, vorausgesetzt, man hat vernünftiges Wetter. Obwohl die Insel weniger als 50 km lang ist, findet man dort eine außergewöhnliche Vielfalt an Landschaften, angefangen von sanften Hügeln bis hin zu rauhen, überhängenden Küstenfelsen. Den Naturgewalten ausgesetzte Bäume sind niedergedrückt vom berühmt-berüchtigten "*Tramuntana*"-Wind, der in regelmäßigen Abständen über die Insel fegt. Unter den auffallendsten Merkmalen der Insel sind die riesigen, meist nicht mehr benutzten Steinbrüche und die Schluchten und Bergkämme aus Kalkstein und rotem Sandstein, und alle diese wurden zu reichen Quellen der Inspiration.

Für Ken und Jean war es Liebe auf den ersten Blick, und bald entschlossen sie sich, die Wohnung ihres Freundes zu kaufen. Von den ersten Steinbrüchen waren sie besonders angetan. Die jüngeren, die vielmehr von Maschinen bearbeitet wurden als von Hand, sind noch nicht verwittert und sind von einer butterweißen Farbe, abgesehen von einem langen rötlichen Fleck hier und da, wo erdfarbenes Regenwasser durchgesickert ist. Inspiriert von der Reichhaltigkeit des Sujets, fertigte Draper, als sie einige Monate später zurückkamen, ein paar Pastellzeichnungen an und arbeitete, zum ersten Male in mindestens 20 Jahren, direkt nach dem Vorbild der Natur.

Überhaupt versuchte er von nun an, wenn er *al fresco* arbeitete, sein Objekt an einem einzigen Tag einzufangen. Hauptsächlich ist das eine Frage des Lichtes, welches höchstwahrscheinlich am folgenden Tag völlig anders sein würde. Also fängt Draper den Effekt an einem Tag ein, oder er beginnt von Neuem. Für Arbeiten, die er im Studio anfertigt, braucht er oft viel länger. Ob drinnen oder draußen, die Methode ist dieselbe. Ölpastellfarben werden über Kreide gelegt und umgekehrt, und eine Menge Fixiermittel wird nach jeder Schicht aufgesprüht. Oft kratzt er eine oder zwei Schichten mit dem Fingernagel oder dem Spachtel wieder ab, um diese einzigartigen Effekte von durchscheinendem Licht zu erzielen.

Von Anfang an war es sein Ziel, die Stimmung und die Energie eines Ortes einzufangen und ein empfindliches Gleichgewicht zwischen dem Physikalischen und dem "Seelischen" dieses Ortes zu schaffen. Der großen, romantischen Tradition verbunden, bemerkt er, daß er auf urzeitliche Landschaften am intensivsten reagiert. Rauh, groß, wettergegerbt, der Erosion ausgesetzt: ein Felsen oder Baum, verwittert, auf einer Seite übergebeugt von mächtigen Winden, ein vom Eis zerschnittenes Tal, ein altes Flußbett, eine kleine Bucht am Meer, Felsen, durch die Kraft des Wassers ausgehöhlt, von der heißen Sonne ausgetrocknetes Land, Schlammbänke und Treibsand, zurückgelassen vom sich zurückziehenden Meer oder Flüssen, und Bergwerke und Steinbrüche mit ihrer wundersamen Enthüllung der Präsenz des Menschen.

Während sich Draper mit diesen Pastellzeichnungen auf neuem Terrain bewegte, fuhr er in den späten 80er Jahren auch mit der Bildhauerei fort, wobei er hauptsächlich galvanisierten Stahl verwendete. Dies wurde nun noch offensichtlicher mit Landschaft verbunden, und zwar über die Farbpigment-gefärbte Harzpaste, die er auf die Oberflächen auftrug.

Aber seine bildhauerischen Leistungen sollten—zumindest zeitweise—in den 90er Jahren an Bedeutung verlieren, und das ausgerechnet, ironischerweise, mehr oder weniger von dem Moment an, als er 1990 in die Royal Academy gewählt wurde, und zwar aufgrund seines Rufes als Bildhauers.

Eine ganz unerwartete Wirkung hatten seine Zeichenexpeditionen auf Menorca insofern, als sie eine Rückkehr Drapers zu den Landschaften seiner Kindheit in Yorkshire auslösten. Als er 1990 Grassington in Yorkshire besuchte, begann er, große Gemälde auf Sperrholzplatten anzufertigen, wobei er dieselbe Mischung aus Ölfarben und mit Farbpigmenten versehenem Harz wie schon bei seinen Skulpturen anwendete. Draper selbst sieht diese Gemälde als ein Bindelied zwischen den Pastellzeichnungen und der Bildhauerei. Allerdings nehmen sie nur einen geringen Teil seines Schaffens ein.

Trotz der großen Bedeutung, die Menorca für die beiden Künstler hatte, verbrachten sie zuerst nur etwa drei Monate im Jahr in ihrer kleinen Wohnung dort, ihr Hauptwohnsitz blieb jedoch das große Studio in Norfolk. 1989 verliebten sie sich jedoch dann in eine weitere kleine, wettergegerbte Insel mit vielen Steinbrüchen: Portland, genauer gesagt eine Halbinsel, dank des Dammes, der sie mit dem Festland in Dorset an der Südküste verbindet. Dort mieteten sie ein Landhaus, von wo aus sie die zauberhaftesten Sonnenuntergänge beobachten konnten, die Kenneth je in seinem Leben gesehen hatte.

Eine zweiwöchige Kreuzfahrt auf dem Nil 1992 sollte sich als folgenreich erweisen. Draper war nicht nur von den Tempeln fasziniert, sondern auch von der Horizontalität der Landschaft, mit einem grünen Streifen, der sich über 300 oder 400 Meter zu beiden Seiten des Flusses ausdehnte. Um dies einzufangen, während sie sich geschwind fortbewegten, kehrte er zu seiner alten Technik der Bleistiftzeichnung zurück, welche er als Ausgangspunkt für Pastellzeichnungen und Gemälde benutzte, sobald er wieder nach Portland zurückgekehrt war–ein Vorgehen, das er seitdem auf weiteren Reisen angewendet hat.

Seine auf der Landschaft basierenden Zeichnungen (wie Pastellzeichnungen technisch klassifiziert werden) und Gemälde setzten den Maßtab dafür, daß seine Werke im Mai 1992 für eine Ausstellung in New York ausgewählt wurden, welche den Titel trug: "Der poetische Weg: Aspekte der britischen Abstraktion seit 1945". Sie fand in der Adelson Gallery in der 77. Straße statt. Unter den anderen vertretenen Künstlern waren zum Beispiel Alan Davie, Ben Nicholson und William Scott.

Zwei weitere Aufenthalte erwiesen sich als besonders fruchtbar. Der eine führte ihn 1993 nach Arizona und New Mexico, der andere im darauffolgenden Jahr in die Provence. Als er im November ankam, befand sich der tiefe Westen in der Hand von außergewöhnlich kaltem Wetter. Dem Ausfall eines Fluges nach heftigem Schneefall hatten sie es zu verdanken, daß sie sich spät am Abend ein Zimmer in einem Hotel sichern konnten, von welchem man auf den Grand Canyon blickte. Am folgenden Morgen öffnete Draper die Tür und erwartete, die berühmten Risse und Spalten zu sehen–aber es sah aus wie daheim in Yorkshire, mit einem grauen Dunstschleier über allem. Dann war da plötzlich ein Loch. Ganz allmählich klarte es auf, Schicht für Schicht, und dann brach die Sonne durch. Eine Wolke nach der anderen löste sich am Himmel auf, und es war, so erinnert sich Draper später, als ob sie Gott beim Malen beobachteten.

Später fuhren sie zum Monument Valley, mit seinen enormen landschaftlichen Gegensätzen, mit den gigantischen, purpurnen Felsen, die sich dramatisch aus einer flachen Wüste heraus erheben. Es gab aber noch mehr aufregende Dinge: die Angemalte Wüste, der Versteinerte Wald, der Glockenfelsen in Sedona, und in New Mexico das Tal des Echos und Bandelier Canyon, woraus einige Arbeiten von versengender Intensität resultierten.

Auf der zweiten, gewinnbringenden Reise wohnten sie bei John und Kit Hart, die inzwischen alle ihre Geschäfte abwickelten, in deren Ferienhaus in der Luberon, und Draper war fasziniert von der Schlucht von Verdon (die einzige in Europa mit nordamerikanischen Ausmaßen), von den roten und gelben Ockersteinbrüchen von Roussillon und der geheimnisvollen Aura von Carluc Abbey — sie alle erwiesen sich als inspirierend, trotz des furchtbaren Wetters.

Das war im Oktober 1994, als sie dabei waren, sich letztendlich ganz in Menorca niederzulassen. Ein weiterer Steinbruch auf dieser zauberhaften Insel wurde zu einem geeigneten Ort für diese Würdigung. Er befindet sich nahe der alten Hauptstadt Ciutadella und war einzigartig in seiner Unzugänglichkeit: ein gigantisches, blendend weißes Grabmal, eingeschnitten in ein Feld, der Boden 100 Fuss oder mehr abwärts und nur zugänglich über eiserne Leitern, die an einer Seite nach unten führen.

An einem klaren, schönen Tag barg der Steinbruch nichts als blendendes, reflektiertes Licht in sich, an seinen von Steinsägen zernarbten Wänden von sich langsam bewegenden Schatten arrangiert. Manchmal verbrachte Draper dort einen ganzen Tag damit, in diesen schaurigen, reinweißen Abrund zu starren und versuchte dabei, dieses Wunder vor seinen Augen auf Papier zu bannen.

Nun, am Ende meines siebentägigen Besuches auf Menorca, freute er sich darauf, mir das alles zu zeigen.

Man stelle sich seinen Schock vor, als sich uns, über die den Steinbruch umgebende Mauer gelehnt, ein Bild der Verwüstung bot: in jeder der beiden uns gegenüberliegenden Ecken war Schutt abgeladen worden. Links Schutt vom Steinbruch, beschädigte Kalksteinblöcke und jede Menge weißer Staub; rechts Baustellenschutt, aus welchem eine Menge roher Felsbrocken und ausrangiertes Holz herausragten. Sogar, als wir niedergeschlagen in die Tiefe sahen, wurde die Stille von einem Lastkraftwagen gestört, welcher eine riesige Ladung auf den Baustellenschutt aufschüttete. Die fallenden Felsen zerstörten Bretter aus nicht mehr gebrauchtem Holz, und dieser donnernde Lärm war wahrhaft schockierend.

Etwas beinahe Perfektes war zerstört worden. Jedoch selbst von dieser Szene des Vandalismus begann sich eine Art Schönheit in Kens Gedankenwelt zu entwickeln. Diese “Zwillingshügel” studierend, einer weiße der andere braun, sah er, daß sie nahezu perfekte Kegel formten. Sie waren wie Licht und Schatten — gegensätzlich und doch am Boden schon miteinander verschmelzend. Sie führten seine Gedanken zurück zu den Schlackehügeln, die sich so gewaltig in der Gedanken-wie auch der wirklichen Welt seiner Kindheit auftürmten. Mit all ihrer verborgenen Energie und Gewalt bekräftigten sie Drapers Überzeugung, daß nichts wirklich stirbt, sondern alles wiedergeboren wird. Bald, so überlegte er, würde diese wunderbare, meditative Kammer des Lichts wohl ganz und gar verschwinden, das Feld würde zu seinem Orginalzustand zurückkehren, und Rinder würden hier grasen wie Wolken auf seiner Erinnerung des Raumes. Der Sündenfall wäre letztendlich getilgt.

Es braucht kaum erwähnt zu werden, daß Draper sich zwei Tage später, als er das visuelle und akustische Drama dieses Nachmittags vollständig verarbeitet hatte, daran machte, diese Kegel und die Wirkung, die sie auf ihn hatten, in seiner Arbeit einzufangen. Nach großen Anstrengungen war eine Pastellzeichnung von großer Subtilitat und Schönheit entstanden. Er nannte sie, ihre Bedeutung herunterspielend, “Nachwirkungen”. Über einen scheinbaren Rückschlag hatte Draper einen symbolischen Sieg errungen.

Diese Episode könnte man als einen Mikrokosmos seines ganzen Lebens ansehen, ein Leben, das die Behinderung der leidvollen Kindheitsmonate, die Draper im Krankenhaus zubringen mußte, in eine treibende Kraft verwandelt hat. Drapers Energie und Enthusiasmus sind ansteckend, seine Persönlichkeit ist größer und großzügiger als das Leben selbst. Es ist ungewöhnlich unter Künstlern, wenn er mit Wärme über seine Berufskollegen spricht, unter denen er viele zu seinen Freunden zählt. Seine Offenheit, gepaart mit seiner Begabung als Geschichtenerzähler und einer großen Vielfalt an Interessen bewirken, daß man mit ihm unwahrscheinlich gern seine Zeit verbringt, obwohl diejenigen, welche Umarmungen nicht mögen, lieber etwas auf Distanz bleiben sollten.

Die Großzügigkeit seines Geistes, seine Energie und seine Liebe zum Leben spiegeln sich in seinen Werken wider. Inmitten von so viel Kunst, die aalglatt ist, trügerisch und geistig leer, sind Drapers Arbeiten hinreißend für das Auge und labend für die Seele.

Ich hoffe, daß dieses Buch dazu beitragen wird, daß ein noch größeres Publikum die Freude teilen wird, welche die vielen Bewunderer Kenneth Drapers schon an seinen Werken gefunden haben.

Transicion Capturada
La vida y arte de Kenneth Draper

por Roger Berthoud

Hay una colina cubierta de arbustos, cactus gigantes y aceituneros salvajes situada a unas cuantas yardas de distancia de la casa de Kenneth Draper en la isla de Menorca. Esta colina, como otras tantas encontradas en la isla, está compuesta por piedra caliza donde en sus bordes de color miel se han tallado unos cortes cuadriculados. Son parte de una antigua cantera abandonada, cuyas proporciones y sutiles tonos quitan la respiración a cualquiera. Es como una catedral, con unas grandes columnas excepto que las columnas que se encuentran en estas canteras son más anchas que las que se encuentran en los sitios grandiosos de adoración. La luz sale de las aperturas, las cuales están rodeadas por cactus y arbustos que parecen mirar hacia adentro.

Las paredes de este gran edificio-tal como parece-todavía muestran las marcas que las herramientas usadas rasparon en ellas, en tiempos pre-mecanizados, para tallar las piedras. Donde la luz golpea la superficie los tonos de color miel parecen casi blancos. Más profundamente la humedad ha creado unos tonos verdes sutiles, predominados por un gris cobrizo y palido.

Esta cantera es típica del mundo que Draper ha hecho suyo. Su interior y la vegetación que lo cubre han inspirado un número de sus pasteles que últimamente han sido su principal preocupación. Pero Menorca tiene muchos tesoros similares, como podemos descubrir, y con su inspiración Draper también añade medio siglo de experiencia muy completa que sale de sus numeroso viajes. De su niñez en Yorkshire y Derbyshire hasta la India, Pakistan, Uganda bajando por el Nilo y por desiertos y cañones de Oeste de los Estados Unidos, los desfiladeros de Provence, él ha sacado y enriquezido su sentido de color y forma.

Tanto su trabajo como pintor o como escultor, este artista celebra el mundo natural y especialmente aquellas partes donde el hombre ha dejado su huella. Aunque él está enterado de los conceptos y modos regentes en el mundo internacional del arte, Draper ha abierto tranquilamente su propio camino. De hecho, el historiador británico Frances Spalding cree que la falta de asociados que Draper ha tenido le ha ayudado a obtener un puesto fijo y duradero en el arte británico.

Sus esculturas y colores llamativos con sus burlantes exploraciones del espacio y "trompe l'oeil" son únicas en su interpretación y concepción, tan parecidos a cuadros en algunos aspectos como esculturas. Muchas de esas mismas técnicas son empleadas en sus cuadros hechos en madera, en los cuales las formas esculturales parecen flotar hacia el espectador. Los pasteles, realizados en el mismo paisaje, o en el estudio de bosquejos en lápiz captan su respuesta a la naturaleza en toda su variedad tan rica. De unas vistas patentes y descriptivas de una cascada o una colina a unas destilaciones casi abstractas inspiradas por el mar, unas rocas, la bruma, o una puesta de sol siguen una gran tradición de la pintura de paisajes en el estilo inglés y particularmente de estilo de Turner, a veces con colores brillantes y apasionadamente intensos, captando suavemente una colina envuelta por la bruma, a veces por contraste casi estilo Klee y alegres en su equilibrio de las formas.

Muestran humor y luz con muchas niveles de sutileza. Aquí, la luz parece brillar por donde se ha raspado un nivel para mostrar lo que yace debajo. Allí una zona rica en efectos texturales quita la vista del punto central de la obra. Estos pasteles no son tan visuales sino líricos, himnos dedicados a la riqueza del mundo. Sin embargo un tipo de tensión mantiene una simple provacación apartada y los mantiene vitales, misteriosos y lentamente rinden su riqueza total.

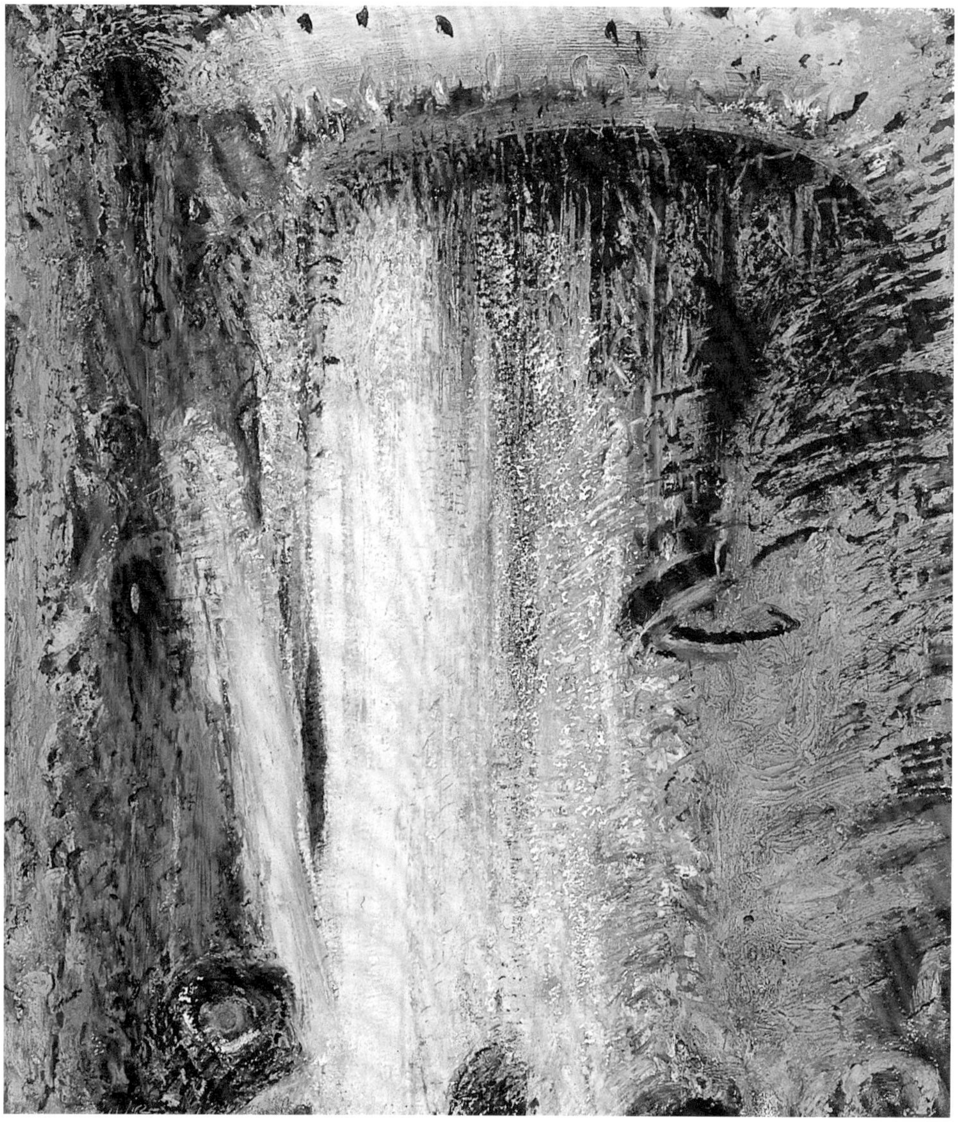

High Fall, Falaise de Buoux 1995
Pastel on Paper
16 × 14 inches (40 × 35 cm)

Kenneth Draper el más joven de tres hijos, nació en 1944 en el pueblo minero del Norte, Killamarsh, cerca de Sheffield en Yorkshire. Su padre Albert Draper, trabajó en la mina local desde una temprana edad (de once años hasta) los sesenta y cinco y poseía un gran talento para el dibujo. Su madre, de soltera Dorothy Lamb, procede de una próspera familia de carniceros de Gainsborough, Lincolnshire. Toda la familia tenía un talento musical. "Nuestro Ken" como le llamaba su madre, empezó a aprender a tocar la corneta y el piano cuando era un niño, pero pronto el arte empezó a tener un lugar predominante en su vida. Se dió cuenta de su talento para el dibujo a una temprana edad de siete años, cuando dibujó un cuadro de una cuadriga romana con sus caballos.

Poco después, cuando tenía ocho años, sus padres fueron avisados que su hijo tenía un caso sospechoso de espina tuberculosa. Durante ocho meses estuvo metido en cama en el hospital de Rivelin Valley en las afueras de Sheffield, siempre boca arriba y atado, su cabeza puesta en un collarín suprimida con dos tablas a cada lado de su cabeza y con unas pesas colgando detrás de su cabeza que la mantenían completamente inmovil. Cuando se recuperó tuvo que aprender a caminar de nuevo, una experiencia que le dió en cuestión de equilibrio una preocupación por vida como artista.

Es imposible averiguar si Draper hubiera llegado a ser artista si no hubiera tendio que aguantar aquellos ocho meses tan traumaticos y debilitadores tumbado de espaldas. El talento siempre estaba allí pero gracias a toda la atención que recibió, especialmente de su inspirada profesora de arte de su escuela Jean Arblaster, le proporcionó un gran sentido de ser diferente, incluso especial.

Sus primeros dibujos eran del extraordinario paisaje que le rodeaba con el hermoso equipo de la mina y unos conos enormes de escoria. Por allí subían unas pequeñas vagonetas que constantemente añadían más escoria a los piramides. Se quedó fascinado por estos traslados tan extraños.

Se trasladó de la escuela secundaria al Colegio Mayor de Arte de Chesterfield, el cuál era pequeño y le venía de percas. Después de tres años de duro trabajo estudiando pintura y escultura, se trasladó a Londres y pasó tres anõs en el Colegio Mayor de Arte de Kingston, donde empezó con la pintura y luego la escultura, entonces pasó tres años más en el departamento de escultura del mismo colegio.

Allí en Kingston desarrolló el concepto de la imagen o figura transitoria, entrando y saliendo de un contexto estático, que durante años le traería de cabeza. También en esta época de mostrar que el espacio era algo que vivía y se movía con su propia fuerza, y que no tenía menos importancia que aquellos objetos que se encontraban en ello. Muchos de sus dibujos de habitaciones y algunas de sus cuadros resultaron y fueron realizados de varios ángulos y generalmente con presencia humana. En su último anõs allí, realizó varias esculturas sustanciales.

Llegó al Colegio Mayor Royal en Octubre de 1965, Draper realizó solo cuatro piezas, todas muy grandes y complejas, y pasó mucho tiempo pintándolas y luego volvió a repintarlas. La primera, con el título de "ARENA", le llevó un año y medio para realizarla y fue expuesta por primera vez en la exposición de Redfern en 1968. La segunda, "TRES MARCOS" dió la sensación que algo se movía entre su marco de madera. Cuando realizó este cuadro Draper se dió cuenta que si dejaba pistas en la parte delantera del cuadro el espectador podía a traves de un tipo de falsa esperanza encontrar lo que quedaba al otro lado, y entonces encontraría un sentido de sorpresa y misterio basados en la memoria.

Con la llegada de su graduación, cogió un trabajo de tiempo parcial como profesor trabajando un día a la semana en el Colegio Mayor de Arte de Hornsey en el norte de Londres. Ya que no era mucho mayor que sus propios alumnos, formó una gran relación con ellos, cosa que no lograría en otras ocasiones cuando fuera mayor. Los estudiantes a menudo le visitaban en el estudio que él tenía alquilado en el barrio de Borough Market, al sur del London Bridge. La enseñanza le ayudó a clarificar sus ideas, hablar con un estudiante un día y el día después trabajar en su estudio le enseñó de repente que él compartía los mismos problemas que sus alumnos.

El año siguiente 1969 llegó su debut en la Galería de Arte de Redfern en el West End de Londres, donde la Asamblea del Arte, un patrón público muy influyente compró dos de sus grandes esculturas en este mismo año viajó a la India y a Pakistan, aquel viaje tendría un impacto duradero en su trabajo. En el norte de Bombay no muy lejos de Aurangabad en el estado de Maharashtra, visitó las asombrosas cuevas que eran templos de Ellora y Ajanta talladas de solida roca y que representaban las cimas de la escultura y pinturas rupestres de Hindú y Budismo. Después de haber visitado el Taj Mahal en Agra, cruzó hasta Pakistan donde la atracción era la ciudad excavada de Mohenjodaro, que una vez formó parte de la civilización extraordinariamente sofisticada del valle de Indus que existió entre 2500–1800 AC. Volando por encima de Pakistan en un pequeño aeroplano le dió a Draper su primera experiencia de un caleidoscopio de un paisaje visto desde una altura baja.

Entre todas las impresiones sacadas de acquel viaje, la más notable fue la manera especialmente en la India que la arquitectura parecía surtir de la tierra: el paisaje y los templos se respondían mutuamente como un eco, formando un total orgánico, con el color como parte integral de la forma. Otra impresión que le causó asombro fue la manera en que los extremos de la luz y la sombra hacían que los objetos sólidos tomaron otra forma, un efecto que más tarde usaria en sus esculturas. También él adquirió un nuevo sentido de espacio y apertura, que el año siguiente usaria en sus enormes piezas sobre muros colgados del techo.

En su primera visita en Abril/Mayo a los Estado Unidos, gracias al Premio Memorial de Mark Rothko, algunas de las impresiones fueron más reforzadas. Su viaje de siete semanas, el itinerario del cuál fue organizado por el secretariado del Premio, le llevó a Nueva York, Boston, Washington, Philadelphia, Chicago, San Francisco y Los Angeles en un época ideal de año.

Aquí se encontró en el centro de una cultura vibrante cuyos pintores habían superado durante más de un cuarto de siglo a París y a una larga y duradera posición como punto focal del Arte Contemporáneo. Draper ya era un admirador ferviente de Rothko, Pollock y Jasper Johns. Ahora que se encontraba en América encontró que su aprecio y comprensión de otros artistas entraba en otra dimensión. En Nueva York conoció a Helen Frankenthaler y a la viuda de Pollock, Lee Krasner Pollock, y en California entre otros a Richard Diebenkorn.

Este sentido de revelación no estaba limitado al arte americano. Los grandes museos virtualmente en cada ciudad que visitaba, tenían mucha más materia de arte europea desde los Impresionistas hasta entonces que cualquier museo británico. Aquellas semanas en los USA tan excitantes enriquecieron sus concocimientos y experiencia visual de los cuales su trabajo de madurez crecería. Su efecto inmediato, él cree, era cambiar su sentido de escala e incrementar su poder y la intensidad de su trabajo.

Hubo evidencia de esta evolución en las grandes piezas sobre muro para colgar en el techo que había realizado para una exposición de escultura contemporánea en la Real Academia en Picadilly en Enero de 1972, donde tenía una sala para él solo. La más grande de estas piezas estaba previsto que flotara por encima del espectador, desafiando la gravedad y dando una sensación de espacio y amplios horizontes. Vista de lejos parecía casi llana. Pero cuando el espectador se acercaba a ella se ampliaba y se abría, adquiriendo de esta manera una calidad ilusoria como el artista había procurado mostrar.

Las primeras grandes piezas se trataban en su propia manera de hechos y encuentros, cada una dentro de una estructura individual. Debían algo para minimalizar la preocupación con cajas y estructuras modulares, y también a la exploración del espacio de Anthony Caro. Draper buscaba la manera de ir más

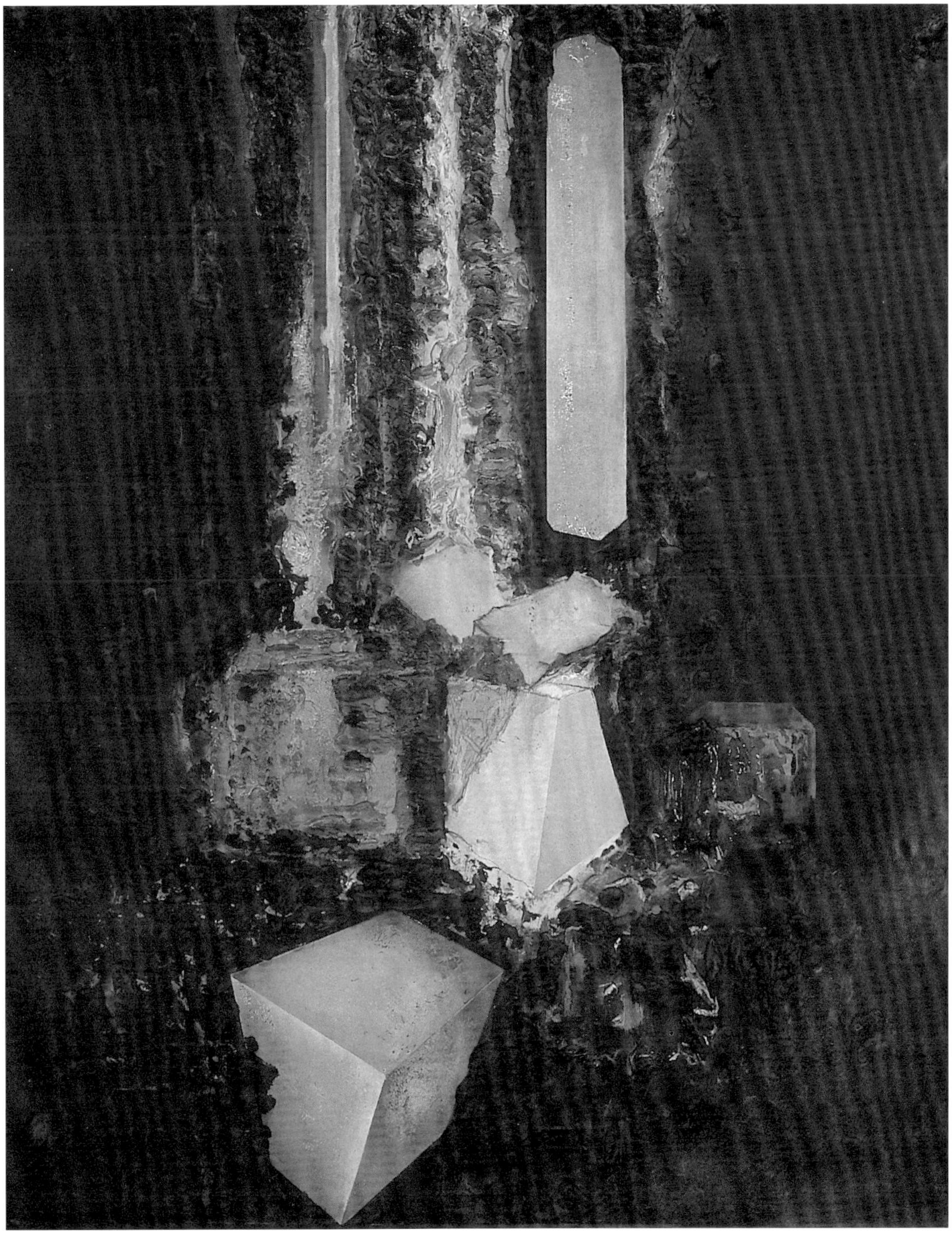

Excavation 1993
Oil and Pigment on Wood
48 × 42 inches (122 × 107 cm)

lejos de la noción de la escultura como un objeto sencillo; aquí que se encuentran esos complots tan ordenados pero al mismo tiempo complejos para sorprender al espectador y engañar al ojo cuando se acercaba o se ponía debajo o giraba a su alrededor de cada pieza.

Alrededor del 1975 su propio trabajo atravesó una metamorfosis hacia obras que incluían un tema de la mar. Estaba harto de pasar tanto tiempo con un gran encargo del Politecnico de Machester, decidió en 1975 concentrarse y destilar su trabajo, por éso empezó a realizar obras más pequeñas. Entre esta encontraban una serie de piezas sobre muros, casi en forma de cajas, diminutas y muy cargadas de unas seis pulgadas de longitud, minimales solo en escala ya que eran basadas en paisajes y sacando mucho de su poder de sus superficies encrustadas y sus brillantes colores. Draper las imaginaba como pegeñas bombas ya que estaban tan concentradas.

Anteriormente él había trabajado principalmente con madera, a la cuál añadía una capa de pintura sombria. Ahora, por contraste mezclaba un pigmento puro de color a sus materiales. Normalmente resina o yeso que luego pegaba a unas superficies de madera o acero. Como en su memoria de la India, el color llegaba a ser parte de la forma, en vez de ser solamente superimpuesto sobre ellas.

Éstas y las pequeñas liezas de cajas fueron incluídas en su segunda muestra el la Galería de Redfern en 1978. Había unos cuantos más de sus antiguos trabajos, esencialmente lineales, incluyendo un encargo para la Universidad de Bradford que basadas en su experiencias en la India y que el artista tardó otra vez casi un año para completarlo antes de su installación en Octubre de 1980. Pero Draper ya estaba bien situado en el camino de los cuadros orientados en paisajes que lleva siguiendo en varios estilos.

Asociados con estos desarrollos llegó otro cambio signifcante. Hasta mediados de los años setenta él había usado sus dibujos hechos con lápiz para explorar sus ideas de escultura montados en un profundo espacio además de sus apuntes de paisajes encontrados en sus viajes. Ahora que estaba produciendo unas esculturas más pequeñas, que se podian hacer y cambiar con relativa rápidez, descubría que quería explorar en sus dibujos ideas que salían al pensar en sus esculturas.

Ya que el color jugaba un papel tan integral en esas obras, los dibujos deberían de ser lógicamente en color. Desde sus comienzos siempre le había gustado usar pasteles, de las variedades de tiza o oleo y se integró en este medio tan veloz e intenso. Gradualmente sus dibujos llegaban a ser menos exploratorios en las ideas de la escultura para ser trabajos más compuestos por derecho propio, inclinados en la dirección de paisajes. Creó un sentido de forma y profundidad por la densidad de las machas oscuras además del uso de lineas. Para Draper el color representaba energia además de la carga emocional que daba al espectador. Cada vez más llegó a ser el enlace entre sus esculturas y sus dibujos.

Trabajando en Norfolk, donde había creado un gran estudio en unos antigua establos y salidas de enseñanza, hacia Londres Draper pasó los primeros cinco años de los ochenta desarrollando su escultura y consolidando su reputación como un practicante original y genuino en aquel medio. Aunque para mucho de sus admiradores él es hoy, primero y ante todo, pintor, sin embargo hasta medianos de los ochenta fue conocido exclusivamente como escultor. No obstante un escultor cuyo trabajo empezaba a ser casi como la pintura y cuyas habilidades como delineante siempre habían sido reconocidos. Sus obras todavía ocupaban una parte pequeña de sus energias y aún no estaban abiertamente basadas en paisajes especifícos y por supuesto no ejeculados afuera o delante del tema.

Una visita a una casa de un amigo en Menorca en el mes de Septiembre de 1985 con su pareja, la fotógrafa Jean Macalpine, sería un punto de cambio. Su reacción a la naturaleza no estropeada de esta pequeña isla le prepara el camino para el consiguiente cambio de enfasis hacia la pintura y dibujo de paisajes.

No es difícil quedarse prendado de Menorca, si uno tiene suerte con el tiempo meteorologico. Aunque la isla tiene menos de 30 millas de longitud, contiene una variedad extraordinaride terreno, desde unos prados suavemente ondulados hasta unos acantilados costales muy desigual, arboles doblados por el feroz viento "La Tramontana" que periodicamente sopla con una gran fuerza. Entre los rasgos más llamativos de la isla uno encuentra varias canteras abandonadas de caliza y sus cimeras y desfiladeros de caliza y sus piedras de arena rojiza, todas estas cosas le serían unas ricas fuentes de inspiración.

Para Ken y Jean fué un caso de amor a primera vista, y pronto decidieron comprar el apartamento de su amigo. Se quedaron prendados particularmente con las primeras canteras que descubrieron. La mayoria de éstas están abiertas al cielo. Las más recientes, tallados con una maquina en vez de a mano, todavía no muestran el paso del tiempo y se han quedado de un color blanco amarillento excepto por una mancha, de vez en cuando, larga y rojiza, donde el agua pluvial ha caído. Draper inspirado por la riqueza de la materia, cuando volvió unos meses después sacó un conjunto de pasteles y trabajó directamente con la naturaleza, cosa que no había hecho durante más de veinte años.

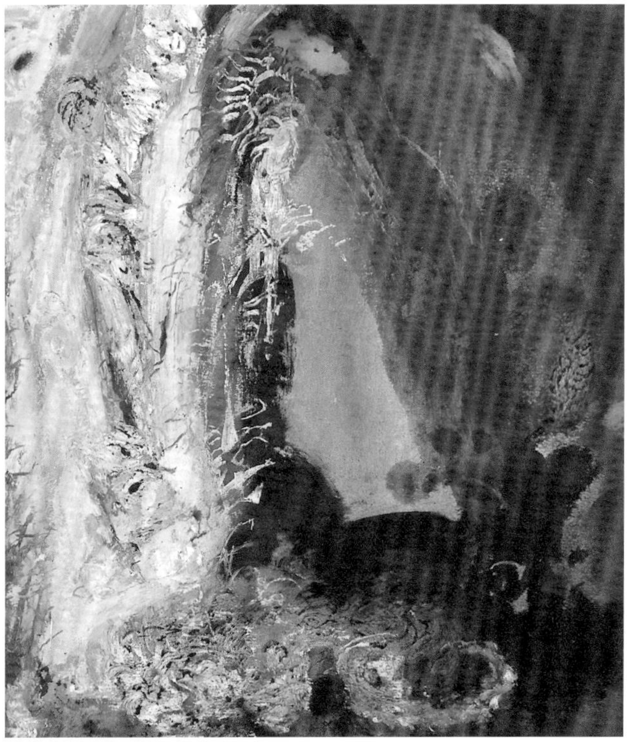

Cave, Golden Light 1996
Pastel on Paper
16 × 14 inches (41 × 36 cm)

Generalamente a partir de entonces, intentó captar su tema en un solo dia cuando trabajaba al aire libre "alfresco" como él lo llama. Principalmente es una cuestión de luz. Probablemente el día siguiente encontraría bastante diferencia del día anterior: o fue capaz de captar el efecto en un día o lo volvía a empezar. En cambio un trabajo hecho en el estudio sobre papel, le llevaba más tiempo aunque a veces el papel no dejaba de aceptar más y se daba por perdido. Dentro o afuera, el metodo es el mismo. Pasteles de oleo están colocados encima de pasteles de tiza y vice versa, con una pulveración de fijador después de cada aplicación. Con frecuencia el artista raspa una o dos capas con una uña o con una espátula para crear esos efectos únicos de luz que las traspasan.

Desde un principio su propósito era captar el espíritu y las energias en un lugar en particular, y hallar un balance entre lo espiritual y lo fisico. Siguiendo la gran tradición Romantica, él conoce que él responde mejor a paisajes rústicos, ásperos y accidentados golpeados por el tiempo, erosionados; sea un árbol inclinado golpeado por unos vientos predominantes o unas rocas gastadas por un lado después de haber sido golpeadas por la mar, una entrada de un río, una cala al lado del mar, tierra secada y agrietada por el caluroso sol, bancos de barro y cieno dejado por las mareas, minas y canteras con surevelación mágica de la presencia del hombre.

Entrando en un nuevo terreno con estos pasteles, Draper continuó esculpiendo sus esculturas durante los últimos años de los ochenta, empleando principalmente acero galvanizado enrollado. Esto se hacía más claramente relacionado a paisajes a traves de la pasta de resina pigmentada con color que el artista fijaba al superficie. Pero su producción de esculturas iba a descender, al menos temporalmente, en los años noventa, ironicamente, más o menos desde el momento que fue elegido Academico Real en el año 1990, gracias a su reputación como escultor.

Un efecto inesperado de sus expediciones de dibujo al aire libre en Menorca le iba a desencadenar un retorno a los paisajes de su niñez de su lugar natal de Yorkshire. Durante un visita en 1990 a Grasington, Yorkshire, empezó a realizar unos cuadros grandes pintados sobre unos paneles de madera contrachapada, usando la misma mezcla de pintura al oleo y resina coloreada con un pigmento que él aplicaba a sus esculturas. Draper concibe estos cuadros como un enlcae entre los pasteles y sus esculturas. Pero han formado solo una pequeña parte de su producción.

Aunque Menorca les empezaba a proponer un gran importancia en sus vidas, solamente pasaban unos tres meses al año allí en su pequeño apartamento, y seguían estando basados en su gran estudio en Norfolk. Entonces en 1989 se quedaron prendados por otra pequeña isla, golpeada por el mar y el viento, y extraida: Portland, casi una peninsula gracias a una elevada que lo junta con Dorset en la costa Sur. Allí alquilaron una casita, desde donde podían contemplar las puestas de sol más magníficas que Ken jamás había visto.

Era una medida de la marca que los dibujos basados en paisajes dejaban (como los pasteles están tecnicamente clasificados) y cuadros de su trabajo que deberían de haber sido incluídos en una exposición en Nueva York en Mayo de 1992 titulada: El Vestigio Poetico: Aspectos de la Abstracción Británica desde 1945, que se celebró en las Galerías de Adelson en la calle 77. Otros artistas incluídos fueron Alan Davie, Ben Nicholson y William Scott.

Un crucero por el Nilo de dos semanas en el otoño de 1992 resultó seminal. Draper quedó prendado no solo por los templos sino por la horizontalidad de los paisajes, con una linea verde que avanzaba tres o cuatrocientas yardas a cada orilla del río. Para captar éso mientras viajaban tan rápidamente, volvió a practicar su antigua manera de hacer dibujos con lápiz, que luego usaba para empezar su cuadros de pasteles cuando regresaba a su casa de Portland, una técnica que adoptó en sus siguientes viajes.

Dos otras salidas fueron especialmente fructíferas. Una era a Arizona y Nuevo Mejico en 1993 y la otra fué a Provence al año siguiente. Cuando llegaron en Noviembre el pofundo Oeste estaba envuelto por un tiempo excepcionalmente frío. Gracias a una cancellación de último momento, debido a una gran nevada, pudieron asegurar tener una habitación en el hotel que daba al Gran Cañón. A la mañana siguiente ellos abrieron la puerta con esperanzas de ver la famosa grieta, y se parecía a Yorkshire, todo cubierto por una bruma gris. De repente apareció un agujero. Gradualmente se empezaba a despejar, capa tras capa, y salió el sol. Una nube tras otra se lenantaba hacia el cielo, y a Draper le dió la impresión que era como mirar a Díos pintando.

Más tarde fueron al Valle Mountain, una antítesis pintoresca, con rocas gigantescas de color púrpura, saliendo dramaticamente de un desierto llano. Había más sorpresas, El Desierto Pintado "The Painted Desert" y El Bosque Petrificado "The Petrified Forest" La Roca Campana "The Bell Rock" en Sedona y en Nuevo Mejico el Cañón el Eco y El Cañón Bandolero, que le ayudaron a realizar algunos trabajos con una gran intensidad.

En su segundo viaje de gran rendimiento se hospedaron con John y Kit Hart, quienes ya eran sus agentes comercíales, en su casa de vacaciones en el Luberon, a Draper le llamó la atención el desfiladero de Verdon (el único cañón europeo con tamaño norteamericano) con sus canteras rojizas y ocres amarillentados de Rousillon y el aura mistica de la Abadía de Carluc, que le inspiraron aunque el tiempo fuera tan pésimo.

Ésto fue en Octubre de 1994 cuando se iban a instalar definitivamen en Menorca. Otra cantera en esta encantada isla le seria un lugar apropiado parta terminar ese aprecio. Está situada cerca de la antigua capital de Ciutadella y fue única en absoluto por su inaccesibilidad una tumba gigante blanca y deslumbrante tallada en un prado, su suelo a unos cien pies más abajo al cuál uno solo podía llegar con la ayuda de unos peldaños de hierro situados en uno de sus lados.

En un dia de buen tiempo sostenía una luz deslumbrante que reflejaba en sus paredes verticales y marcadas por una sierra, causando unas sombras que se movían lentamente. Draper a veces pasario un día entero observando este espacio de un puro blanco casi escalofriante, intentando captar su magia en la hoja que tenía delante de él. Ahora hacia el final de mi visita de siete dias él esperaba con ilusión enseñármelo.

Imagínensé su horror, cuando apoyados en una pared de piedra que rodeaba la cantera, conteplandola vimos una escena de profanación. En cada una de las dos esquinas frente a nosotros se habían vertido unos escombros, a nuestra izquierda escombros de la cantera compuesto de bloques de caliza dañados y una enorme cantidad de polvo blanco, a la derecha unos escombros de unos constructores donde se encontraban unas rocas y trozos de madera desechados. Incluso mientras que mirábamos hacia abajo, el silencio fue roto por el sonido de un camión descargando una gran carga encima del montón de los constructores. Cuando las rocas que caían sobre los paneles de madera el sonido de los golpes causaba un gran estruendo, que era de lo más espantoso.

Algo casi perfecto había sido destruído. Pero incluso de esta escena dejada por un acto de vandalismo, un tipo de belleza empezó a formarse en la mente de Ken. Estudiando los dos pilotes gemelos, uno blanco y el otro marrón, él veía que formaban unos conos casi perfectos. Eran la luz y la oscuridad, contrarios directos que ya se unían al fondo. Se acordaba de los conos de escoria que surgían tan grandes en los paisajes físicos y mentales de su niñez. Con toda su energia latente y violencia confirmaban la convicción de Draper que nada muere de verdad sino que todo renace. Pronto él reflejó que la maravillosa camara de luz llegaría a desparecer por completo. El prado volvería a su estado original y el ganado pasturaría como nubes arriba de su memoria del espacio. Por fin LA CAIDA sería cumplida.

No es necesario explicar que dos dias más tarde, cuando él había asimilado totalmente los dramas aurales y visuales, se puso a trabajar para captar esos conos y el impacto que le habían causado. Después de mucho trabajo salió un cuadro en pastel de gran belleza y sutileza él lo llamó, no señalado, "AFTERMATH" "SECUELAS". De un aparente contratiempo Draper había marcado una victoria simbólica.

Este episodio podía haber sido considerado como un microcosmo de su vida en si, una vida que ha transformado la menusvalía de aquellos meses de su niñez de sufrimiento con la cabeza oprimida en una fuerza propulsante. La energia y entusiasmo de Draper siguen siendo contagiosos, su personalidad es más grande y más generosa que la vida en si. Él es inusual entre artistas cuando habla con cariño sobre sus compañeros del arte, entre los cuales tiene muchos amigos. Su franqueza combinada con sus dones como anecdotista, y a una amplia gama de entusiasmo le hacen una copañia excepcionalmete agradable, aunque aquellas personas a las cuales no les gustan ser abrazadas, deberían mantenerse lejos de él. Su generosidad de espíritu su energia y su amor por la vida están reflejados en su trabajo. Entre tanto arte que es meretricios, egañoso y espiritualmente vacío, Draper está produciendo un trabajo que cautiva el ojo y llena el alma. Espero que este libro ayude a un público más amplio a compartir el placer que muchos de sus admiradores ya han encontrado en sus obras.

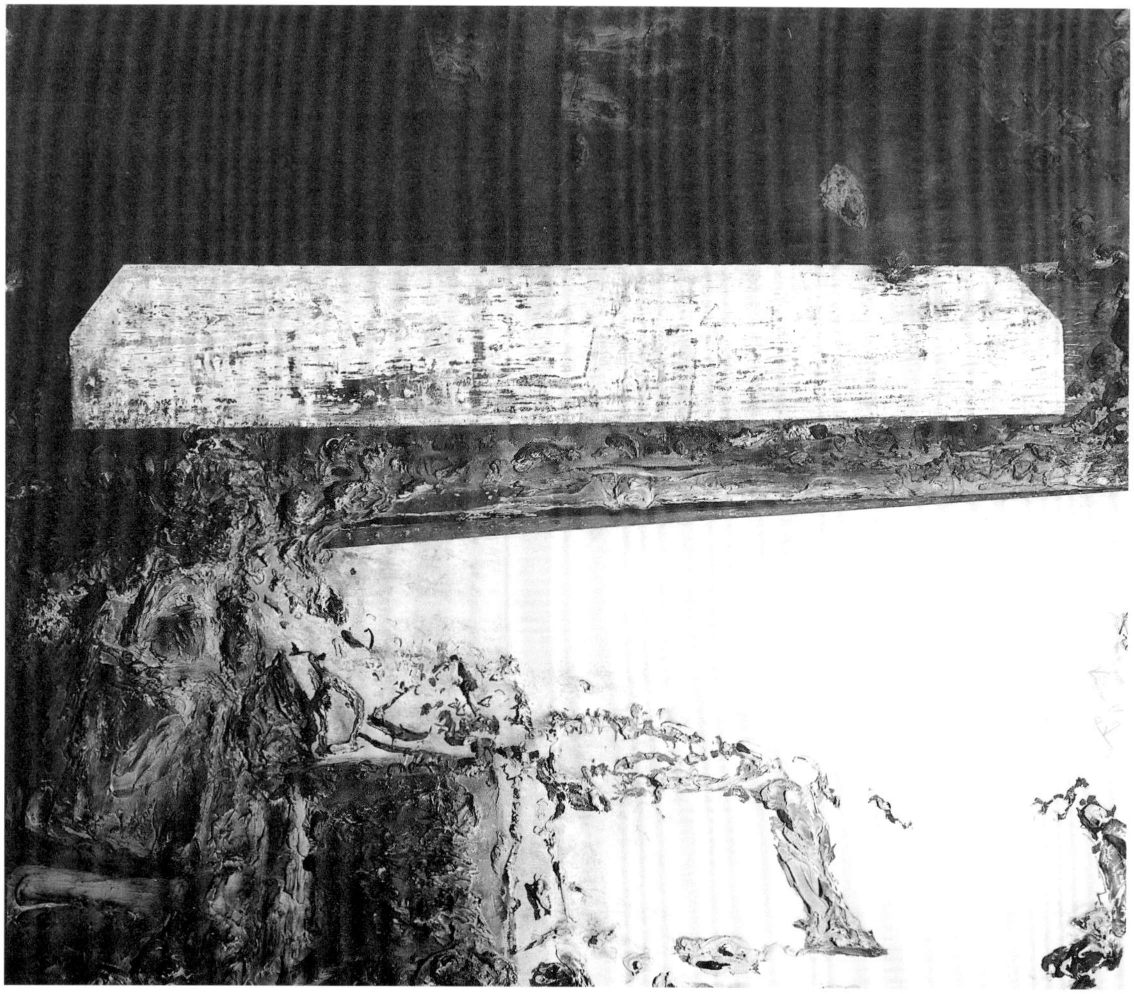

Overlay 1993
Oil and Pigment on Wood
42 × 48 inches (107 × 122 cm)

List of Colour Plates
Farbbilder
Lista de las Ilustraciones de color

Plate 1
Yellow Composition 1964
Komposition in Gelb 1964
Composición amarilla 1964
Gouache on Paper
$8\frac{1}{4} \times 6\frac{3}{4}$ inches (22 × 17 cm)

Plate 2
Evolve 1964
Entwicklung 1964
Evolución 1964
Wood, Glass, Steel, Paper, Oil Pigment
48 × 36 × 12 inches (122 × 90 × 30 cm)

Plate 3
Passages 1964
Übergänge 1964
Pasillos 1964
Gouache and Pencil on Paper
$8\frac{3}{4} \times 14$ inches (22 × 35 cm)

Plate 4
Second Implication 1970
Zweite Bedeutung 1970
Segunda implicación 1970
Pastel on Paper
20 × 28 inches (51 × 71 cm)

Plate 5
Overhang V Sounds 1971
Überhang versus Klänge 1971
Sonidos colgantes V 1971
Wood, Steel and Oils
15 × 16 × 28 feet (457 × 488 × 584 cm)

Plate 6
Foundation 1975
Fundament 1975
Fundación 1975
Mixed Media
5 × 7 × 5 inches (12 × 18 × 12 cm)

Plate 7
Blue Enclosure 1978
Blaues Grundstück 1978
Envuelto en azul 1978
Pastel on Paper
30 × 44 inches (76 × 112 cm)

Plate 8
Blue Veil 1984
Blauer Schleier 1984
El velo azul 1984
Steel, Resin, Oil Pigment
$23\frac{1}{2} \times 7 \times 23\frac{1}{2}$ inches (59 × 12 × 59 cm)

Plate 9
Ascend 1981
Aufstieg 1981
La Subida 1981
Aluminium, Resin, Oil Pigment
19 × 22 × 9 inches (48 × 56 × 23 cm)

Plate 10
February 1988
Februar 1988
Febrero 1988
Pastel on Paper
12 × 14 inches (30 × 35 cm)

Plate 11
Monks Moor 1988
Das Mönchsmoor 1988
El Prado de los Frailes 1988
Pastel on Paper
$18 \times 19\frac{1}{2}$ inches (46 × 49 cm)

Plate 12
Glacier 1989
Gletscher 1989
Glaciar 1989
Pastel on Paper
16 × 14 inches (41 × 35 cm)

Plate 13
Mountain 1989
Berg 1989
Montaña 1989
Steel, Wood, Resin, Oil Pigment
$29 \times 30 \times 6\frac{1}{2}$ inches (74 × 76 × 16 cm)

Plate 14
November 1990
November 1990
Noviembre 1990
Pastel, Pigment on Wood
16 × 14 inches (41 × 36 cm)

Plate 15
Distant Fall 1991
Fall in der Ferne 1991
Caída Distante 1991
Pastel, Pigment, Mixed Media on Wood
16 × 14 inches (41 × 36 cm)

Plate 16
Dark Lagoon 1992
Dunkle Lagune 1992
El Lago oscuro 1992
Pastel on Paper
16 × 14 inches (41 × 36 cm)

Plate 17
Quarry, St Austell 1990
Steinbruch, St Austell 1990
Cantera, St Austell 1990
Pastel on Paper
20 × 18 inches (51 × 46 cm)

Plate 18
Dark Interlude 1992
Dunkles Zwischenspiel 1992
Intermedio oscuro 1992
Pastel on Paper
26 × 22 inches (66 × 56 cm)

Plate 19
Impact 1991
Wirkung 1991
Impacto 1991
Pastel on Paper
16 × 14 inches (41 × 36 cm)

Plate 20
Dark Edge 1992
Dunkler Rand 1992
El borde oscuro 1992
Pastel on Paper
20 × 18 inches (51 × 46 cm)

Plate 21
Gordale Double Image 1992
Doppelbildnis 1992
Imagen Doble de Gordale 1992
Pastel on Paper
26 × 22 inches (66 × 56 cm)

Plate 22
Light Fall 1993
Lichtfall 1993
Caida Ligera 1993
Mixed Media on Wood
48 × 42 inches (122 × 107 cm)

Plate 23
Stones 1990
Steine 1990
Piedras 1990
Pastel on Paper
26 × 22 inches (66 × 56 cm)

Plate 24
Awakening 1992
Erwachen 1992
El despertar 1992
Pastel and Pigment on Wood
42 × 48 inches (107 × 122 cm)

Plate 25
Spring Tide 1984
Springflut 1984
Marea primaveral 1984
Steel, Resin, Oil Pigment
30 × 22 × 12 inches (76 × 56 × 30 cm)

Plate 26
Vessel 1991
Gefäß 1991
Barco 1991
Pastel on Paper
14 × 16 inches (36 × 41 cm)

Plate 27
Eclipsed Labyrinths 1978
Labyrints im Schatten 1978
Laberintos eclipsados 1978
Wood, Concrete, Resin, Oil Pigment
20 × 20 × 20 inches (51 × 51 × 51 cm)

Plate 28
Reflections on a Quiet Place 1992
Reflektionen an einem ruhigen Ort 1992
Reflexiones de un lugar tranquilo 1992
Pastel, Pigment, Mixed Media on Wood
48 × 42 inches (122 × 107 cm)

Plate 29
High Ledge, Falaise de Buoux, Provence 1994
Hoher Fenstersims, Falaise de Buoux, Provence 1994
Desfiladero Alto, Falaise de Buoux, Provence 1994
Pastel on Paper
20 × 18 inches (51 × 46 cm)

Plate 30
Divided Encounter 1990
Geteilte Begegnung 1990
Encuentro dividido 1990
Pastel on Paper
20 × 18 inches (51 × 46 cm)

Plate 31
Divided Encounter 1978
Geteilte Begegnung 1978
Encuentro dividido 1978
Steel, Wood, Resin, Oil Pigment
22 × 28 × 10 inches (56 × 71 × 25 cm)

Plate 32
Stones 1992
Steine 1992
Piedras 1992
Pastel, Pigment, Mixed Media on Wood
48 × 42 inches (122 × 107 cm)

Plate 33
Light Quarry 1994
Heller Steinbruch 1994
Cantera con luz 1994
Oil and Pigment on Wood
42 × 48 inches (107 × 122 cm)

Plate 34
Blue Stone 1993
Blauer Stein 1993
Piedra azul 1993
Oil and Pigment on Wood
42 × 48 inches (107 × 122 cm)

Plate 35
Evening Quarry 1993
Steinbruch am Abend 1993
Cantera al atardecer 1993
Oil and Pigment on Wood
21 × 26 inches (53 × 66 cm)

Plate 36
Mirage 1993
Luftspiegelung 1993
Espejismo 1993
Mixed Media on Wood
26 × 22 inches (66 × 56 cm)

Plate 37
Transient Light 1993
Vergängliches Licht 1993
Luz transiente 1993
Mixed Media on Wood
26 × 22 inches (66 × 56 cm)

Plate 38
Light Through Dark 1993
Licht durch Dunkelheit 1993
Luz a traves de la oscuridad 1993
Pastel, Pigment, Mixed Media on Wood
48 × 42 inches (122 × 107 cm)

Plate 39
Darkness and Light 1993–4
Dunkelheit und Licht 1993–4
Oscuridad y luz 1993–4
Oil and Pigment on Wood
48 × 42 inches (122 × 107 cm)

Plate 40
Sunset, Pricili 1994
Sonnenuntergang, Pricili 1994
Puesta del sol, Pricili 1994
Pastel on Paper
13¾ × 11½ inches (35 × 29 cm)

Plate 41
Night Fall 1994
Nachteinbruch 1994
La caida de la noche 1994
Pastel on Paper
14 × 16 inches (36 × 41 cm)

Plate 42
Light Through Dark (The Fall) 1990
Licht durch Dunkelheit 1990
Luz a traves de la oscuridad (La Caida)1990
Steel, Wood, Resin
50 × 40 × 24 inches (127 × 112 × 61 cm)

Plate 43
High Fall 1994
Fall aus der Höhe 1994
La Alta caida 1994
Pastel on Paper
34 × 29 inches (86 × 74 cm)

Plate 44
First Snow, Arizona 1994
Erster Schnee, Arizona 1994
La Primera nieve, Arizona 1994
Pastel on Paper
14 × 16 inches (36 × 41 cm)

Plate 45
Monument Rock, Arizona 1994
Monument Felsen, Arizona 1994
Monument Rock, Arizona 1994
Pastel on Paper
20 × 18 inches (51 × 46 cm)

Plate 46
Nile Temple 1993
Tempel am Nil 1993
El Templo del Nilo 1993
Pastel on Paper
18 × 20 inches (46 × 51 cm)

Plate 47
Valley of The Kings, Egypt 1994
Das Tal der Könige, Ägypten 1994
El Valle de los Reyes, Egipto 1994
Pastel on Paper
22 × 26 inches (56 × 66 cm)

Plate 48
High Cave, Evening 1995
Hohe Höhle, Abend 1995
La Alta cueva, atardecer 1995
Pastel on Paper
20 × 18 inches (51 × 46 cm)

Plate 49
High Cave, First Light 1995
Hohe Höhle, Erstes Licht 1995
La Alta cueva, primera luz 1995
Pastel on Paper
20 × 18 inches (51 × 46 cm)

Plate 50
Rustrel 1995
Rustrel 1995
Rustrel 1995
Pastel on Paper
14 × 16 inches (36 × 41 cm)

Plate 51
Rustrel, Noon 1995
Rustrel am Mittag 1995
Rustrel, mediodia 1995
Oil and Pigment on Wood
42 × 48 inches (105 × 122 cm)

Plate 52
Waterfall, Rustrel, Provence 1995
Wasserfall, Rustrel, Provence 1995
Cascada, Rustrel, Provence 1995
Pastel on Paper
16 × 14 inches (41 × 36 cm)

Plate 53
Mitjana Cliff, Menorca 1995
Mitjana Cliff, Menorca 1995
Desfiladero de Mitjana, Menorca 1995
Pastel on Paper
16 × 14 inches (41 × 36 cm)

Plate 54
Hidden Cactus 1996
Versteckter Kaktus 1996
El Cactus escondido 1996
Pastel on Paper
20 × 18 inches (51 × 46 cm)

Plate 55
Secret Garden 1996
Geheimer Garten 1996
El jardin secreto 1996
Pastel on Paper
20 × 18 inches (51 × 46 cm)

Plate 56
Sacred Stones 1996
Heilige Steine 1996
Piedras sagradas 1996
Pastel on Paper
20 × 18 inches (51 × 46 cm)

Plate 57
Deep Cave, Noon 1995
Tiefe Höhle am Mittag 1995
La Cueva profunda, mediodia 1995
Pastel on Paper
20 × 18 inches (51 × 46 cm)

Plate 58
Aftermath 1996
Nachwirkungen 1996
Secuelas 1996
Pastel on Paper
20 × 18 inches (51 × 46 cm)

Plate 59
Below Ground 1996
Unterirdisch 1996
Bajo tierra 1996
Pastel on Paper
20 × 18 inches (51 × 46 cm)

Plate 60
Golden Edge, Mitjana 1996
Goldene Grenze, Mitjana 1996
Borde dorado, Mitjana 1996
Pastel on Paper
20 × 18 inches (51 × 46 cm)

Plate 61
Cactus, Bryce, Utah 1996
Kaktus, Bryce, Utah 1996
Cactus, Bryce, Utah 1996
Pastel on Paper
14 × 16 inches (36 × 41 cm)

Plate 62
Mojave Dawn 1996
Morgendämmerung in Mojave 1996
Un Amanecer Mojave 1996
Pastel on Paper
18 × 20 inches (46 × 51 cm)

Plate 63
Weeping Moss Fall, Zion Canyon 1996
Weeping Moss Fall, Zion Canyon 1996
La Caida Del Musco Lloròn
Pastel on Paper
20 × 18 inches (51 × 46 cm)

Plate 64
Palm, Florida 1996
Palme, Florida 1996
Palmera, Florida 1996
Pastel on Paper
14 × 16 inches (36 × 41 cm)

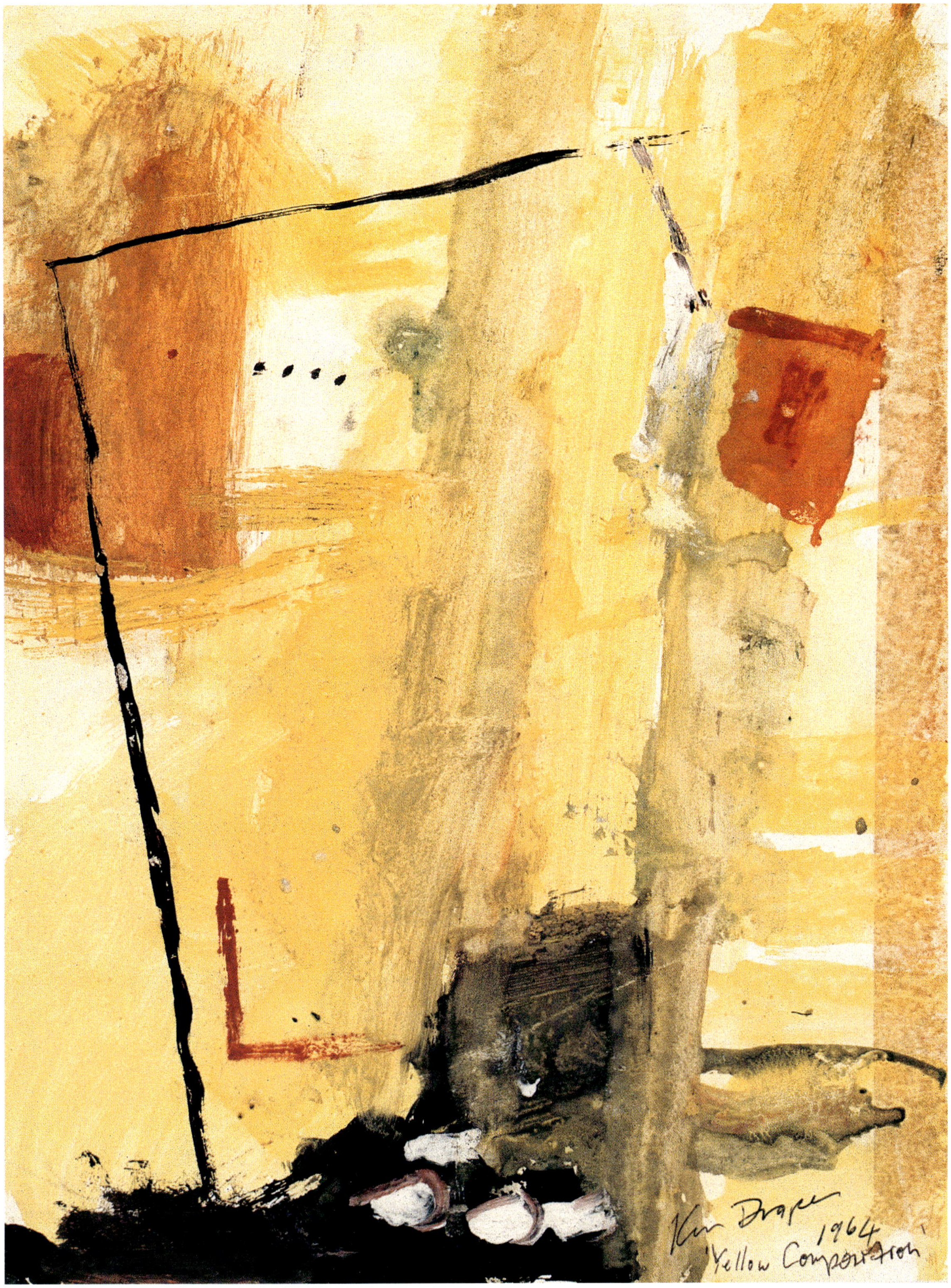

Plate 1

Yellow Composition 1964

Gouache on Paper

$8\frac{3}{4} \times 6\frac{3}{4}$ inches (22×17 cm)

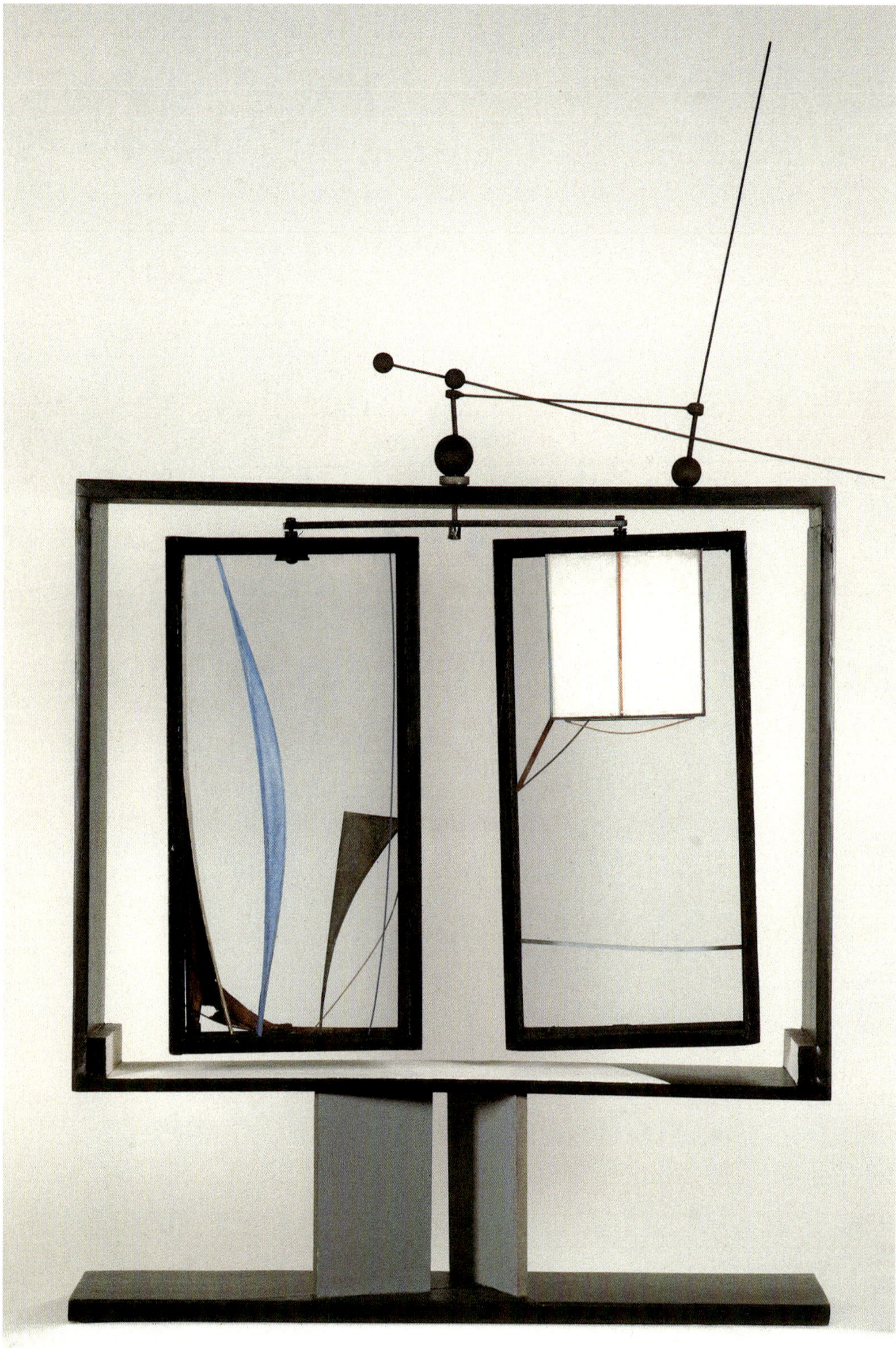

Plate 2

Evolve 1964
Wood, Glass, Steel, Paper, Oil Pigment
48 × 36 × 12 inches (122 × 90 × 30 cm)

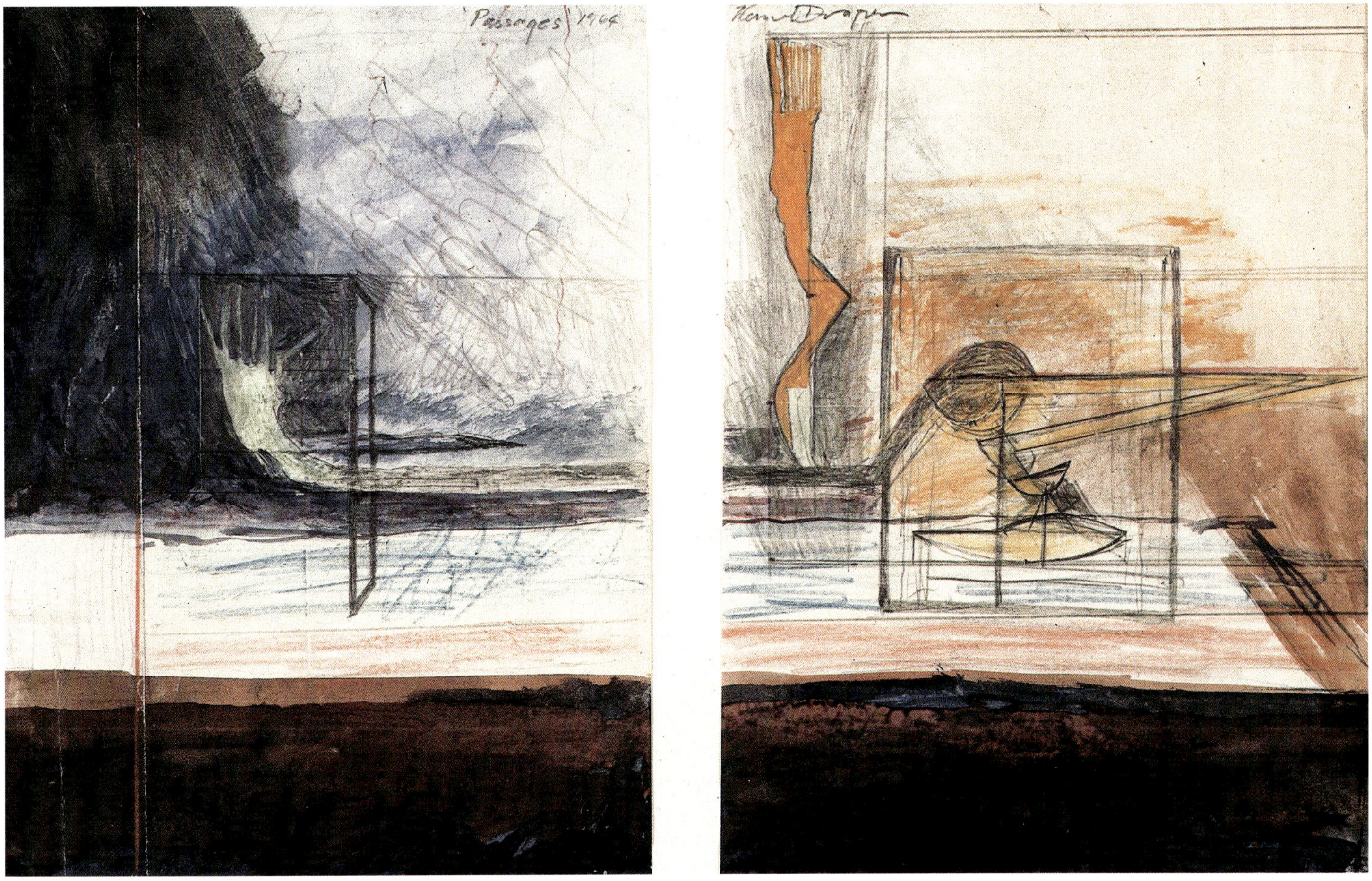

Plate 3

Passages 1964

Gouache and Pencil on Paper

8¾ × 14 inches (22 × 35 cm)

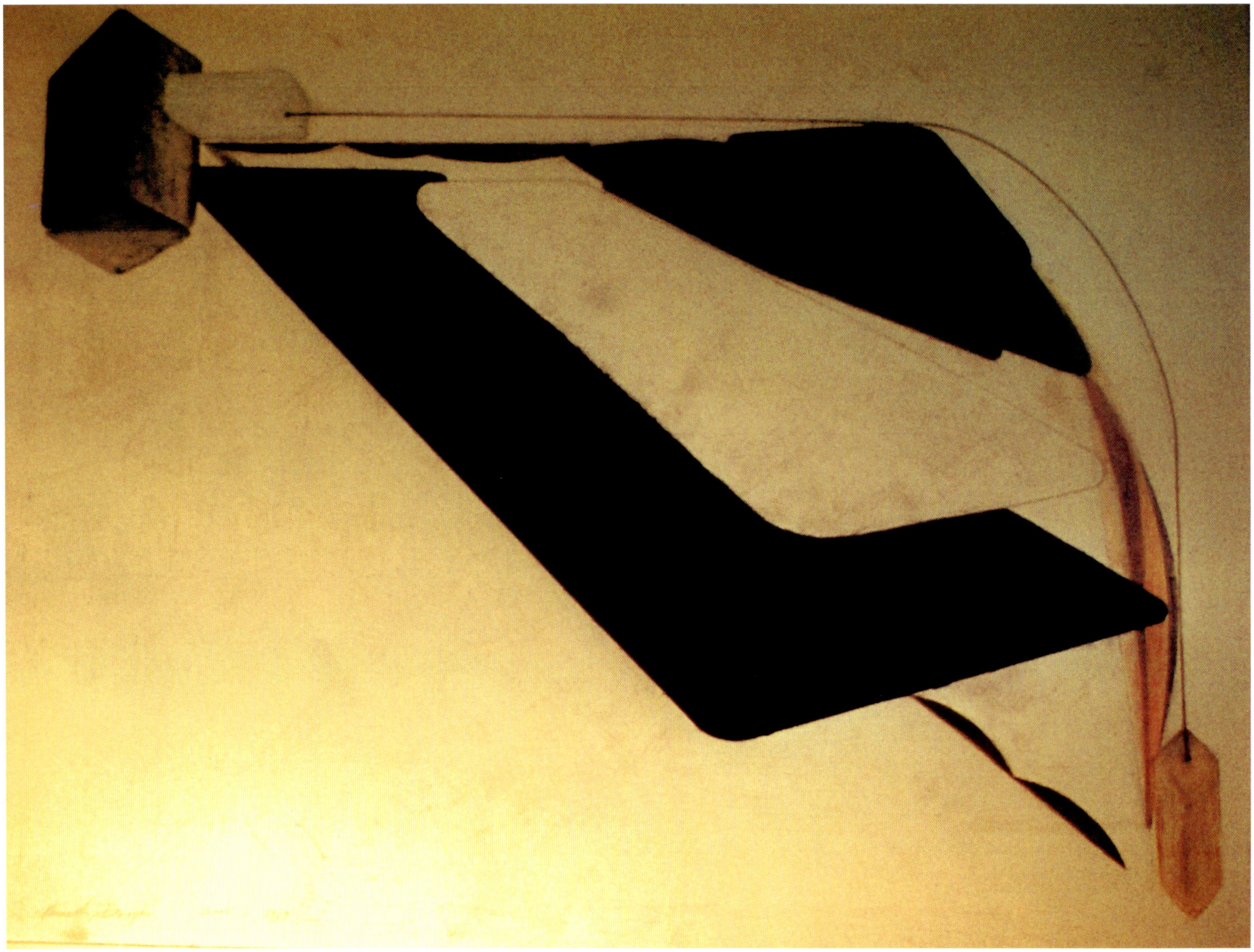

Plate 4

Second Implication 1970
Pastel on Paper
20 × 28 inches (51 × 71 cm)

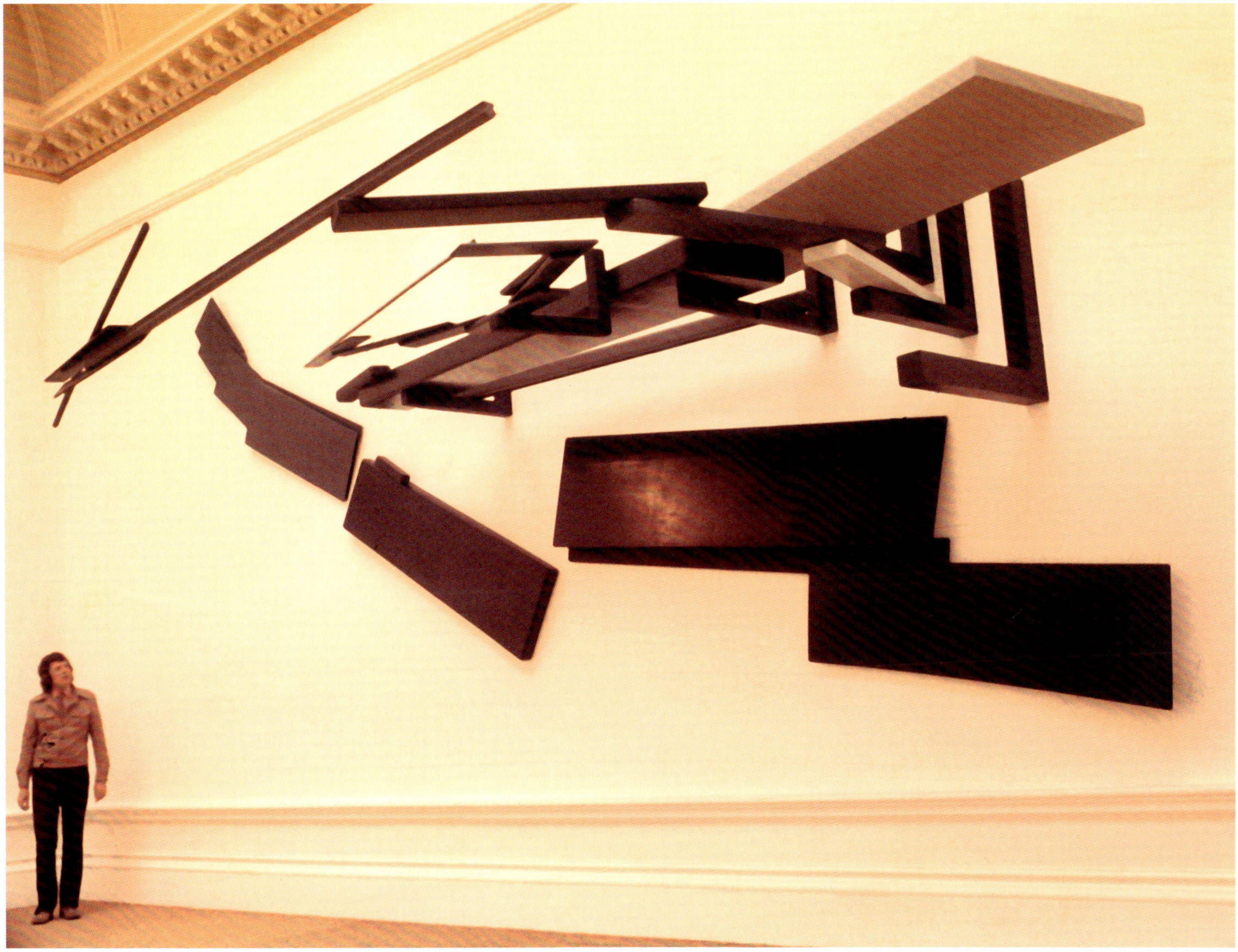

Plate 5

Overhang V Sounds 1971
Wood, Steel and Oils
15 × 16 × 28 feet (457 × 488 × 584 cm)

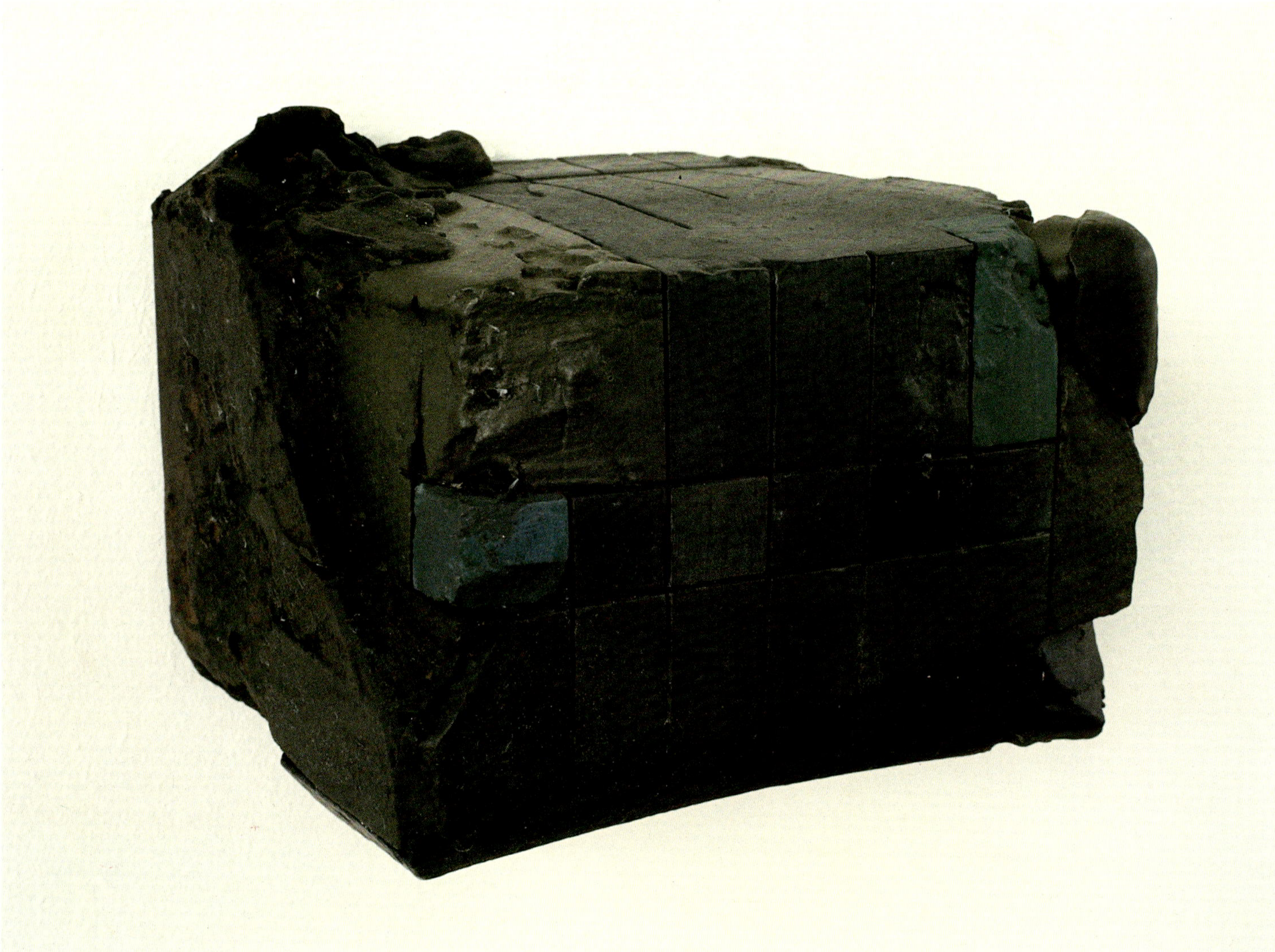

Plate 6

Foundation 1975
Mixed Media
5 × 7 × 5 inches (12 × 18 × 12 cm)

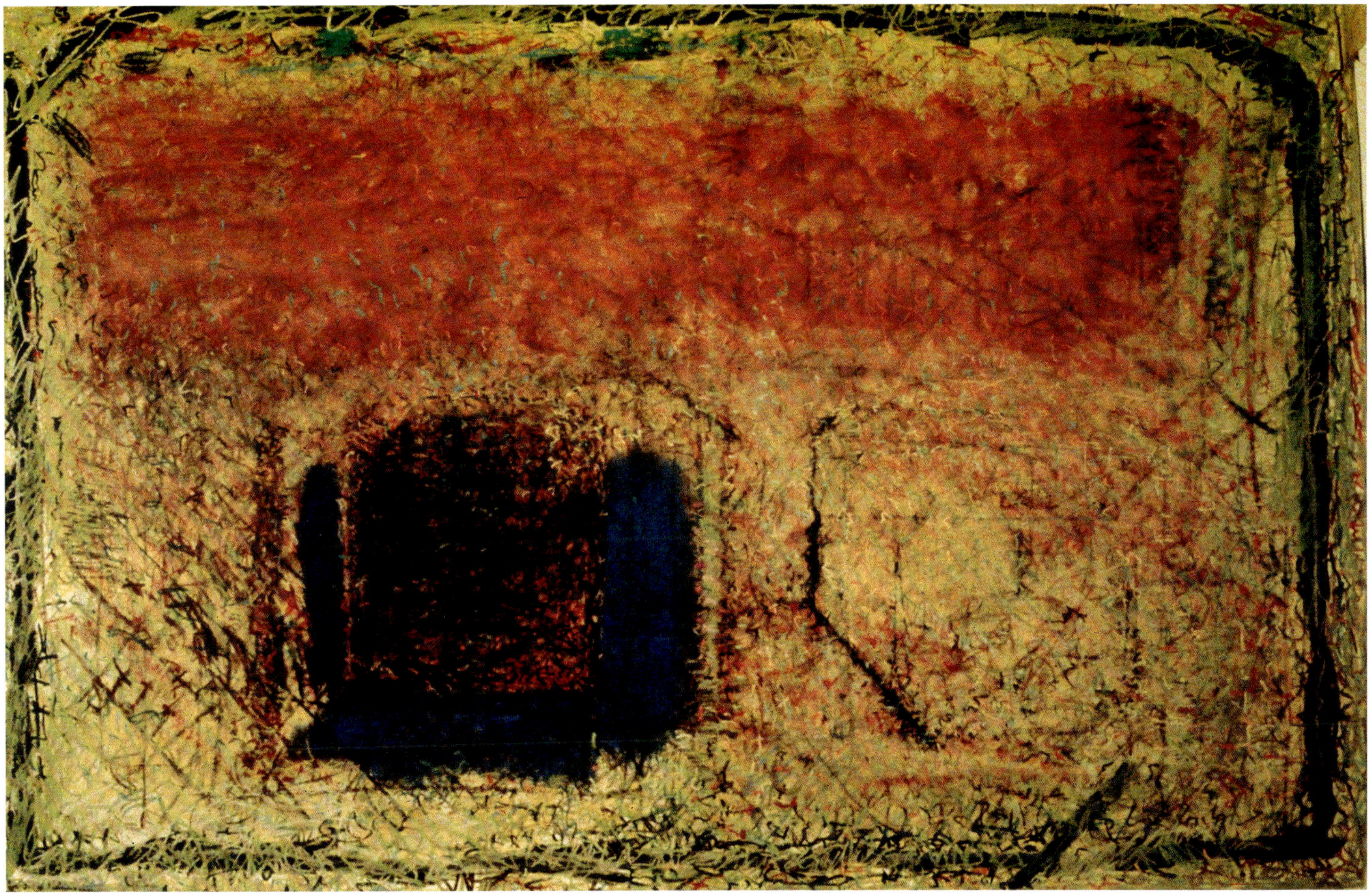

Plate 7

Blue Enclosure 1978
Pastel on Paper
30 × 44 inches (76 × 112 cm)

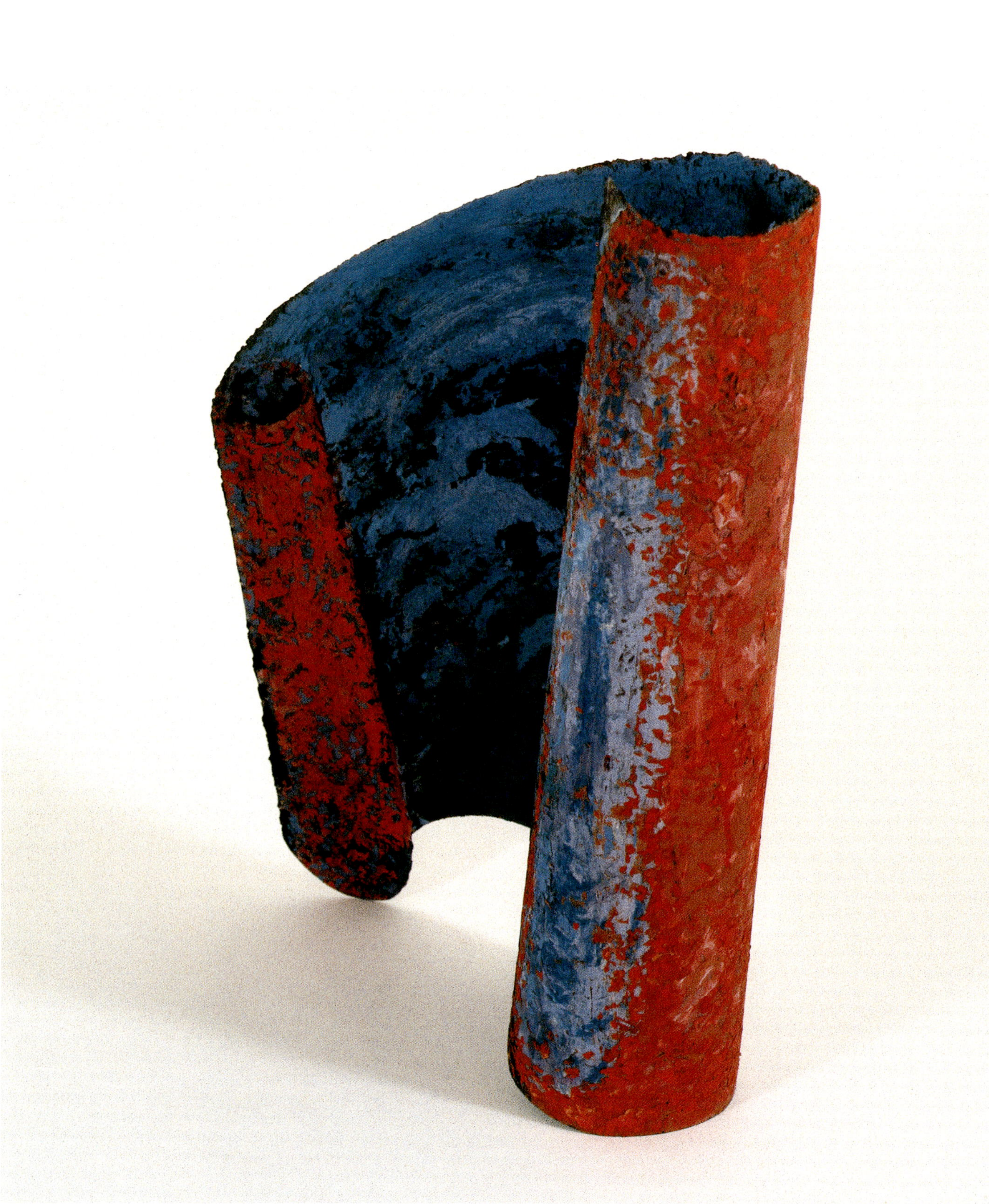

Plate 8

Blue Veil 1984
Steel, Resin, Oil Pigment
$23\frac{1}{2} \times 7 \times 23\frac{1}{2}$ inches (59 × 12 × 59 cm)

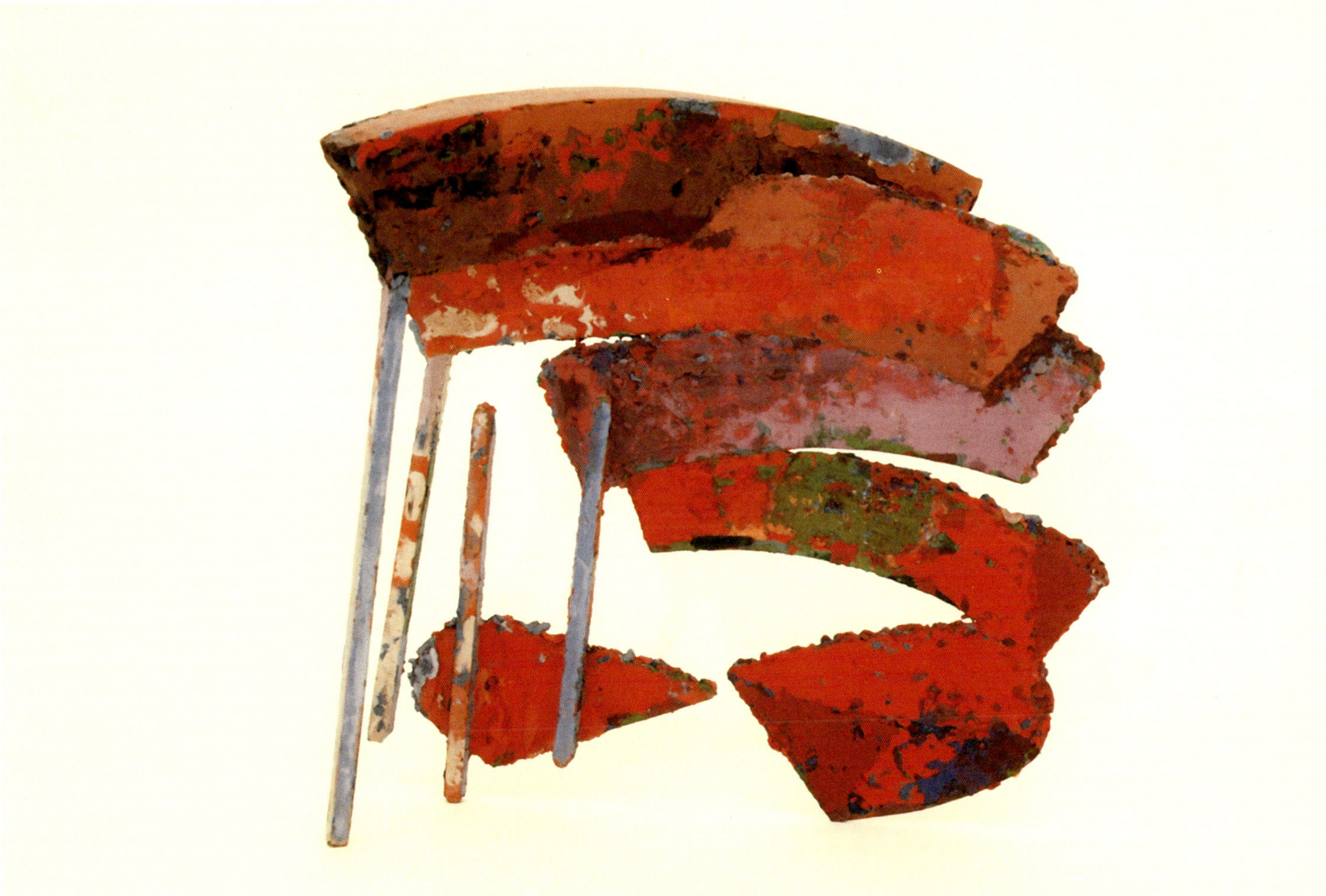

Plate 9

Ascend 1981
Aluminium, Resin, Oil Pigment
19 × 22 × 9 inches (48 × 56 × 23 cm)

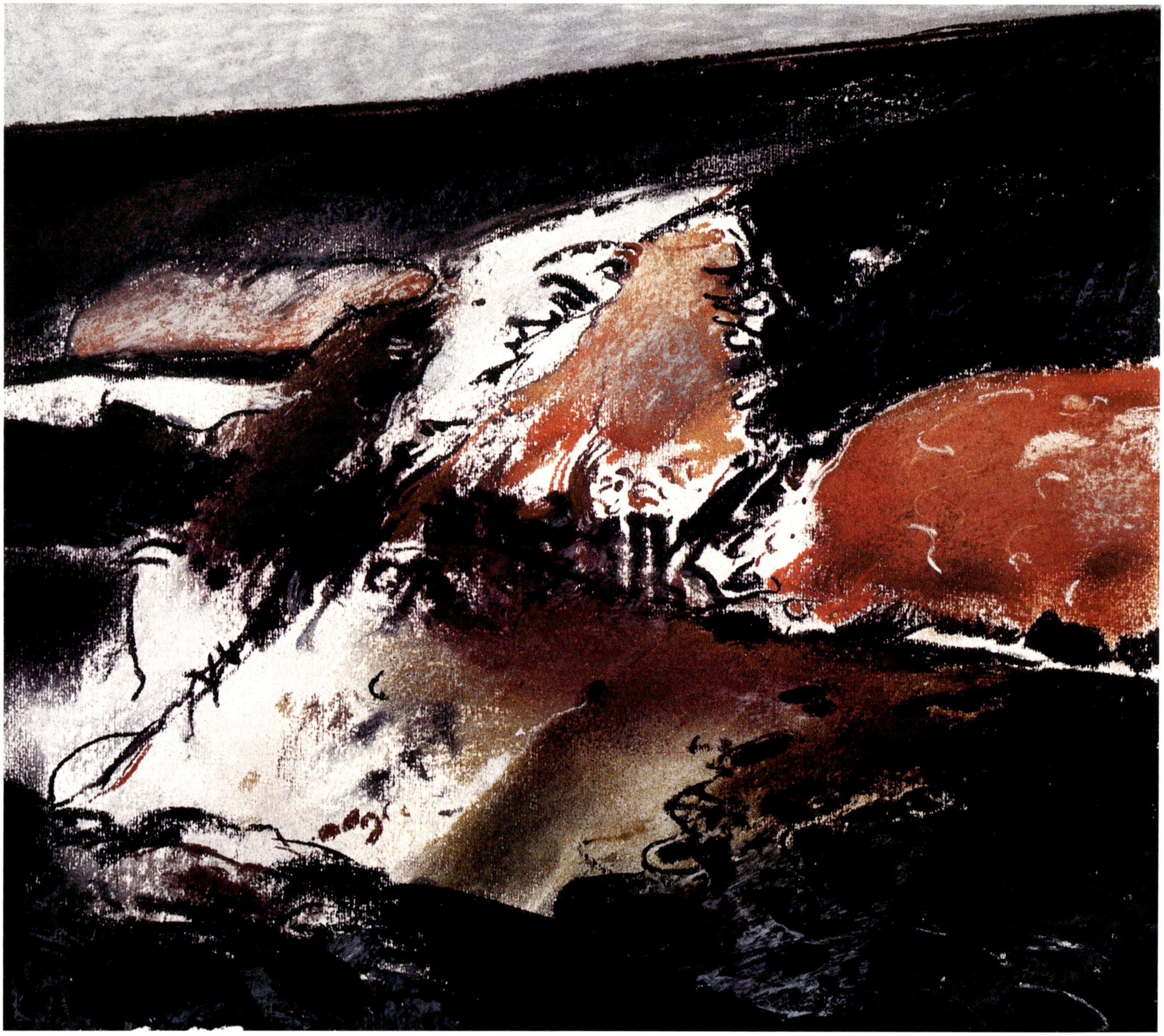

Plate 10

February 1988
Pastel on Paper
12 × 14 inches (30 × 35 cm)

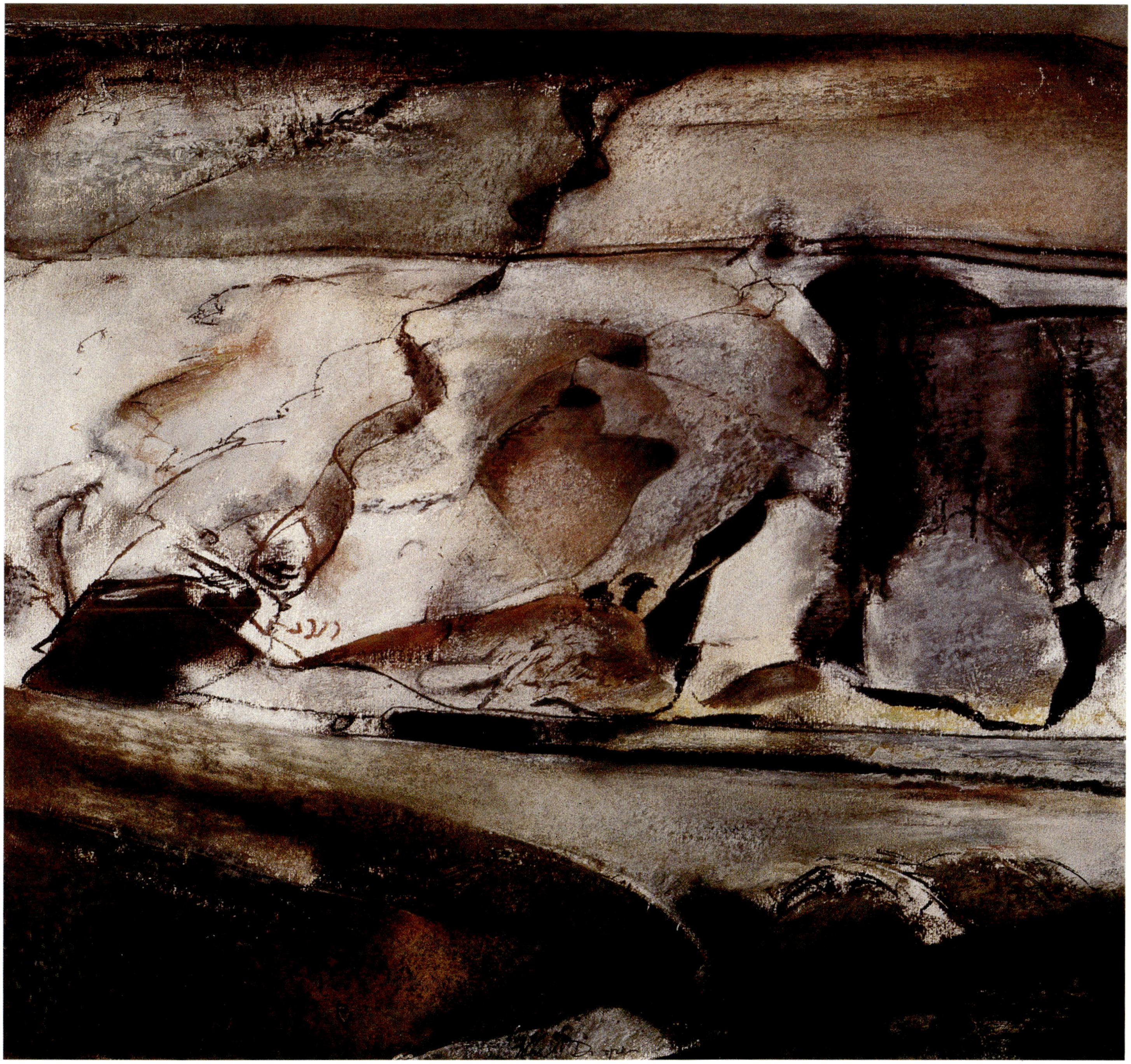

Plate 11

Monks Moor 1988
Pastel on Paper
18 × 19½ inches (46 × 49 cm)

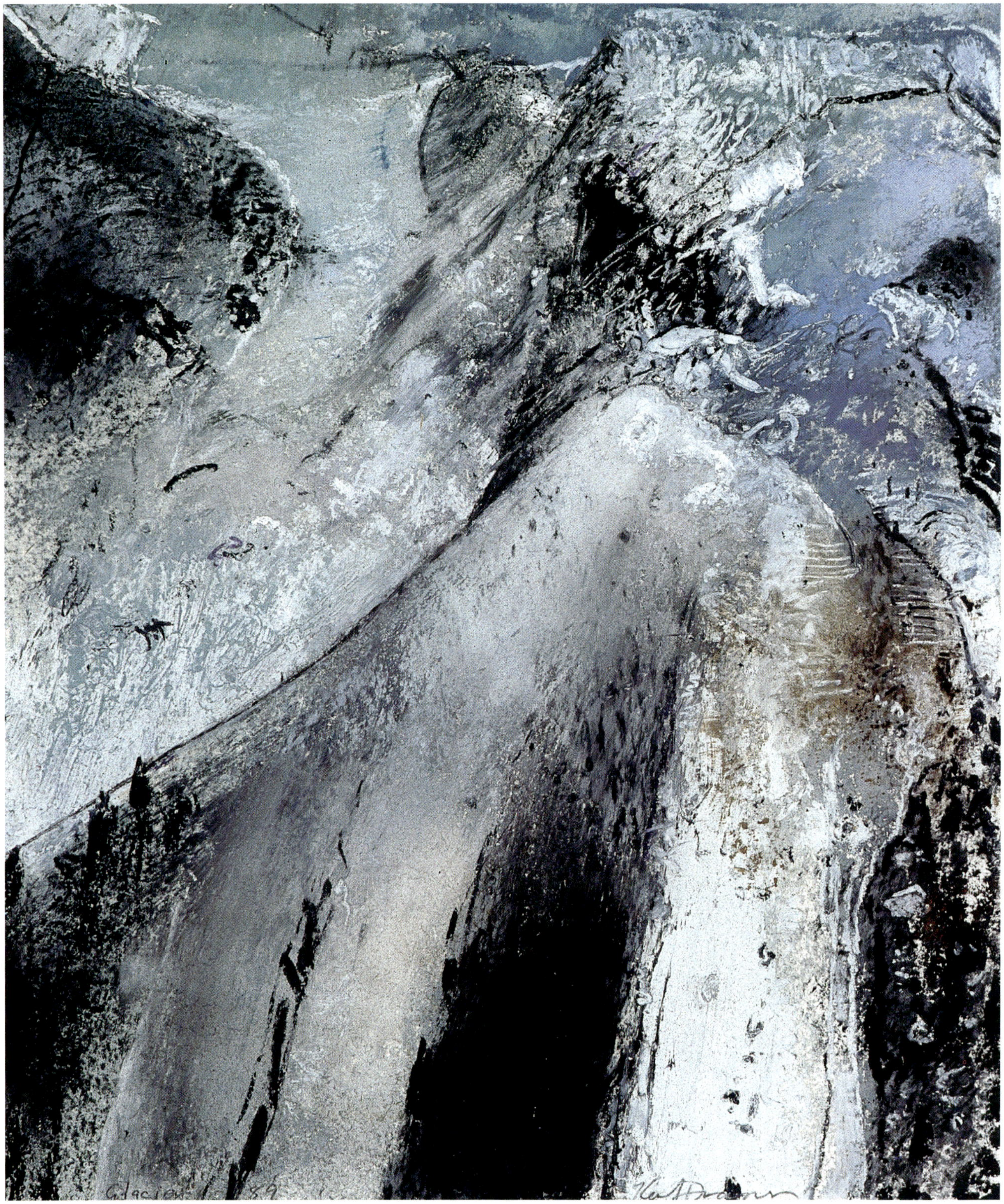

Plate 12

Glacier 1989
Pastel on Paper
16 × 14 inches (41 × 35 cm)

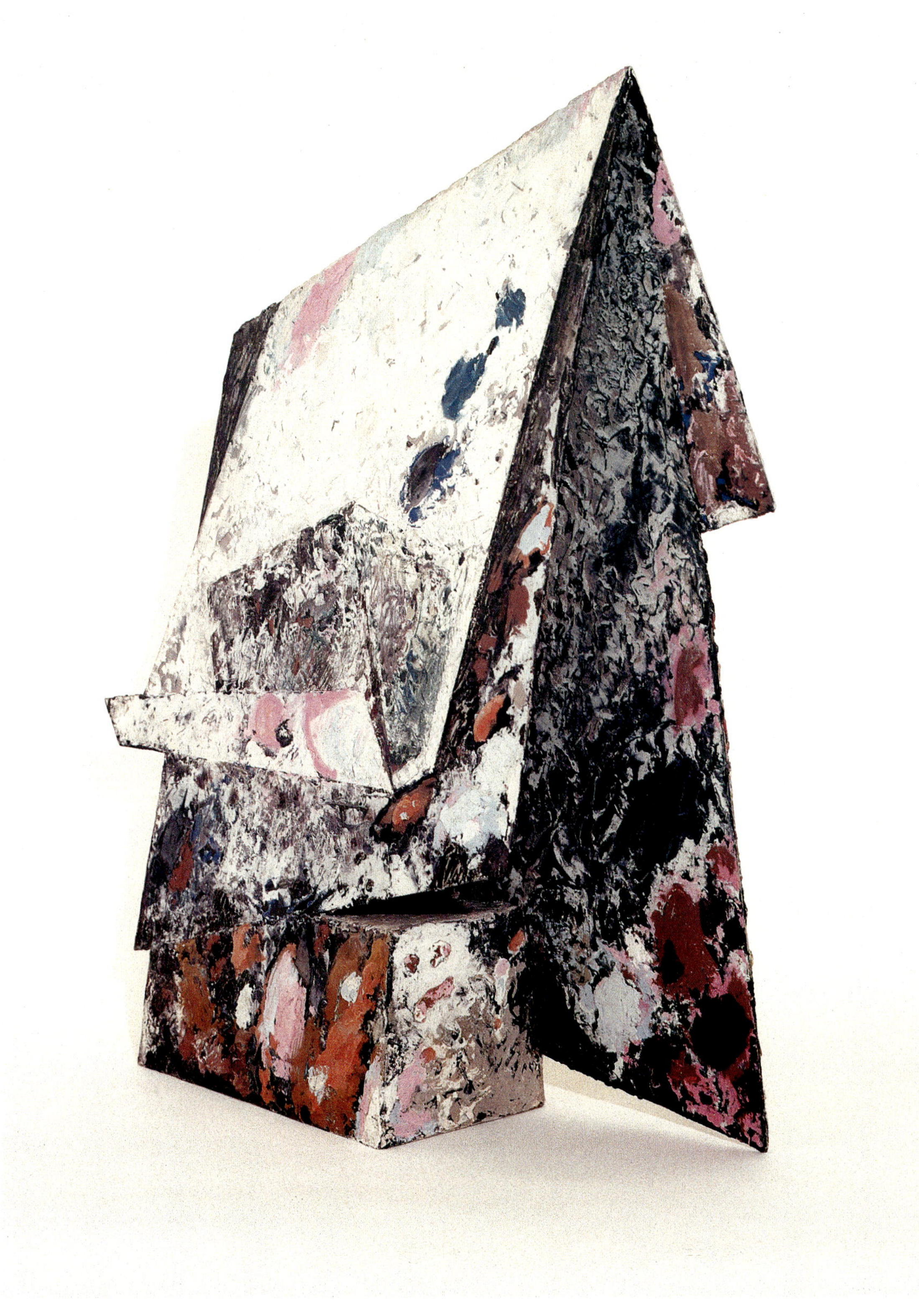

Plate 13

Mountain 1989
Steel, Wood, Resin, Oil Pigment
29 × 30 × 6½ inches (74 × 76 × 16 cm)

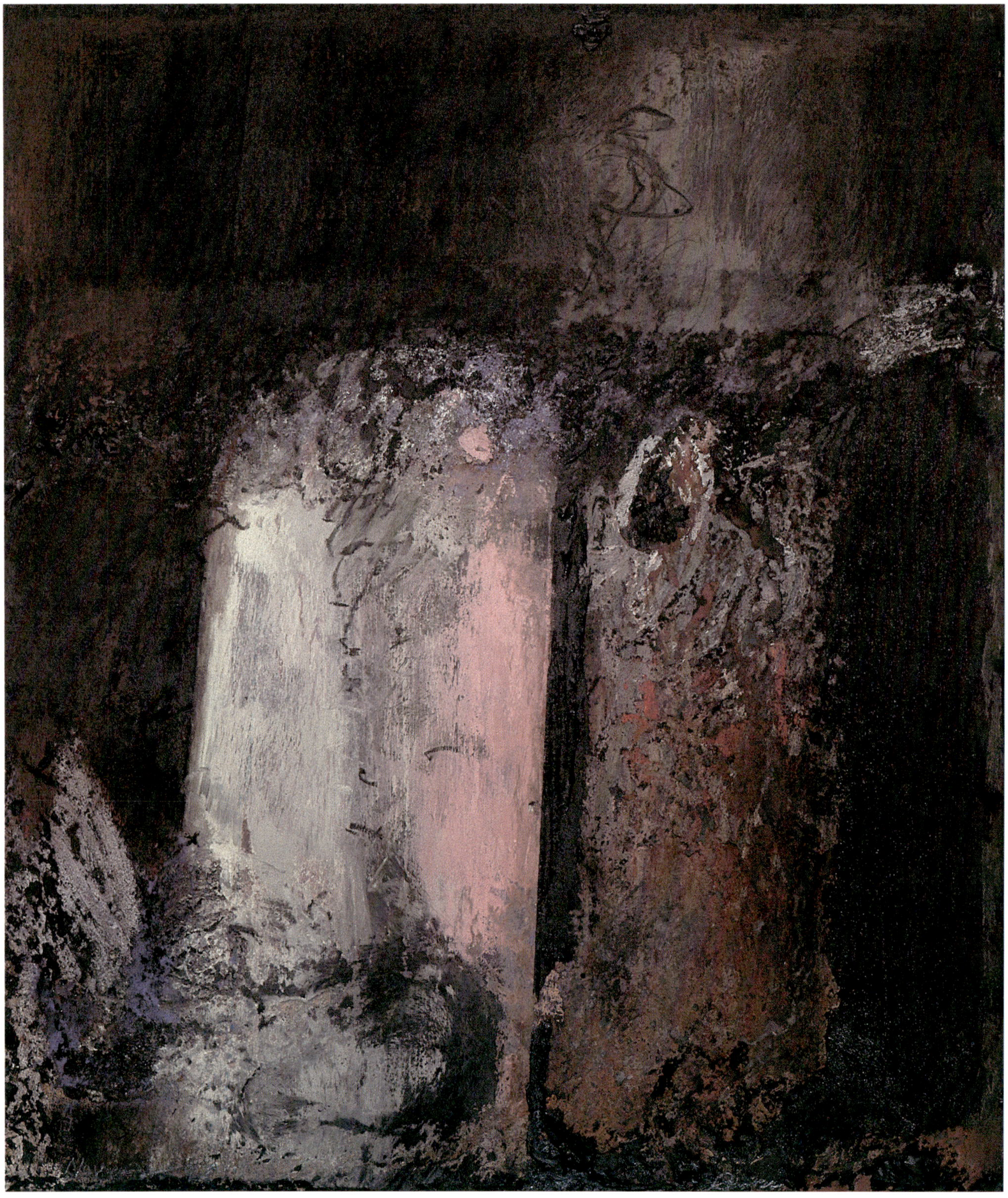

Plate 14

November 1990

Pastel, Pigment on Wood

16 × 14 inches (41 × 36 cm)

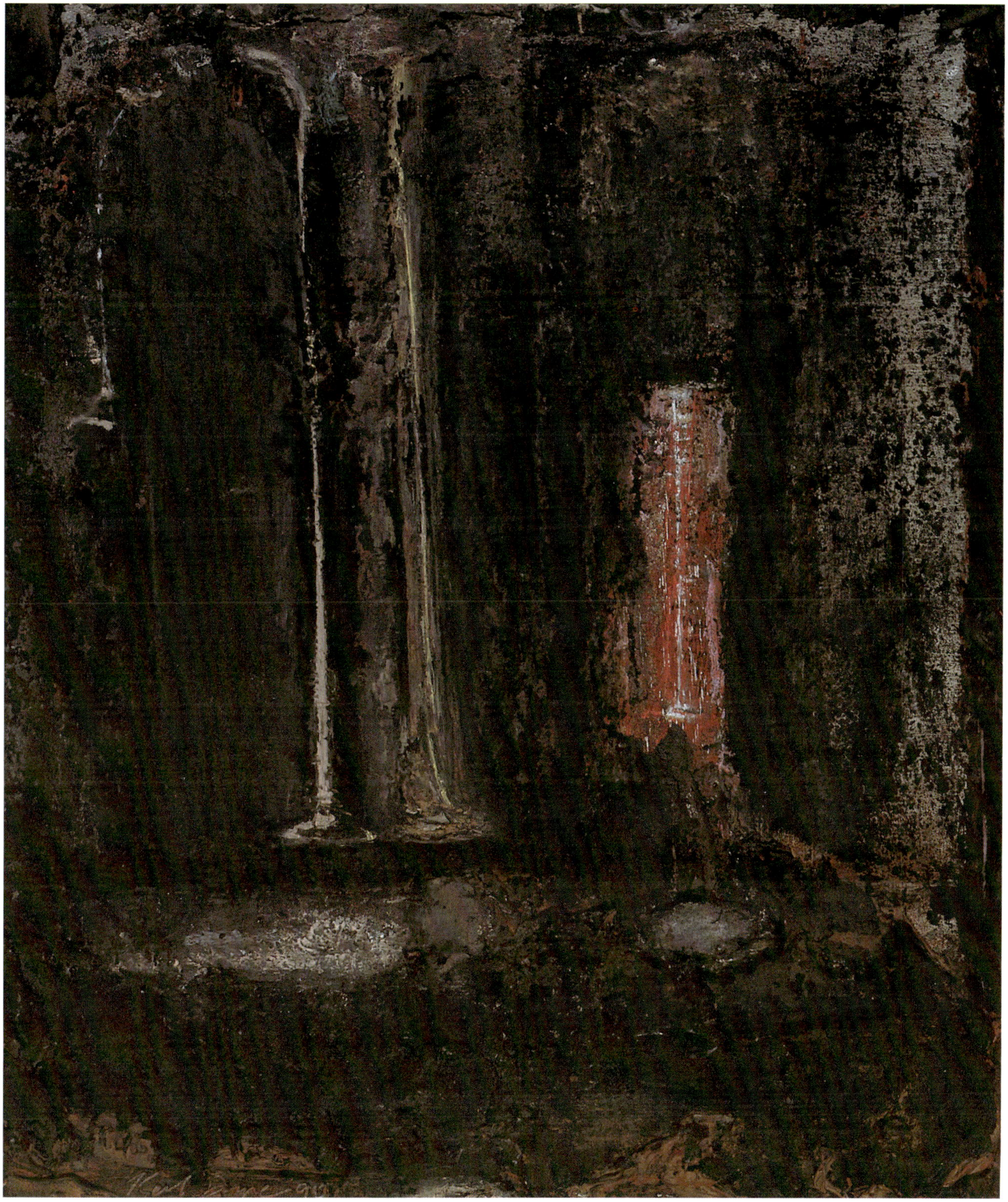

Plate 15

Distant Fall 1991
Pastel, Pigment, Mixed Media on Wood
16 × 14 inches (41 × 36 cm)

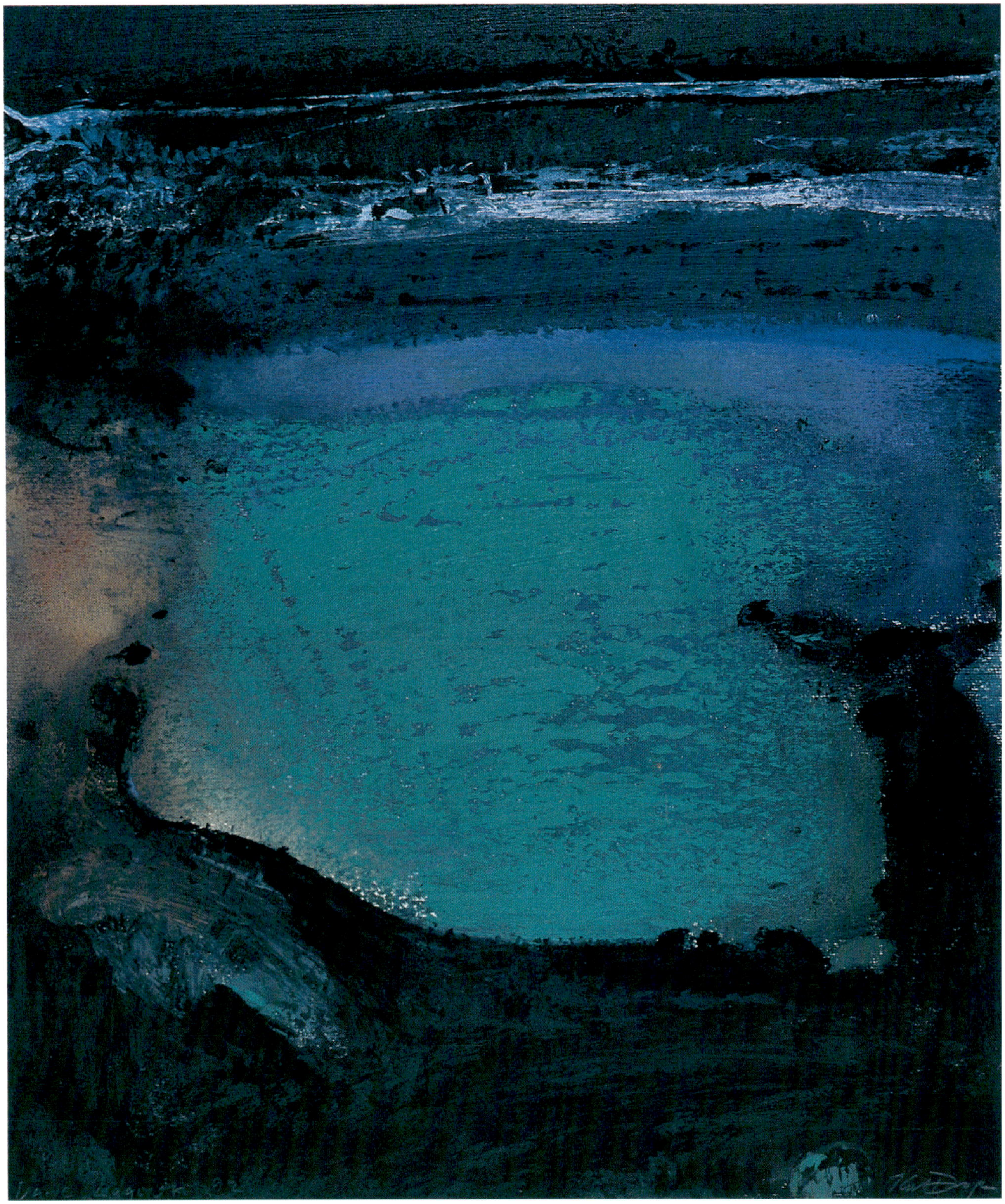

Plate 16

Dark Lagoon 1992
Pastel on Paper
16 × 14 inches (41 × 36 cm)

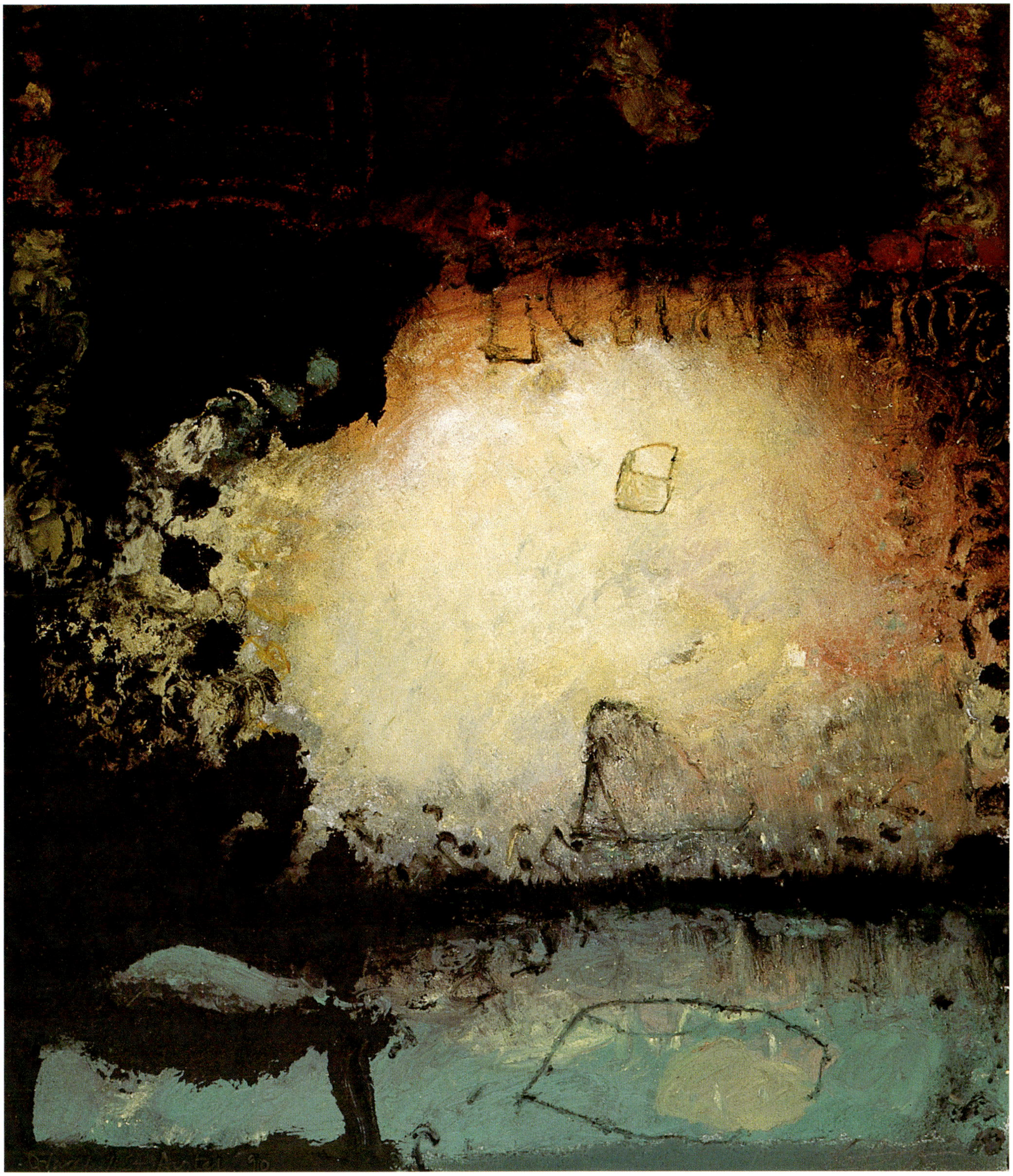

Plate 17

Quarry, St Austell 1990
Pastel on Paper
20 × 18 inches (51 × 46 cm)

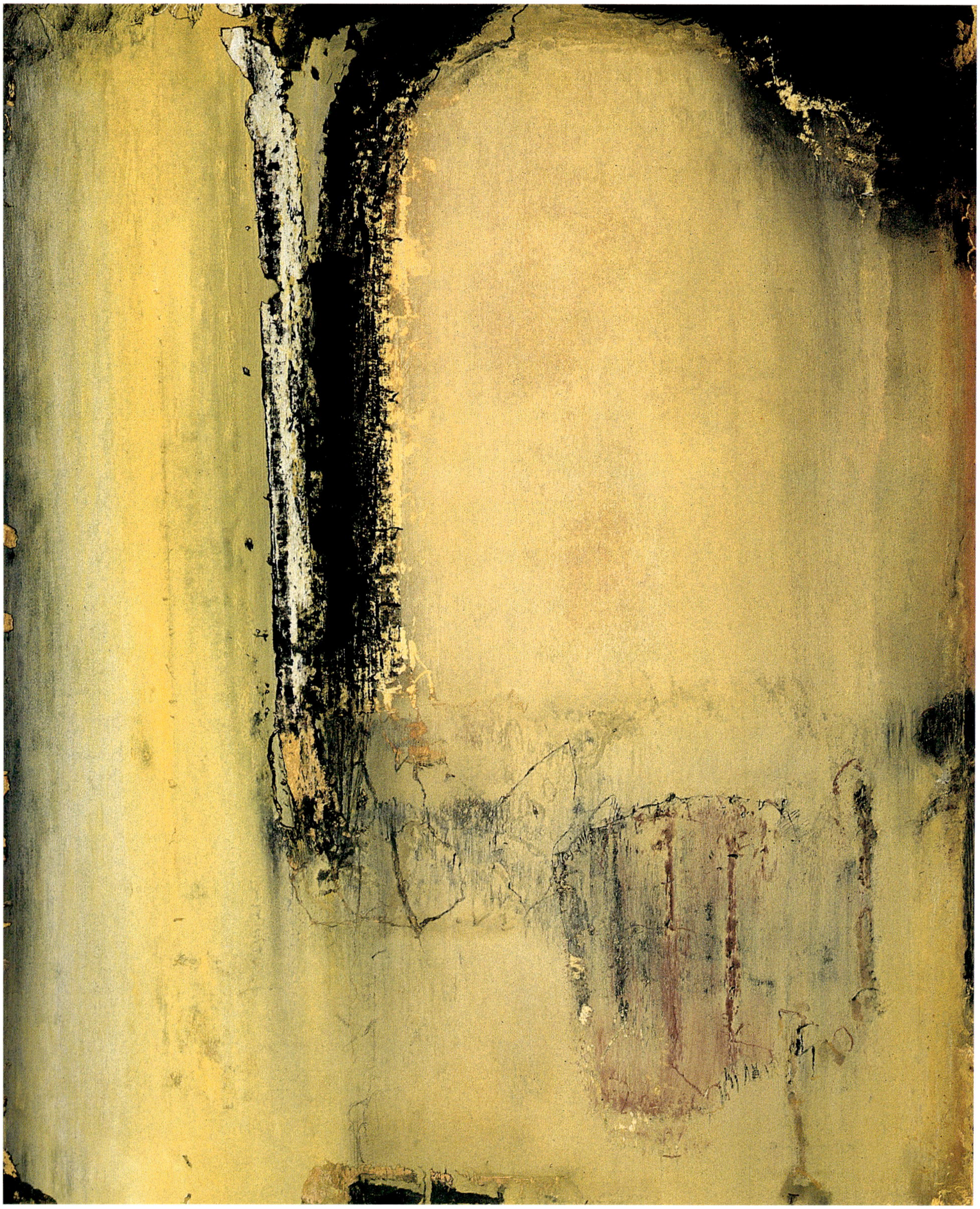

Plate 18

Dark Interlude 1992
Pastel on Paper
26 × 22 inches (66 × 56 cm)

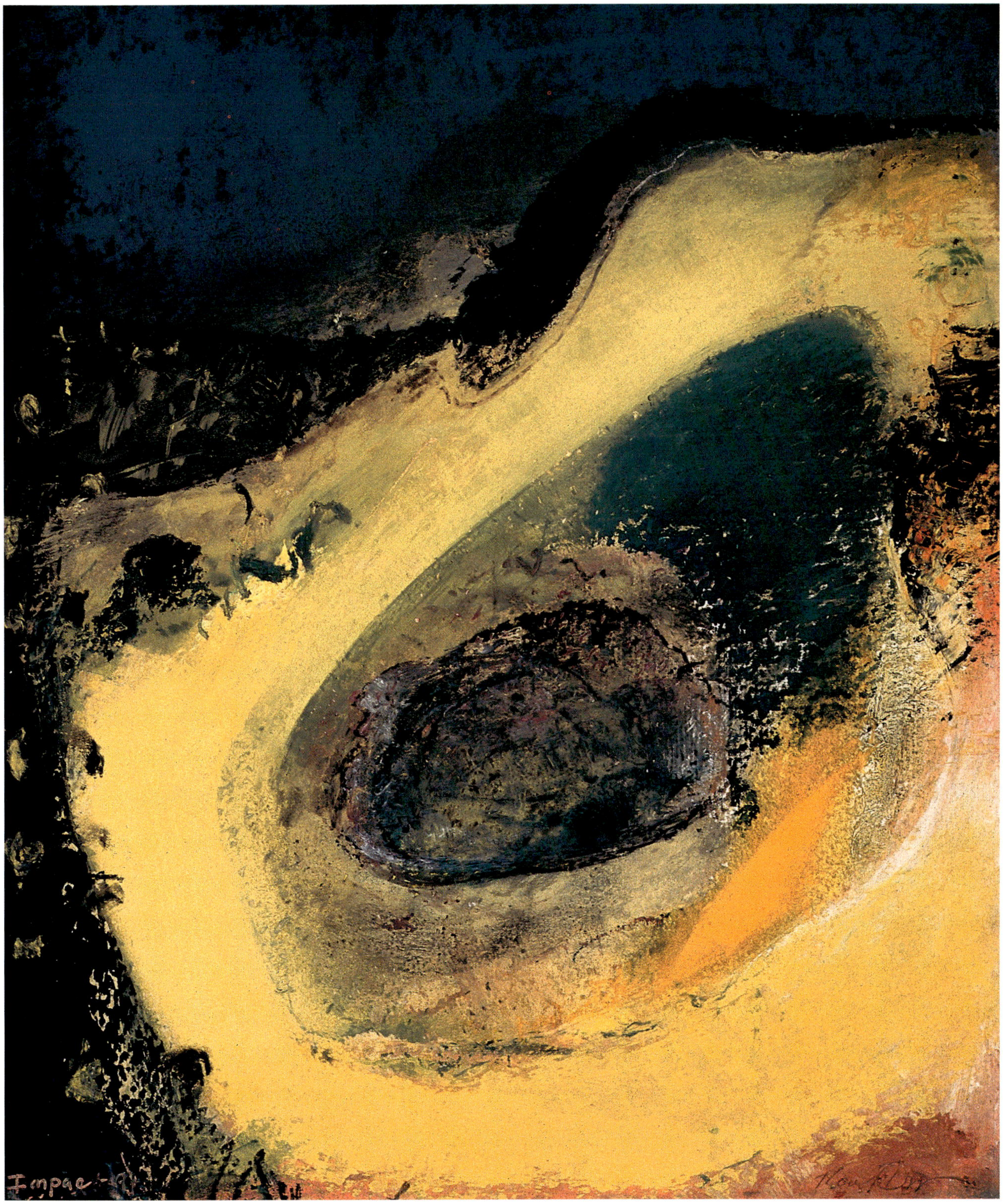

Plate 19

Impact 1991

Pastel on Paper

16 × 14 inches (41 × 36 cm)

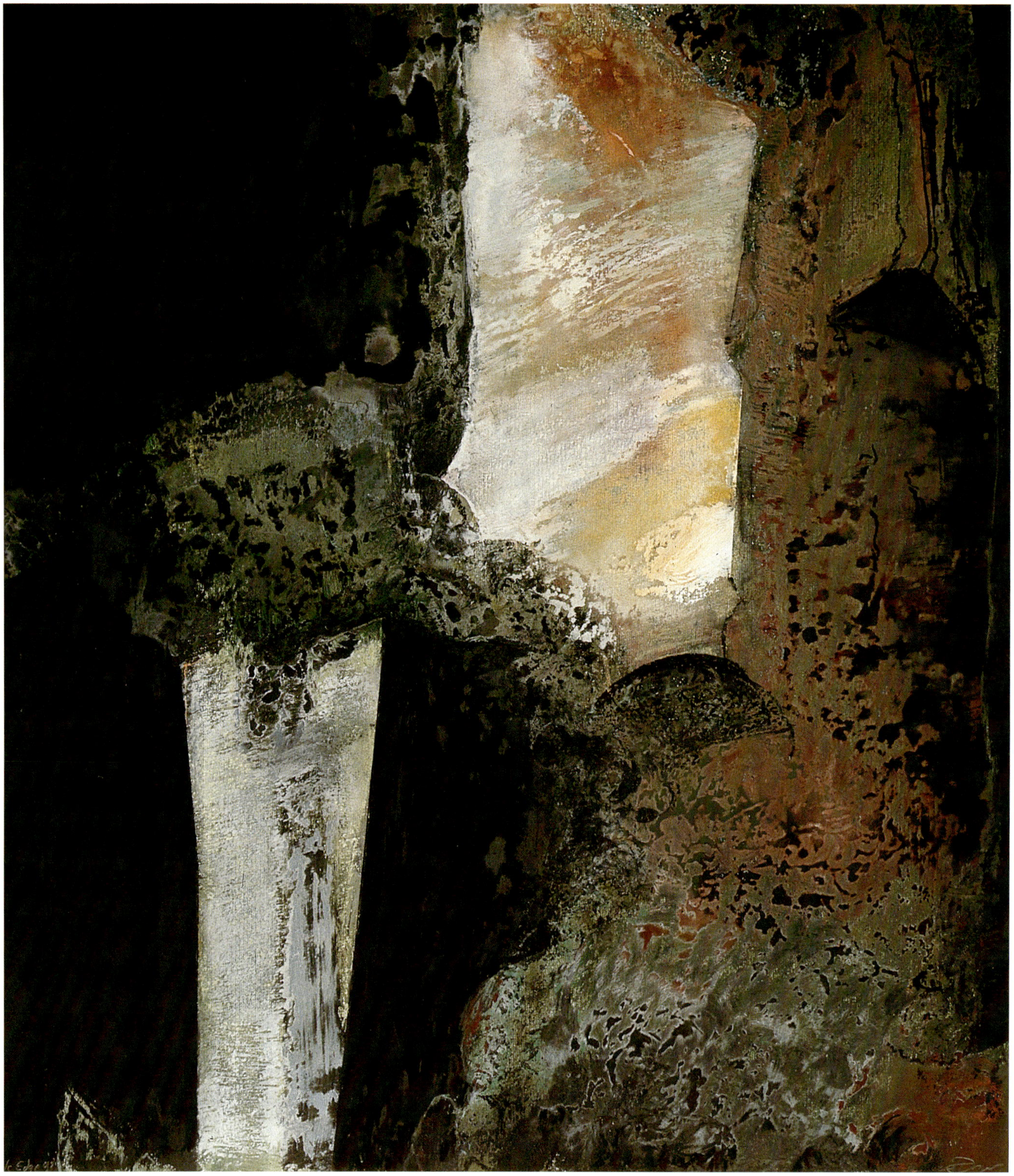

Plate 20

Dark Edge 1992
Pastel on Paper
20 × 18 inches (51 × 46 cm)

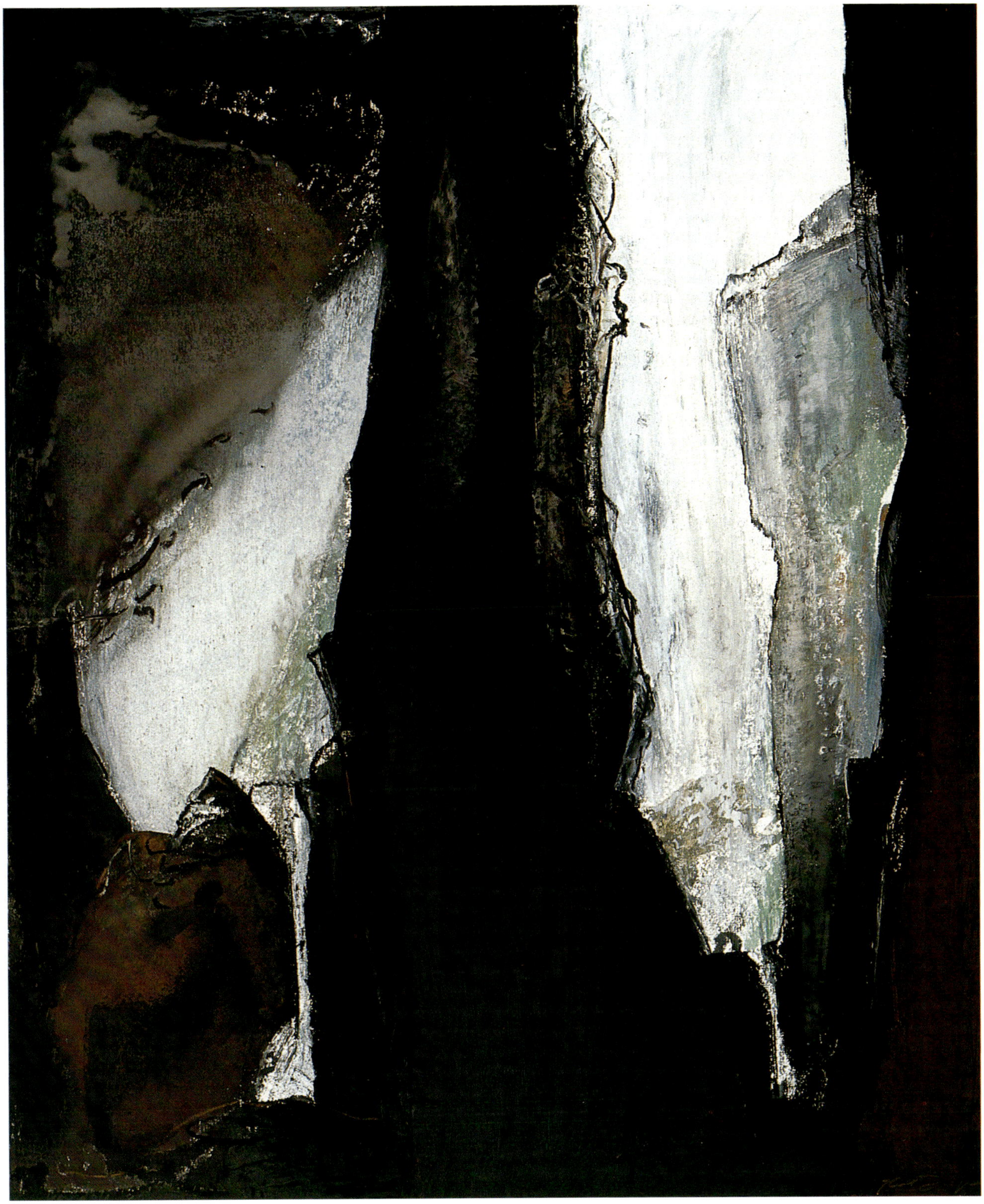

Plate 21

Gordale Double Image 1992

Pastel on Paper

26 × 22 inches (66 × 56 cm)

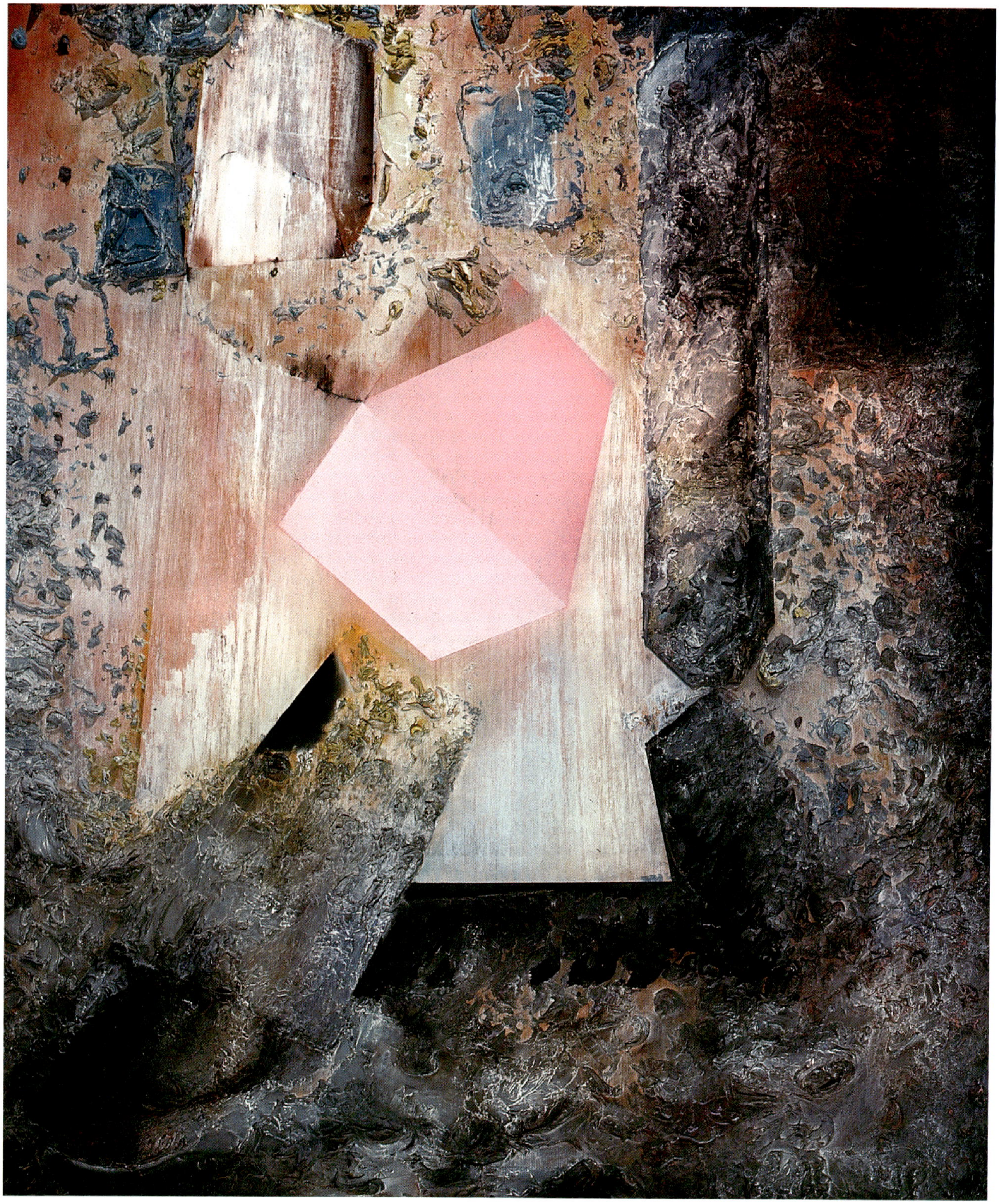

Plate 22

Light Fall 1993
Mixed Media on Wood
48 × 42 inches (122 × 107 cm)

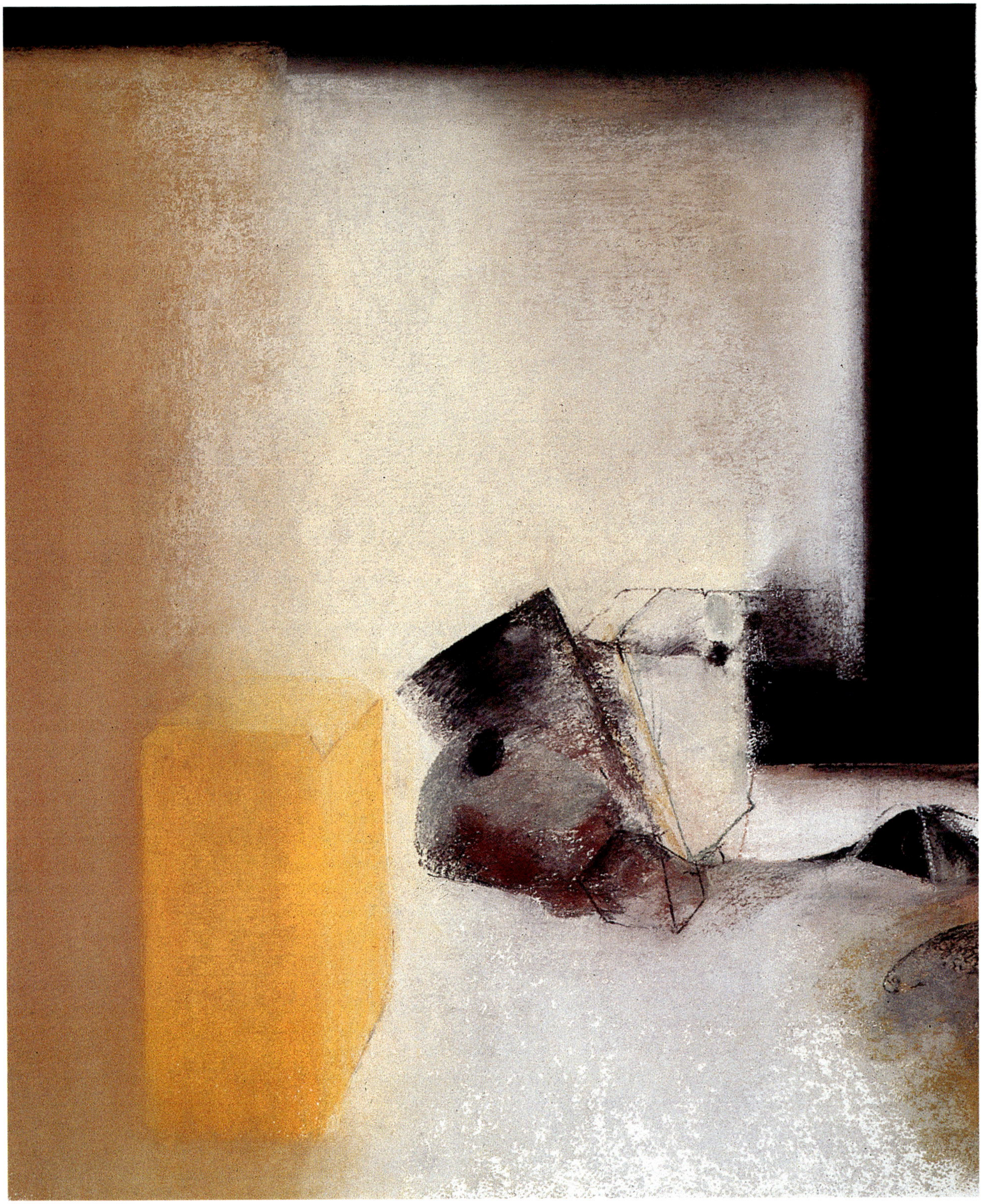

Plate 23

Stones 1990
Pastel on Paper
26 × 22 inches (66 × 56 cm)

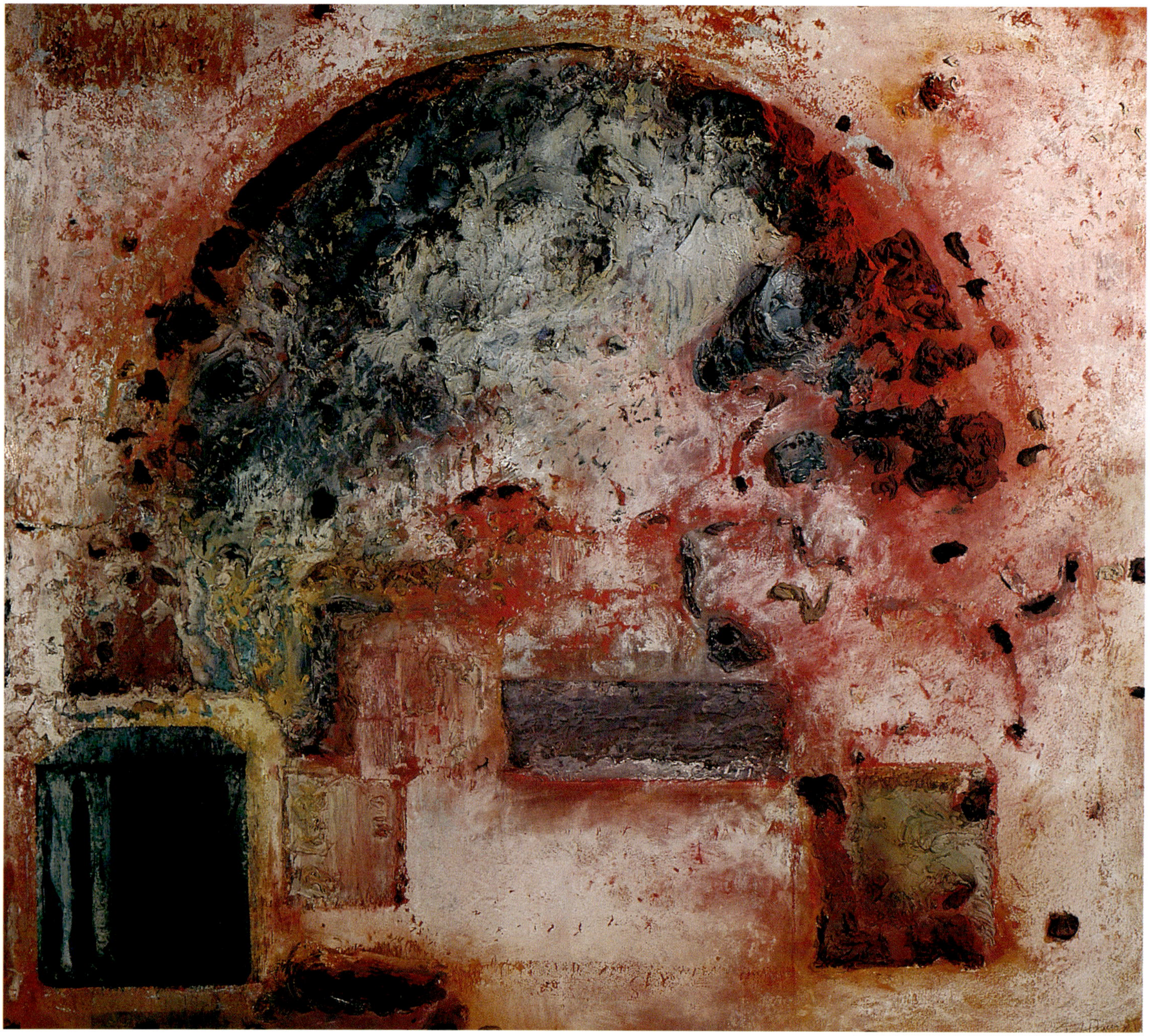

Plate 24

Awakening 1992
Pastel and Pigment on Wood
42 × 48 inches (107 × 122 cm)

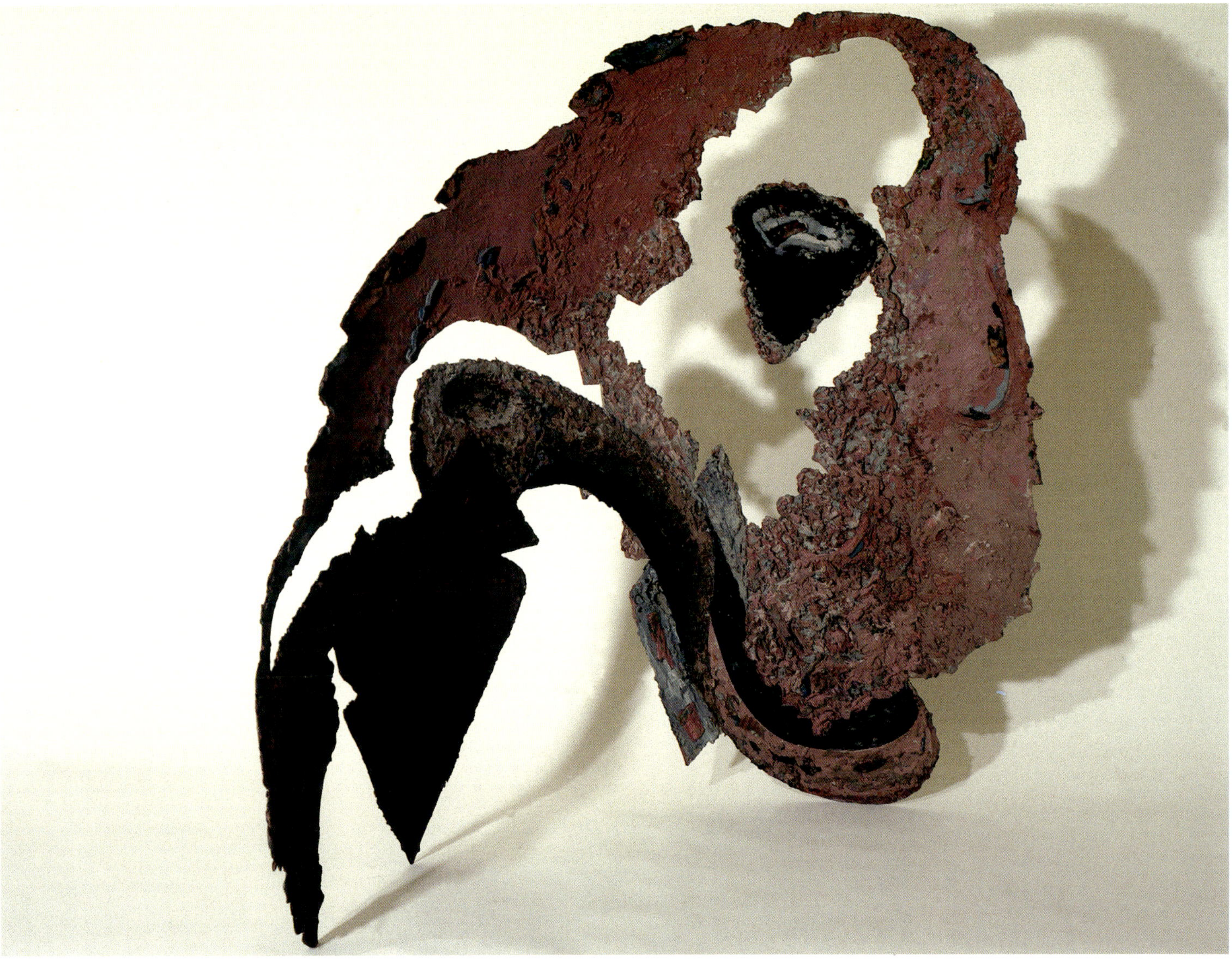

Plate 25

Spring Tide 1984
Steel, Resin, Oil Pigment
30 × 22 × 12 inches (76 × 56 × 30 cm)

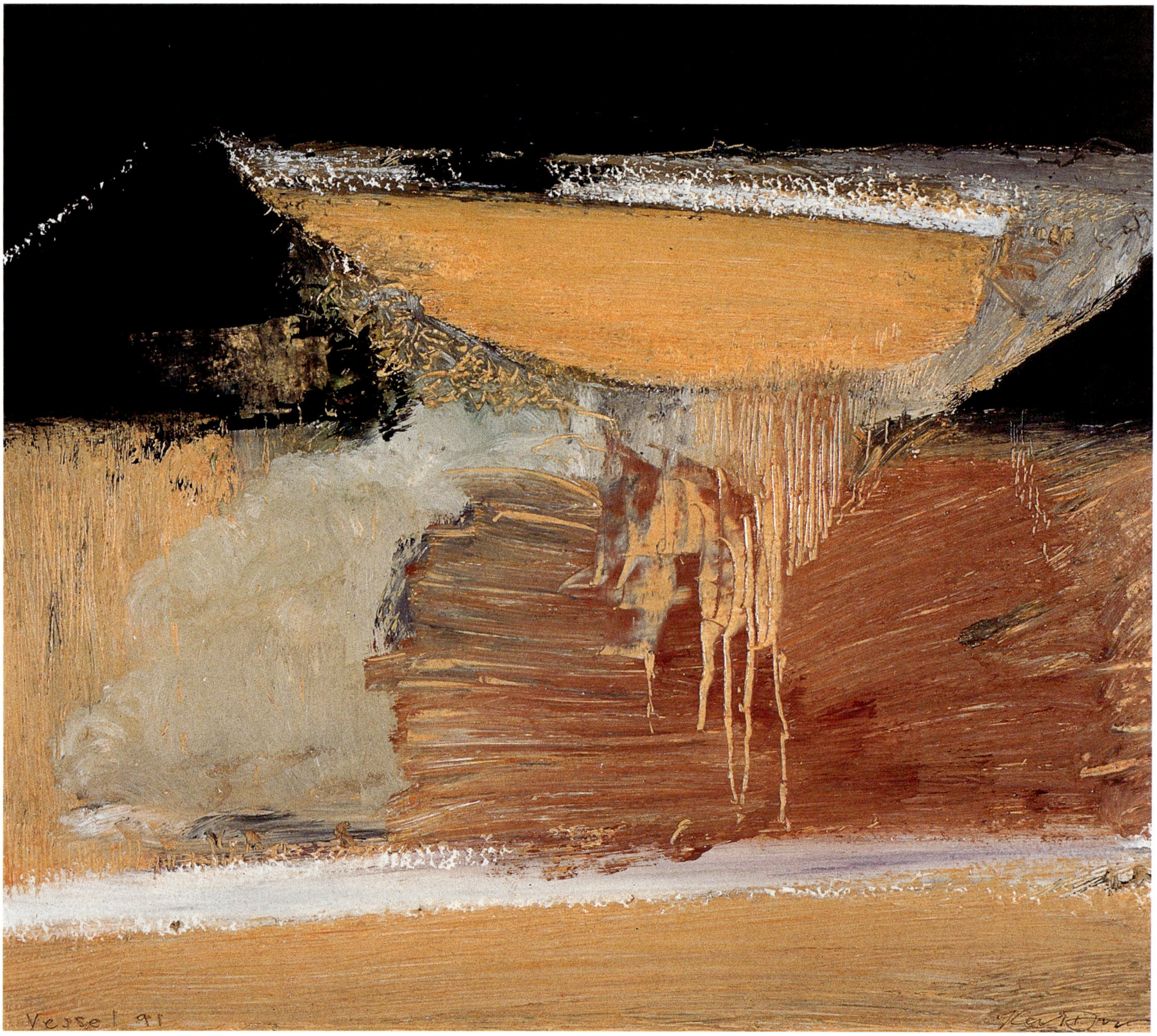

Plate 26

Vessel 1991

Pastel on Paper

14 × 16 inches (36 × 41 cm)

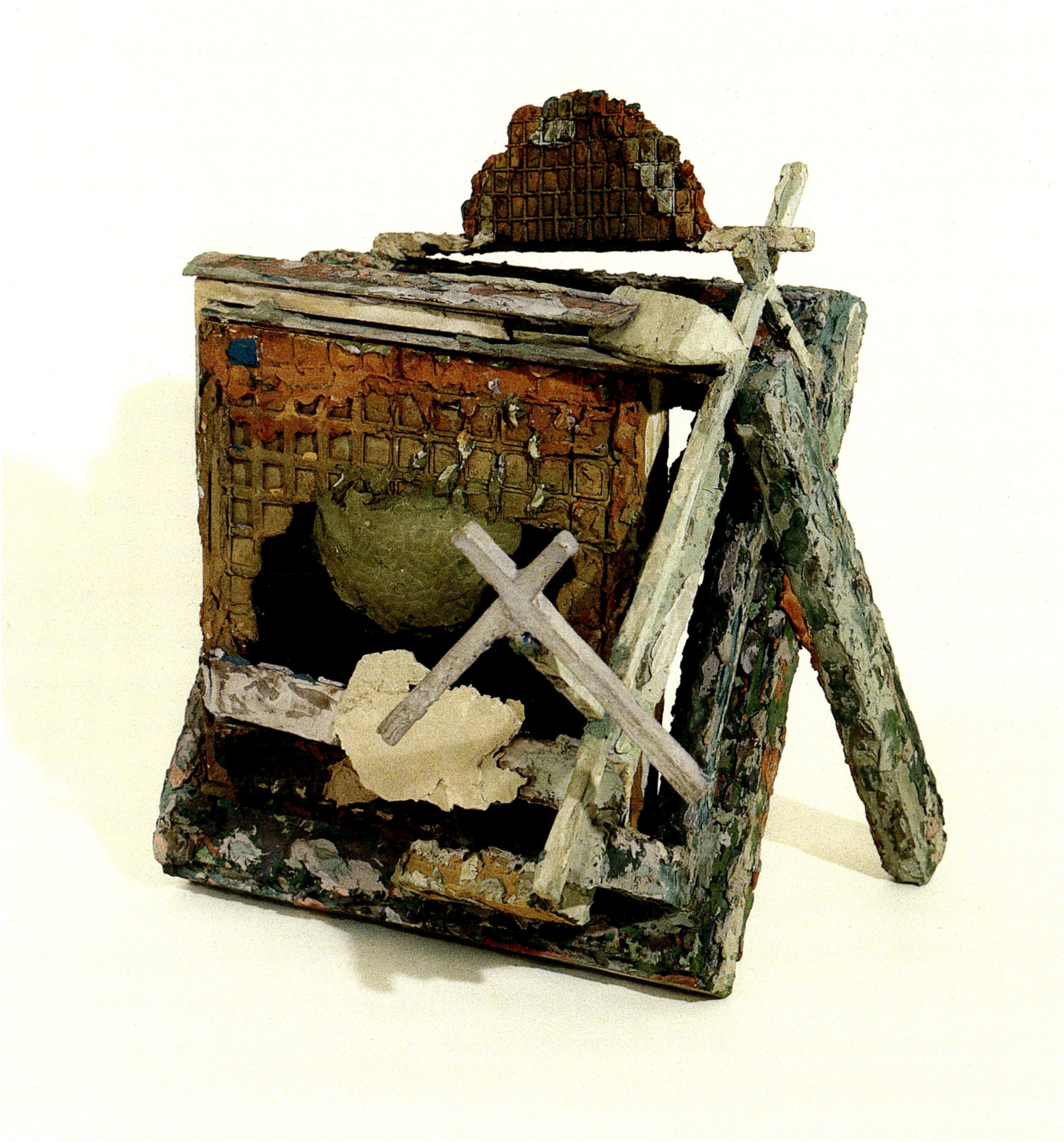

Plate 27

Eclipsed Labyrinths 1978
Wood, Concrete, Resin, Oil Pigment
20 × 20 × 20 inches (51 × 51 × 51 cm)

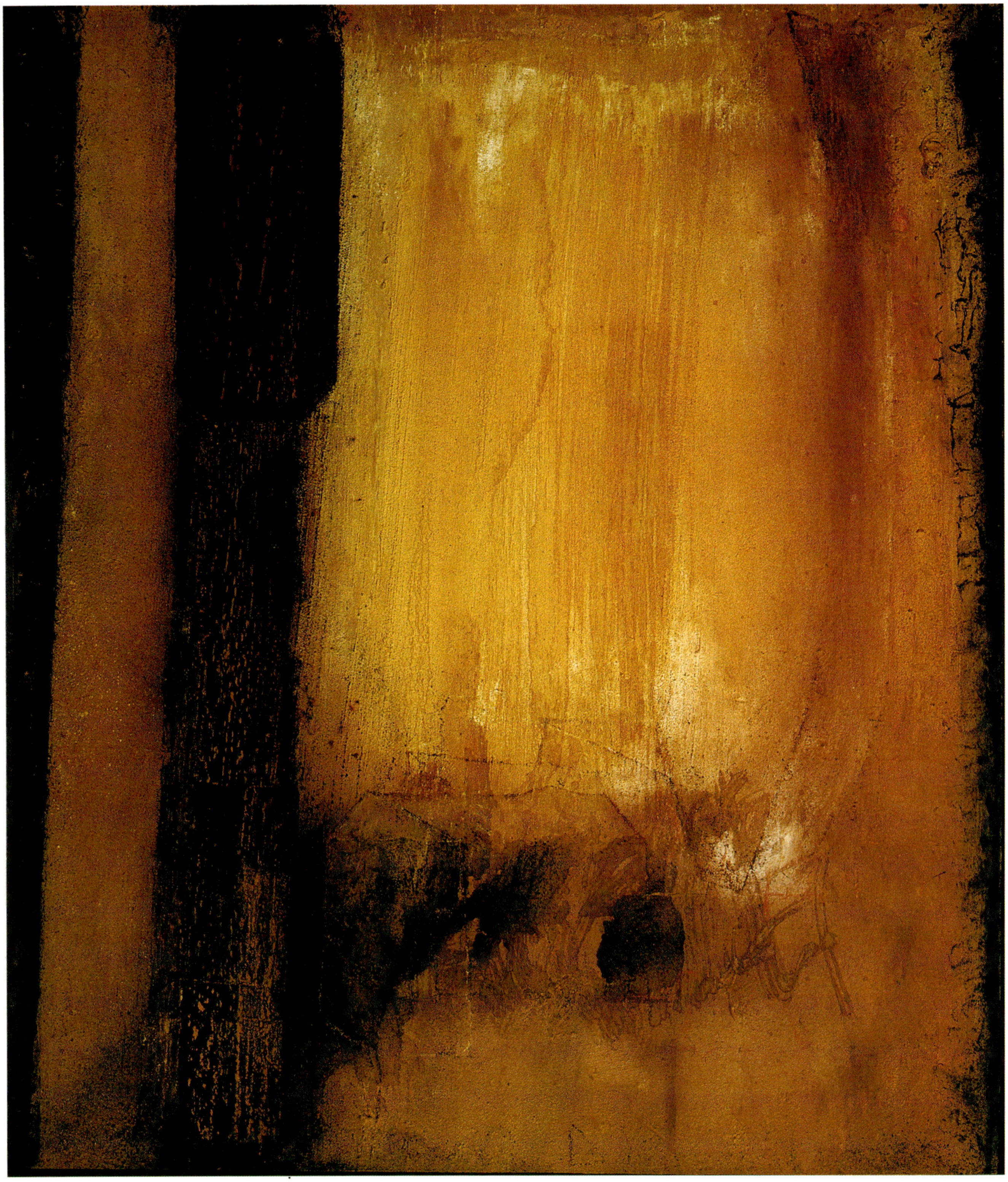

Plate 28

Reflections on a Quiet Place 1992
Pastel, Pigment, Mixed Media on Wood
48 × 42 inches (122 × 107 cm)

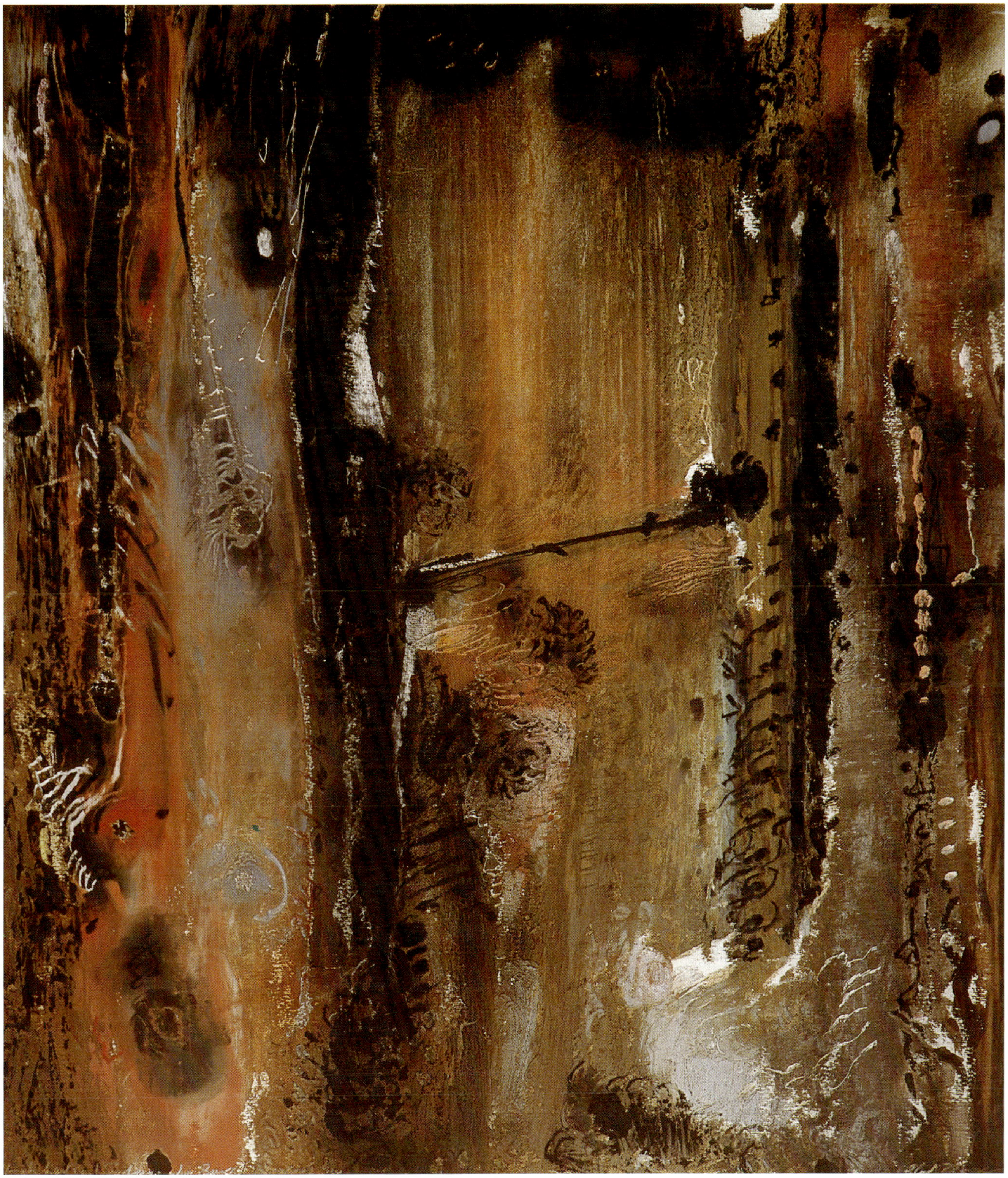

Plate 29

High Ledge, Falaise de Buoux Provence 1994
Pastel on Paper
20 × 18 inches (51 × 46 cm)

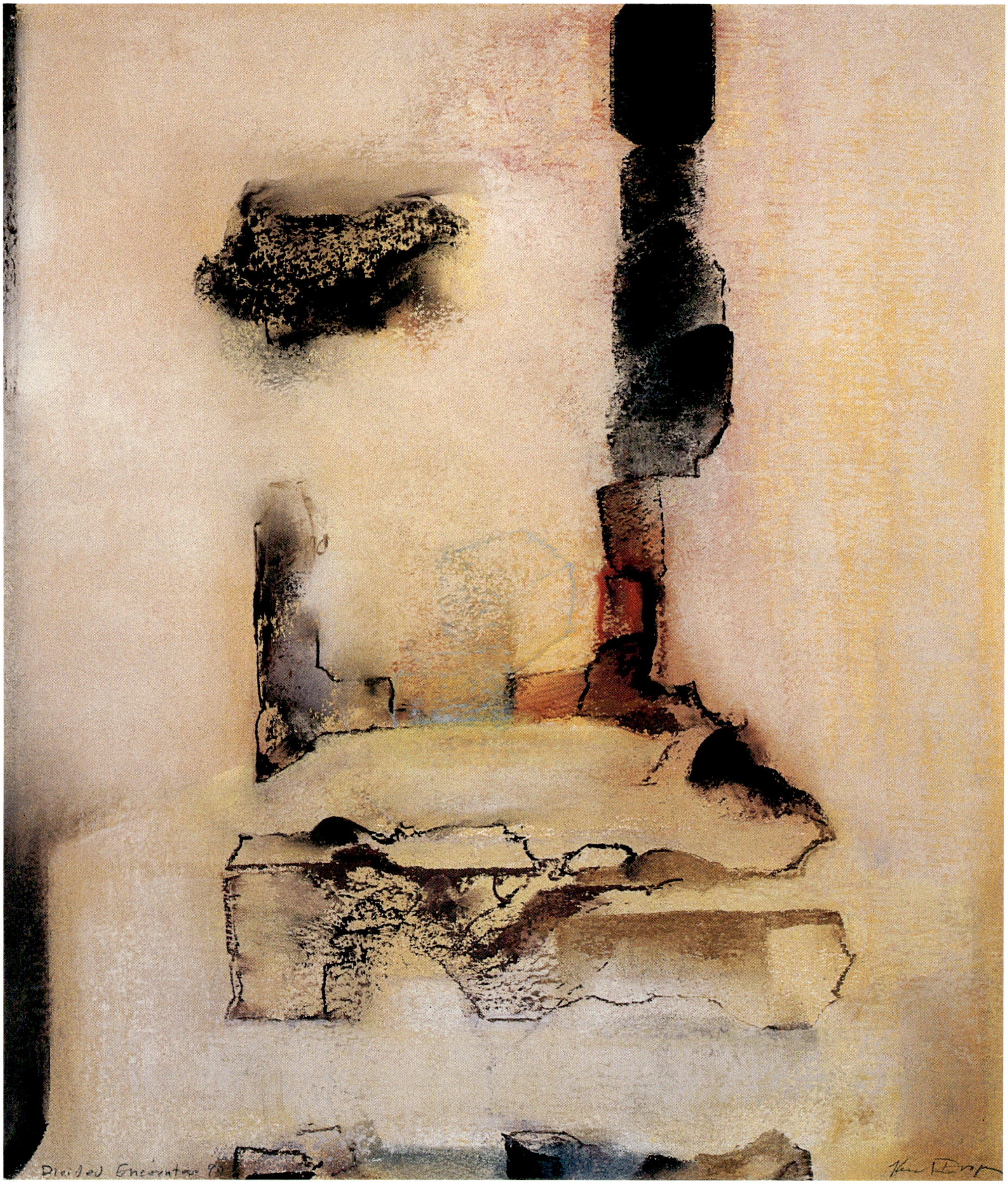

Plate 30

Divided Encounter 1990

Pastel on Paper

20 × 18 inches (51 × 46 cm)

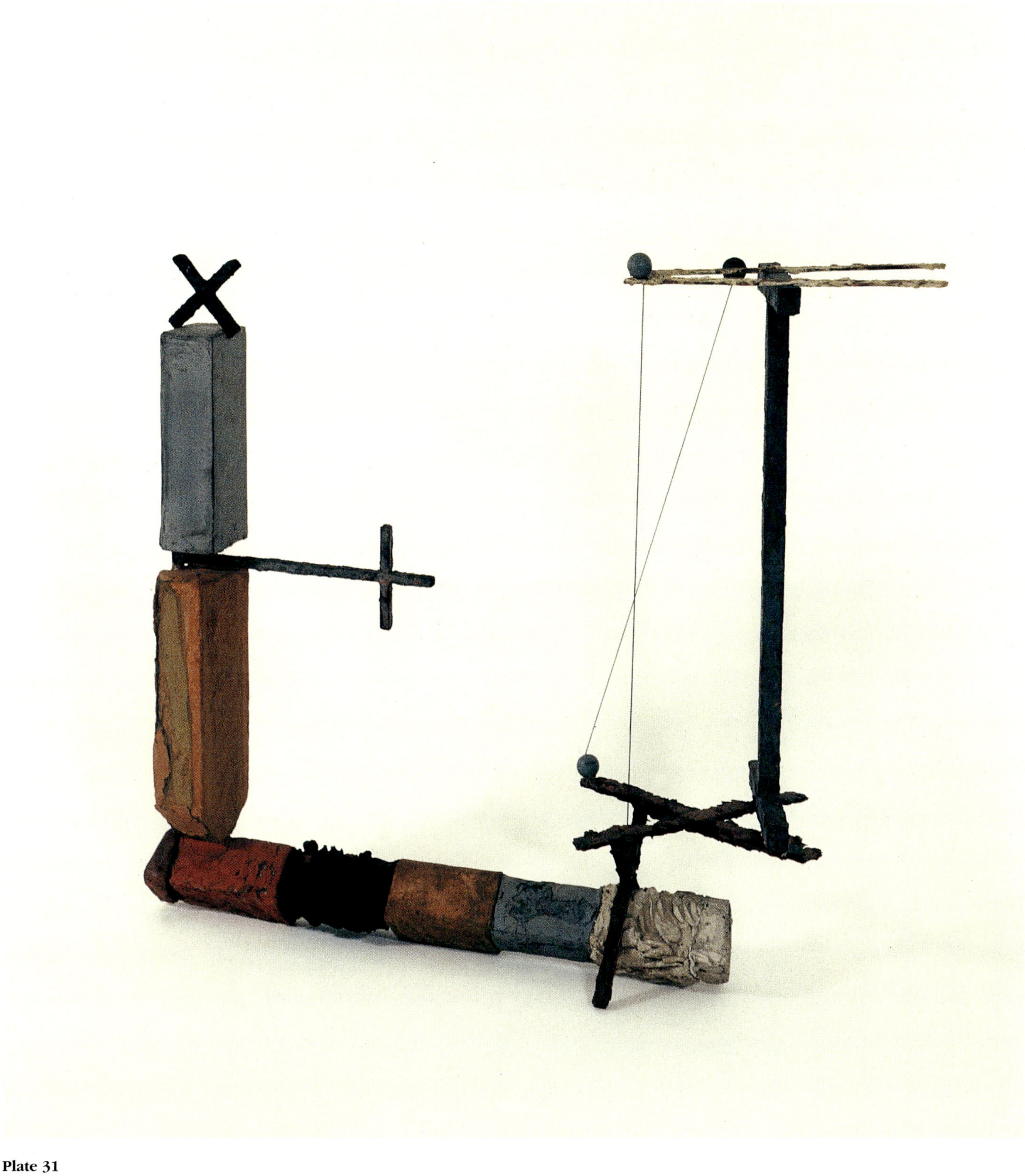

Plate 31

Divided Encounter 1978
Steel, Wood, Resin, Oil Pigment
22 × 28 × 10 inches (56 × 71 × 25 cm)

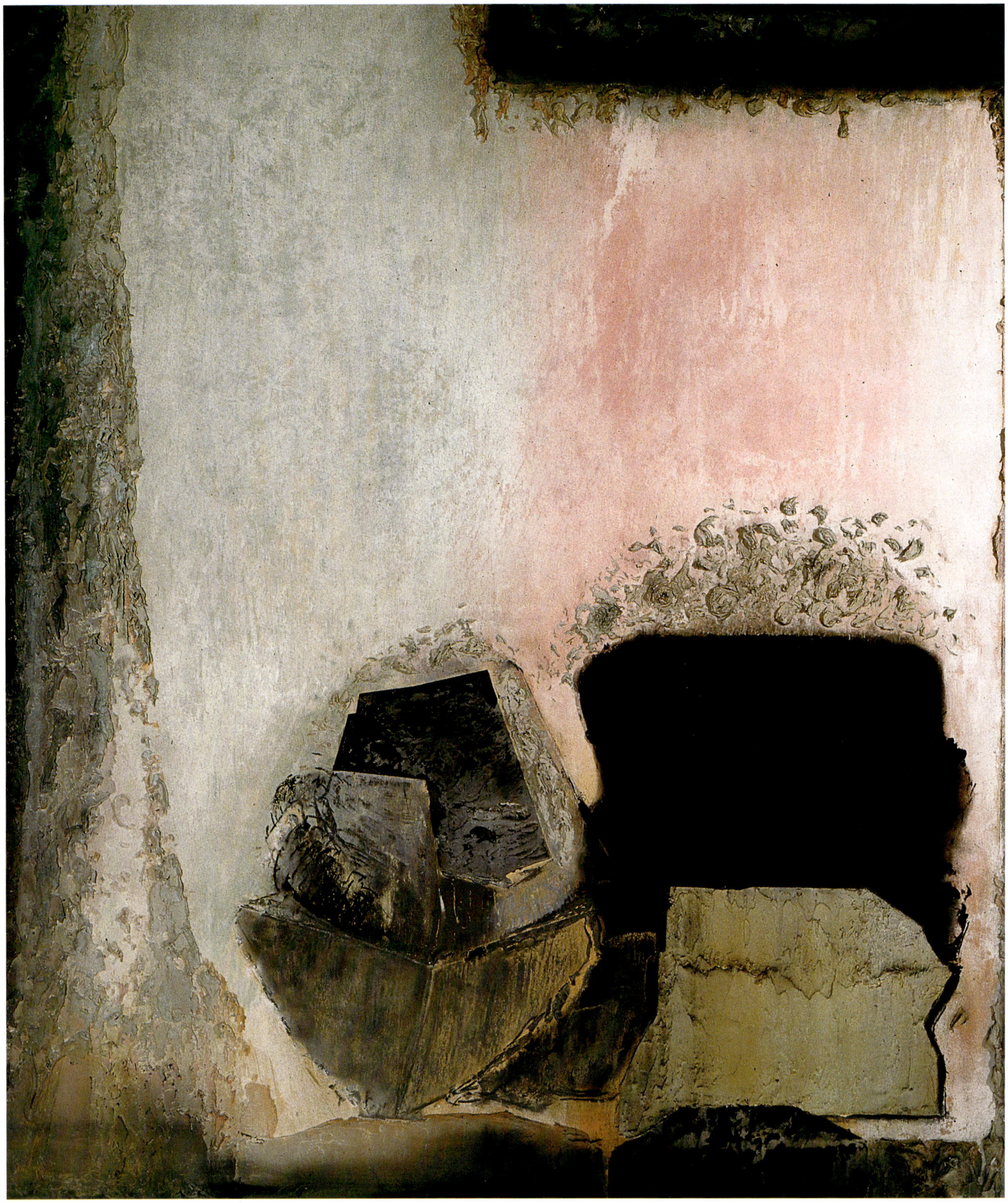

Plate 32

Stones 1992
Pastel, Pigment, Mixed Media on Wood
48 × 42 inches (122 × 107 cm)

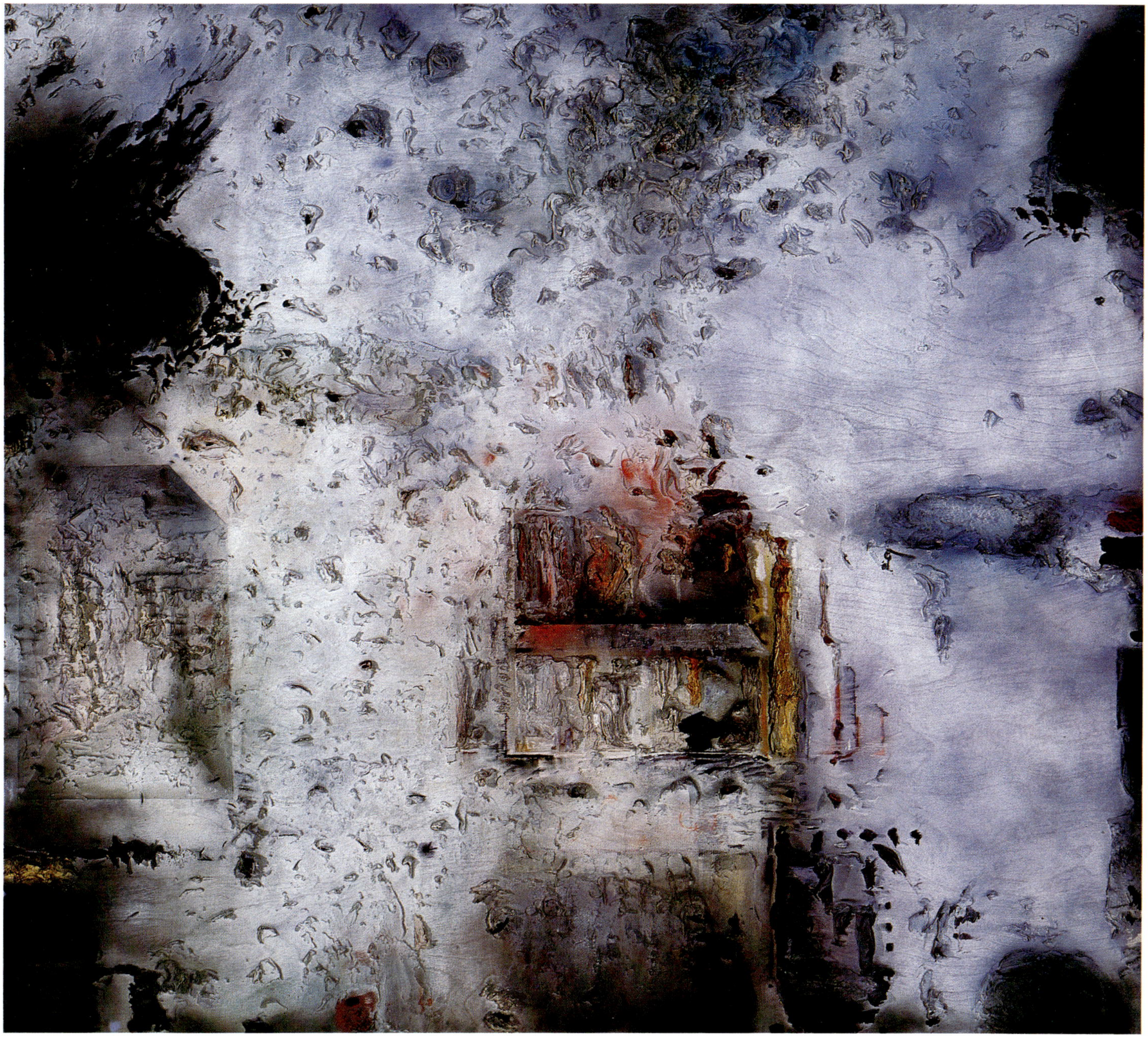

Plate 33

Light Quarry 1994

Oil and Pigment on Wood

42 × 48 inches (107 × 122 cm)

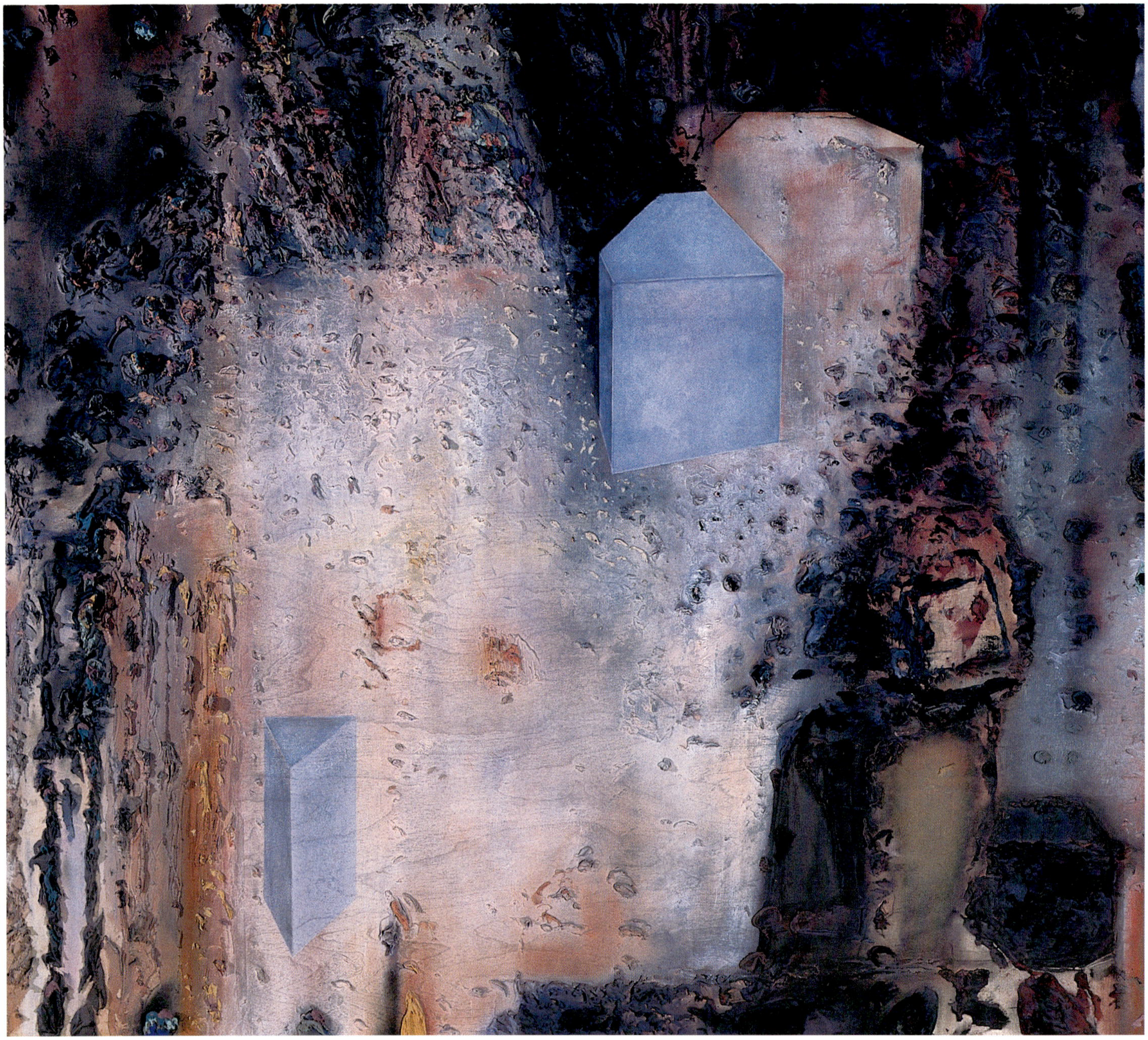

Plate 34

Blue Stone 1993
Oil and Pigment on Wood
42 × 48 inches (107 × 122 cm)

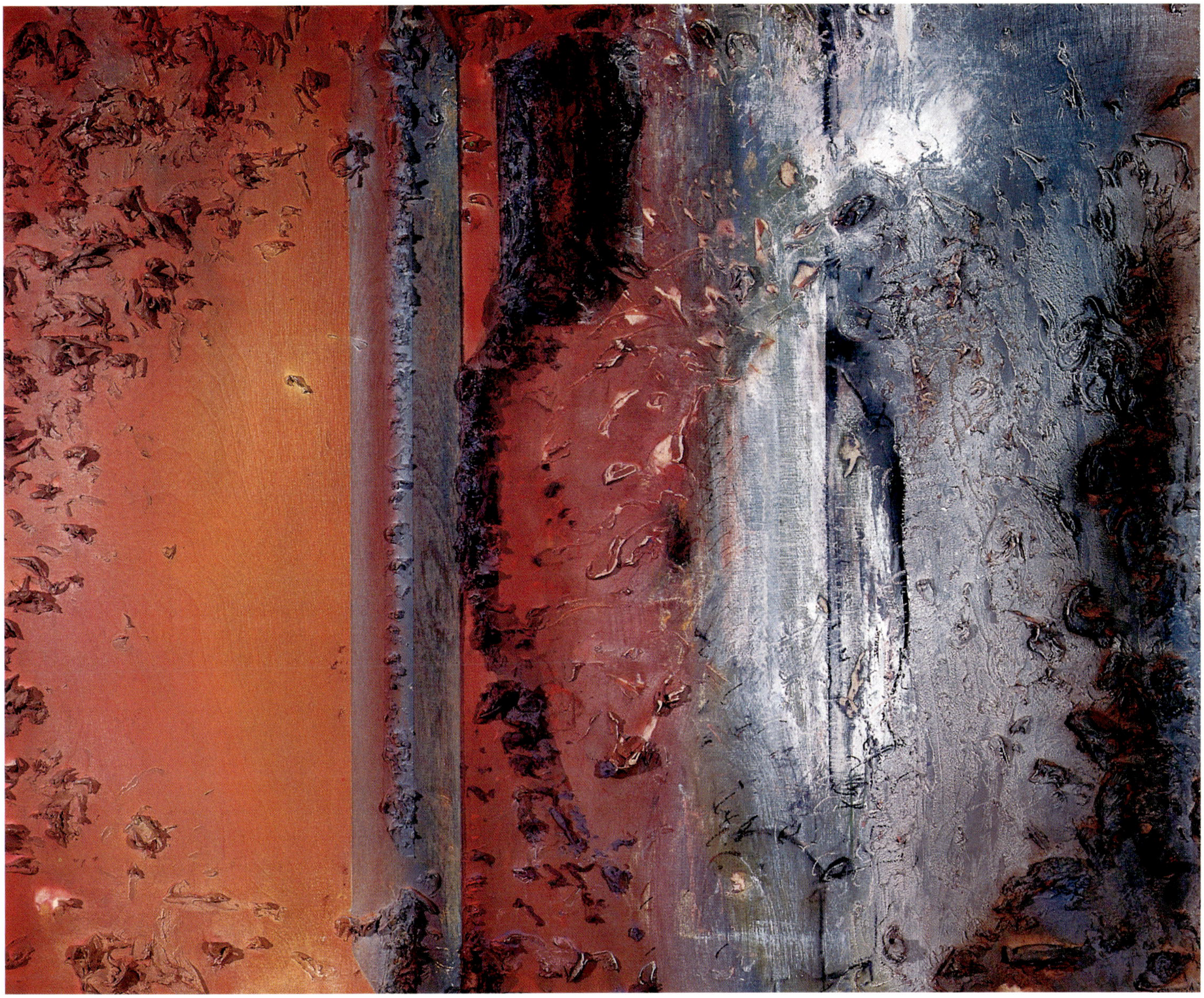

Plate 35

Evening Quarry 1993
Oil and Pigment on Wood
21 × 26 inches (53 × 66 cm)

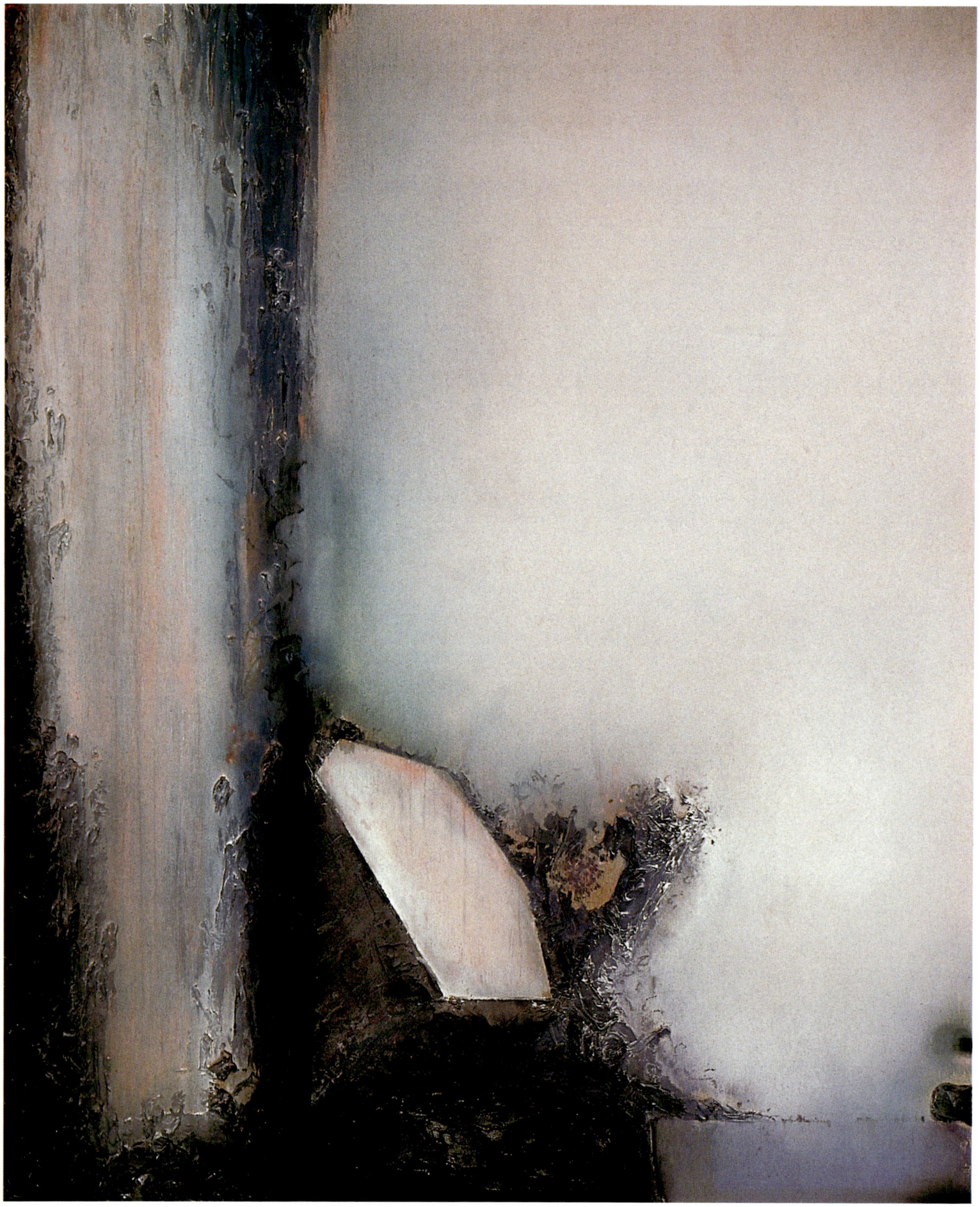

Plate 36

Mirage 1993
Mixed Media on Wood
26 × 22 inches (66 × 56 cm)

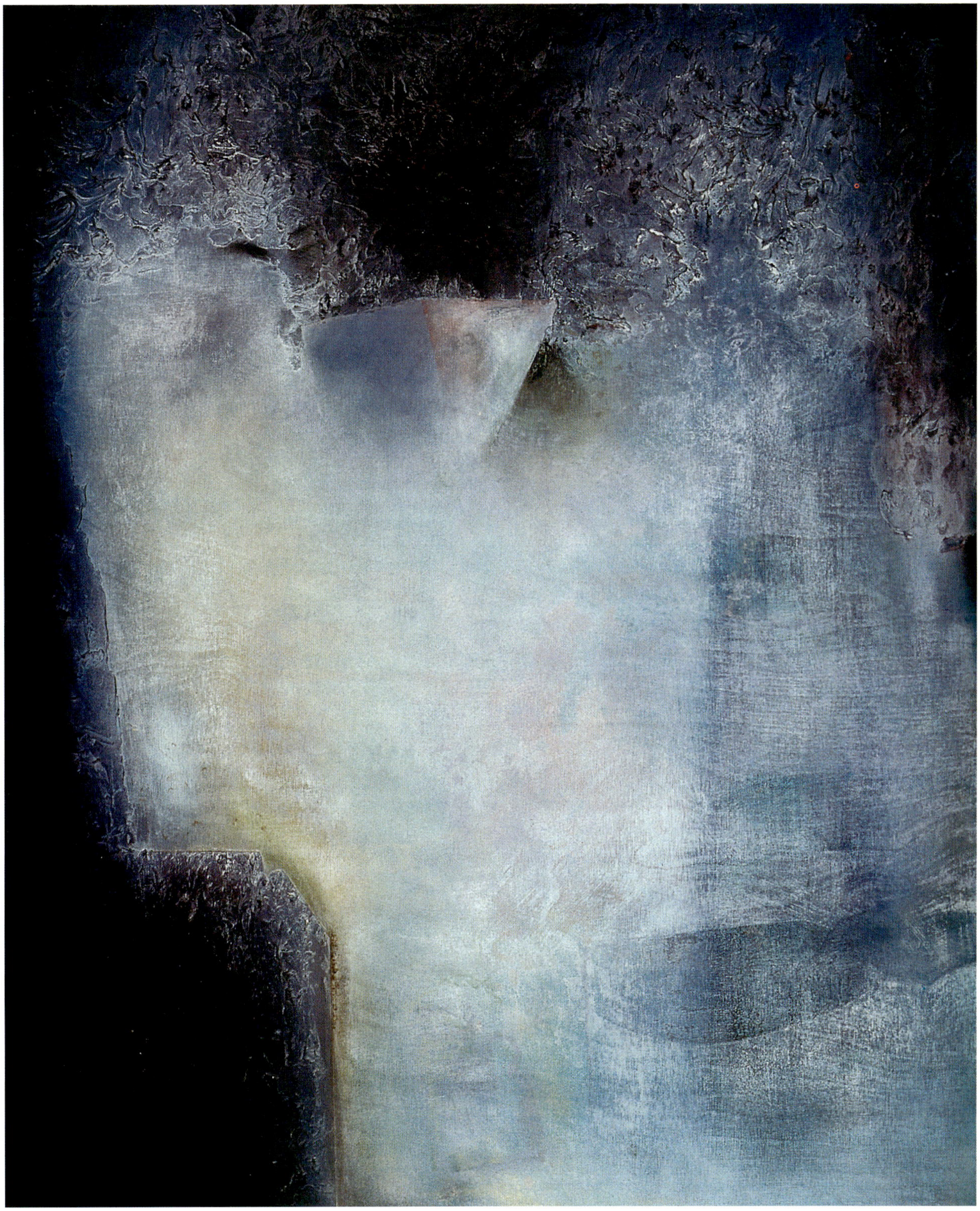

Plate 37

Transient Light 1993
Mixed Media on Wood
26 × 22 inches (66 × 56 cm)

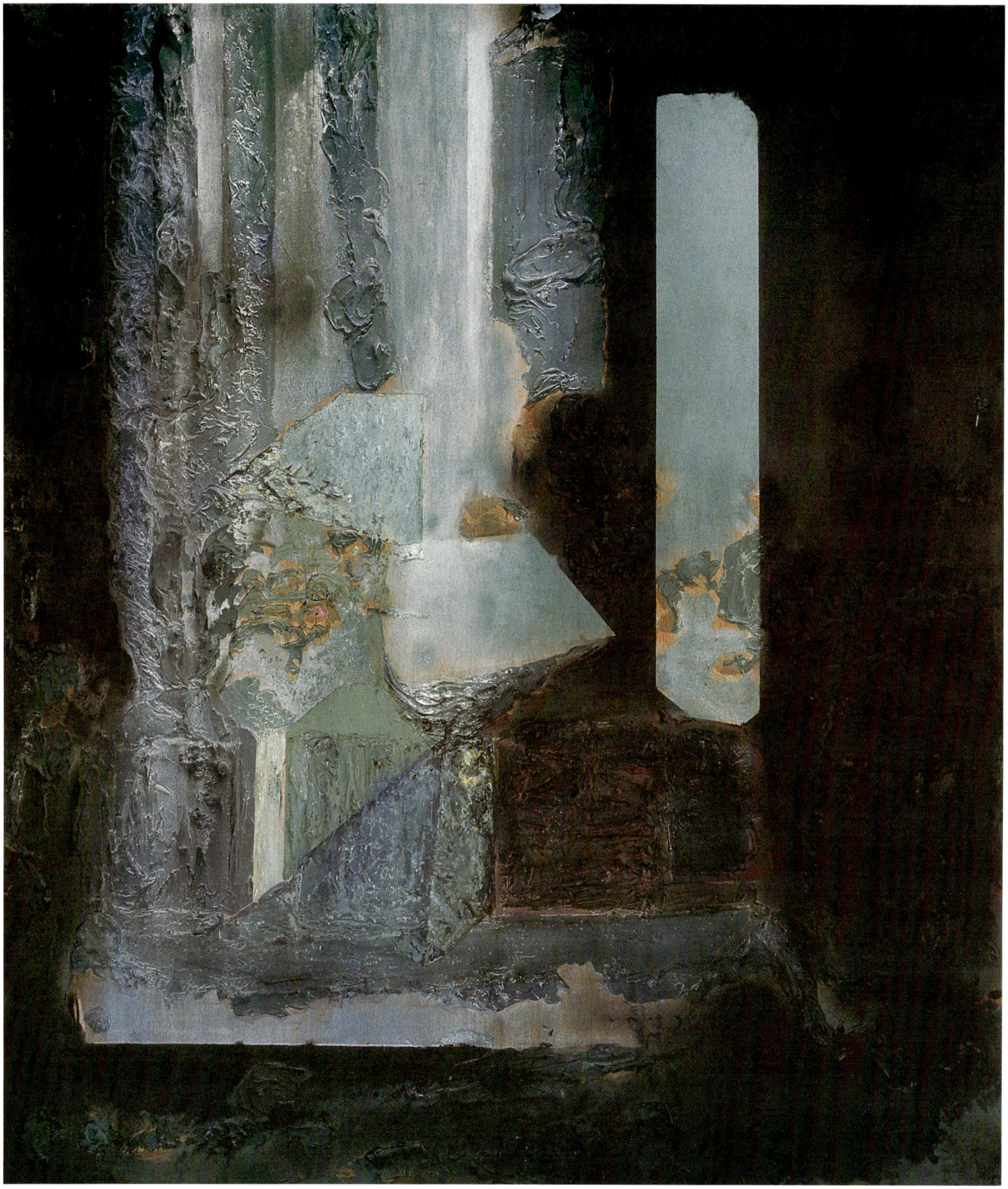

Plate 38

Light Through Dark 1993
Pastel, Pigment, Mixed Media on Wood
48 × 42 inches (122 × 107 cm)

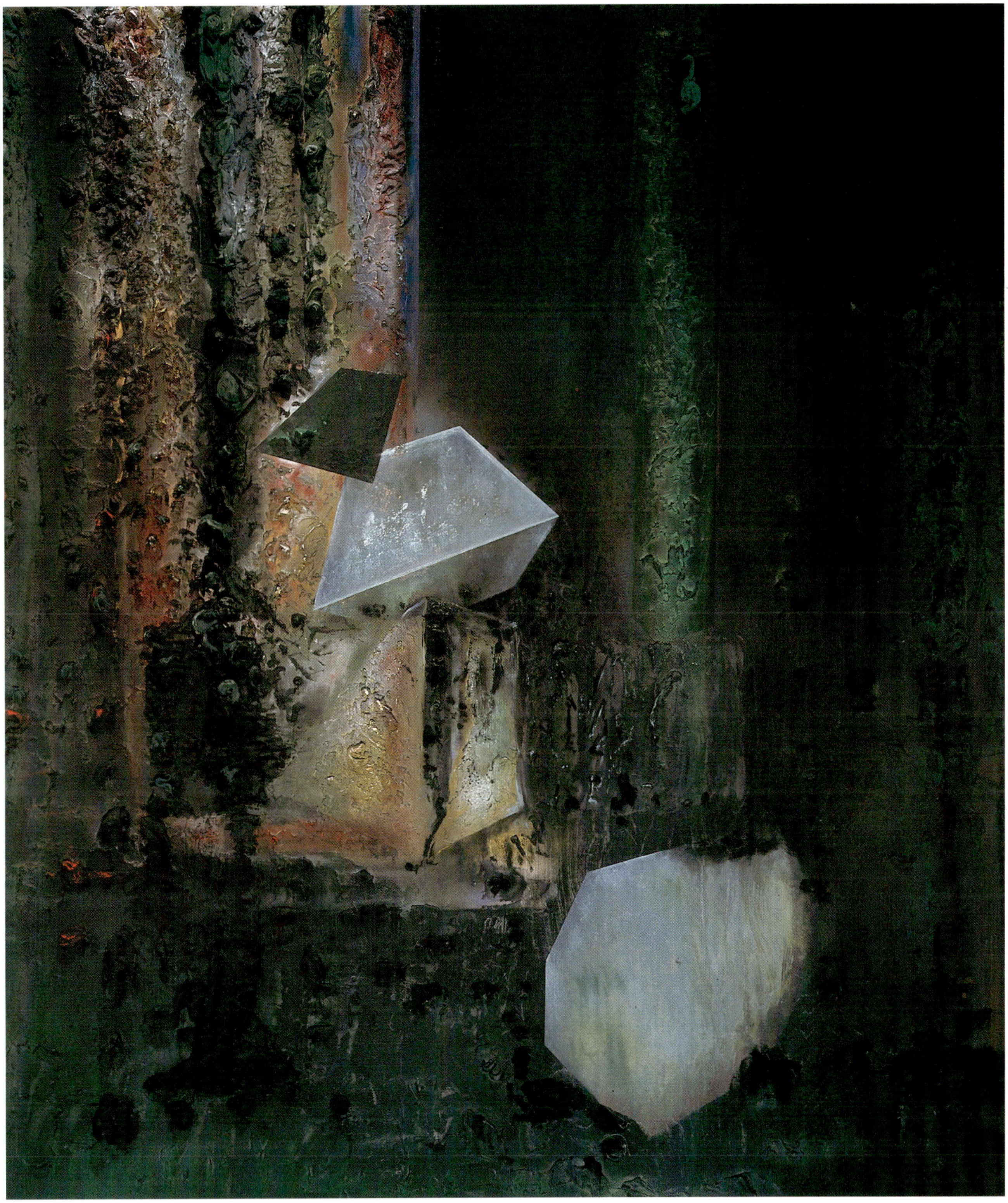

Plate 39

Darkness and Light 1993–4
Oil and Pigment on Wood
48 × 42 inches (122 × 107 cm)

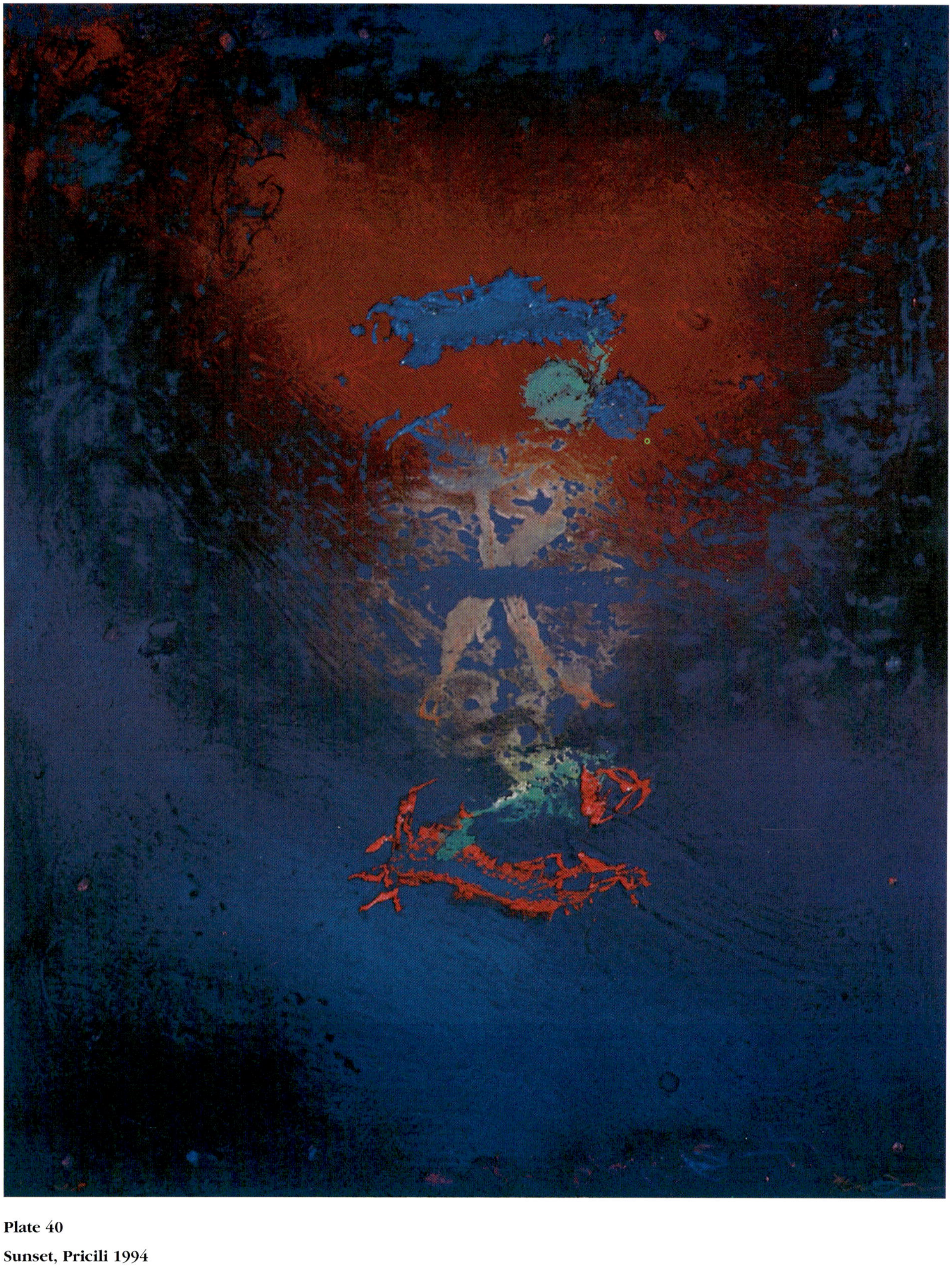

Plate 40

Sunset, Pricili 1994
Pastel on Paper
13¾ × 11½ inches (35 × 29 cm)

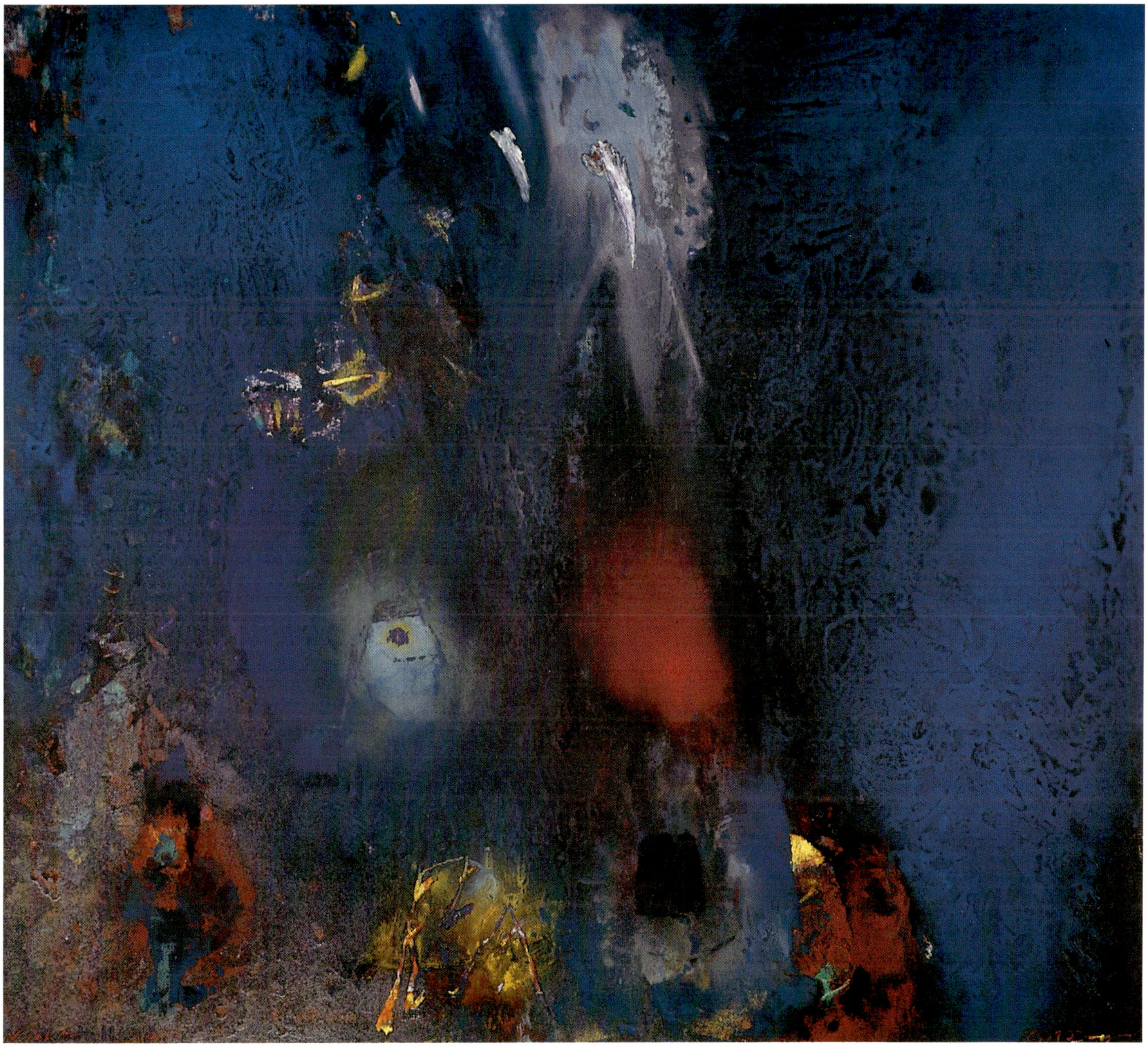

Plate 41

Night Fall 1994
Pastel on Paper
14 × 16 inches (36 × 41 cm)

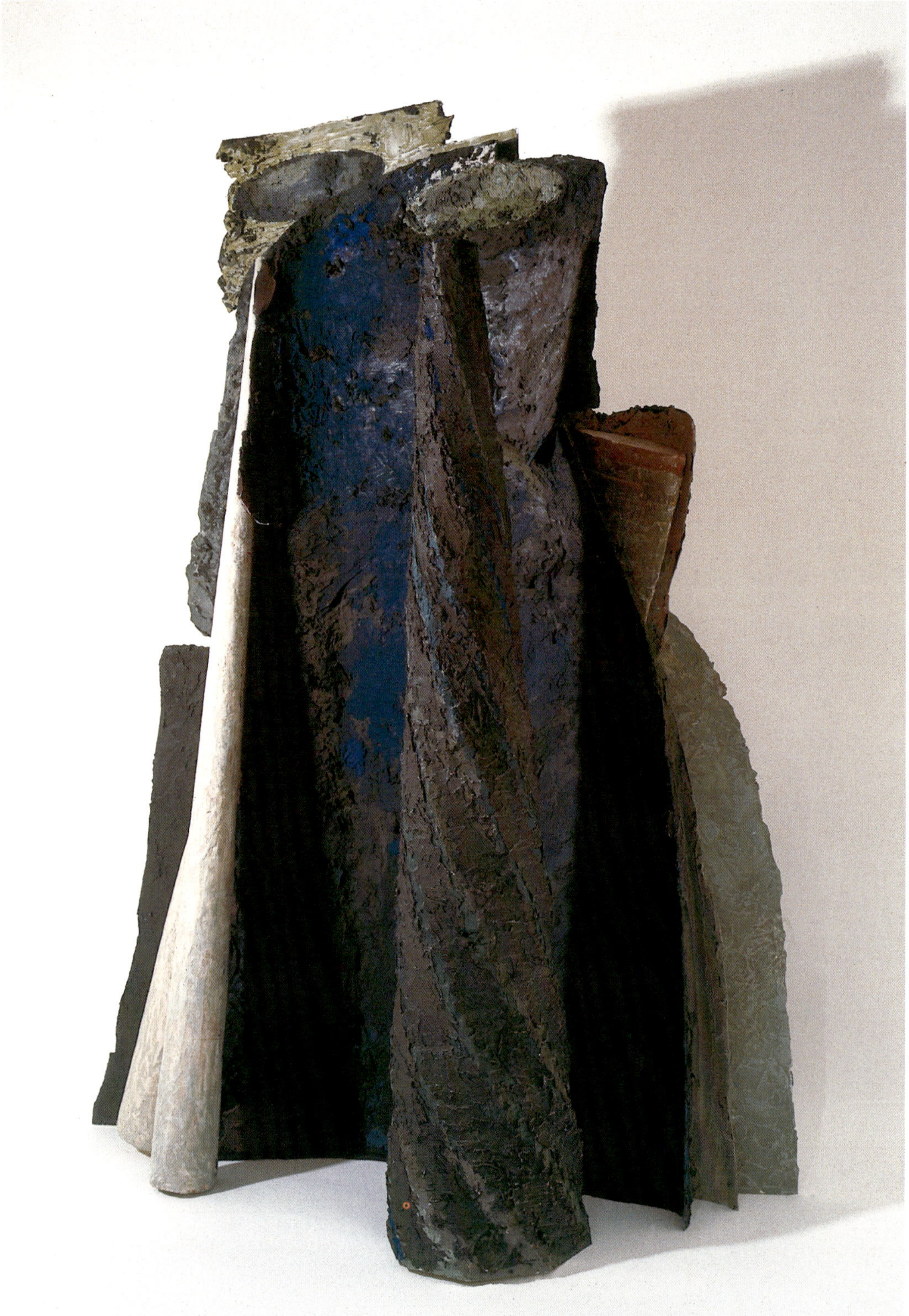

Plate 42

Light Through Dark (The Fall) 1990
Steel, Wood, Resin
50 × 40 × 24 inches (127 × 112 × 61 cm)

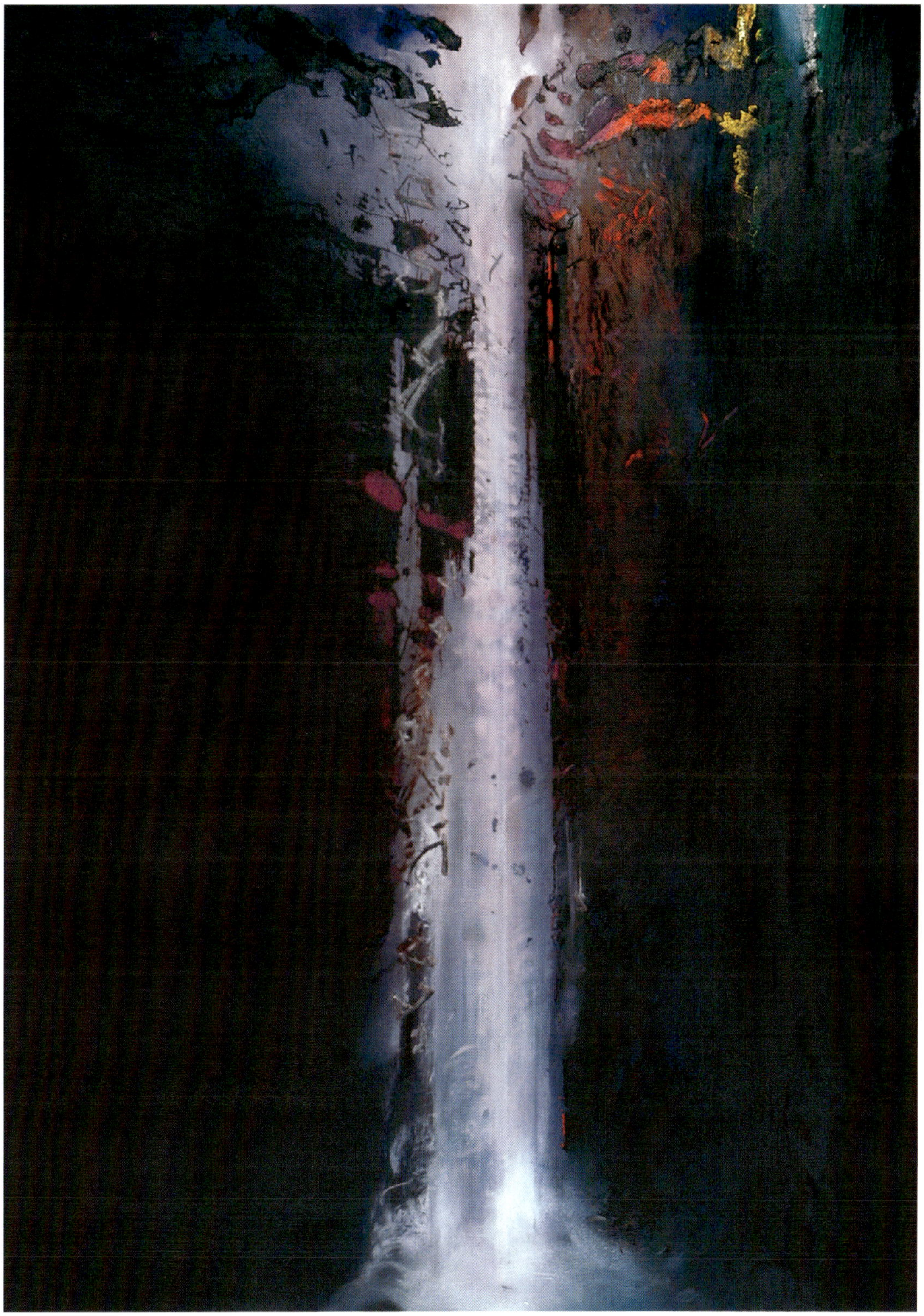

Plate 43

High Fall 1994
Pastel on Paper
34 × 29 inches (86 × 74 cm)

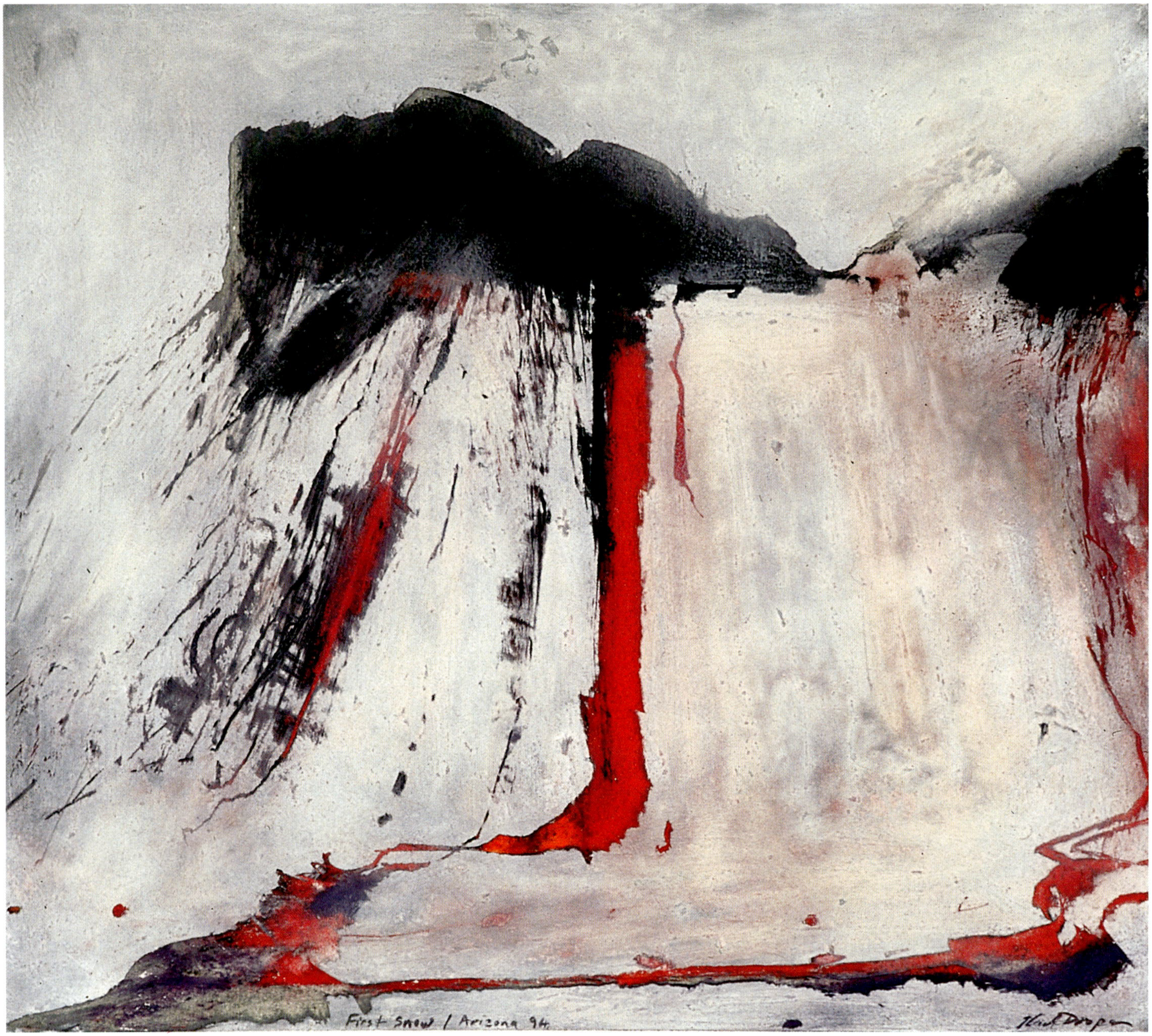

Plate 44

First Snow, Arizona 1994

Pastel on Paper

14 × 16 inches (36 × 41 cm)

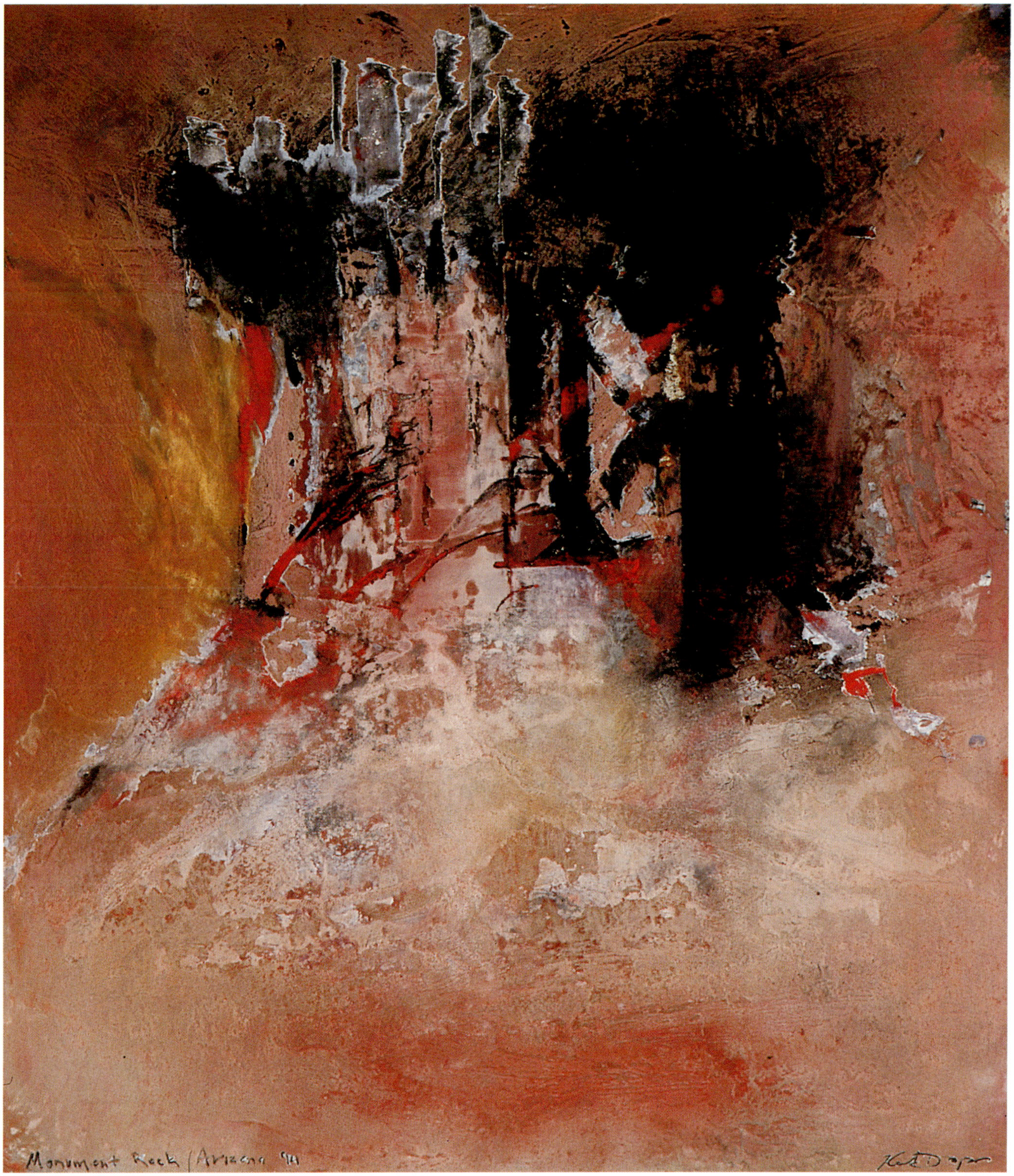

Plate 45

Monument Rock, Arizona '94
Pastel on Paper
20 × 18 inches (51 × 46 cm)

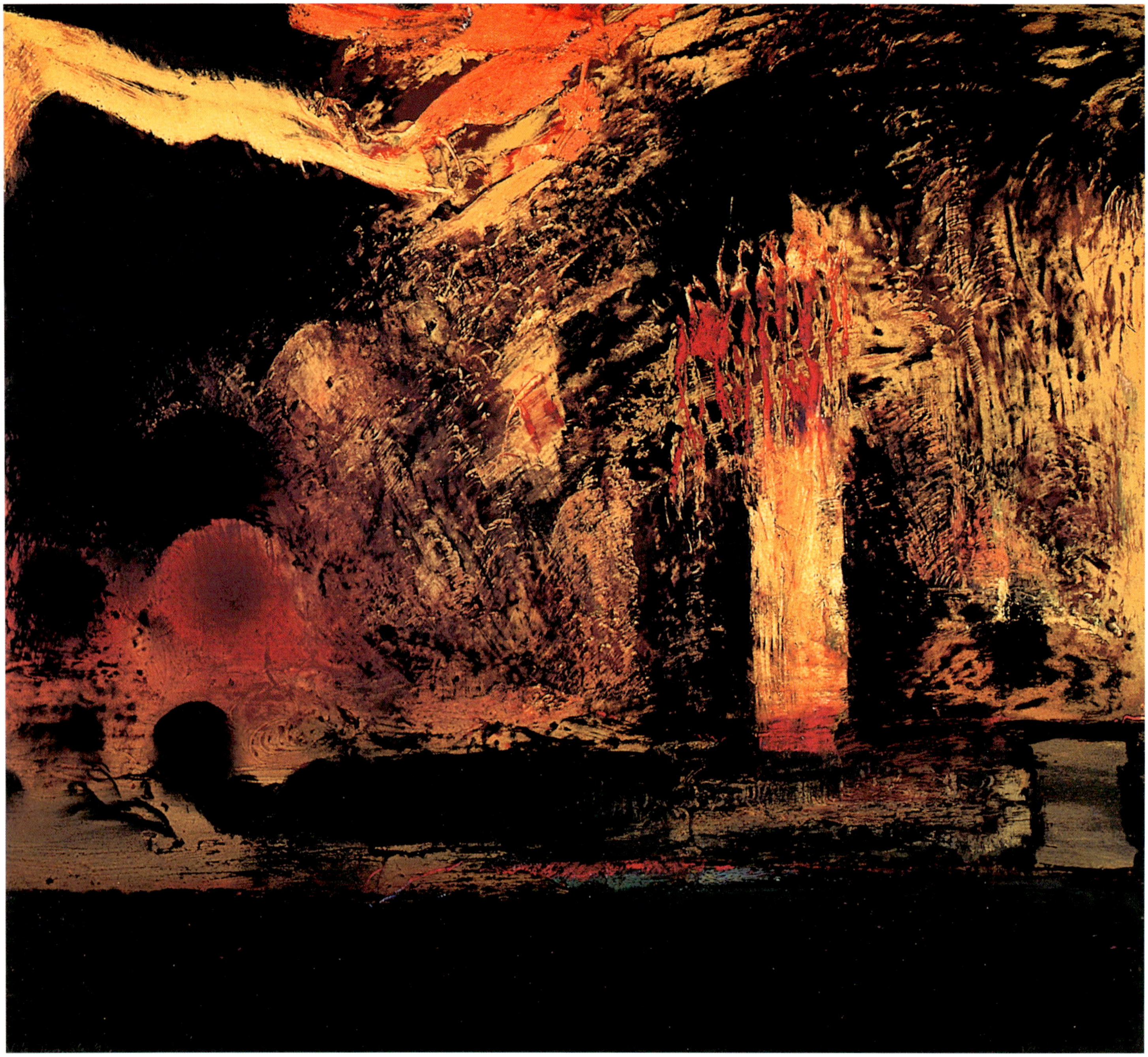

Plate 46

Nile Temple 1993
Pastel on Paper
18 × 20 inches (46 × 51 cm)

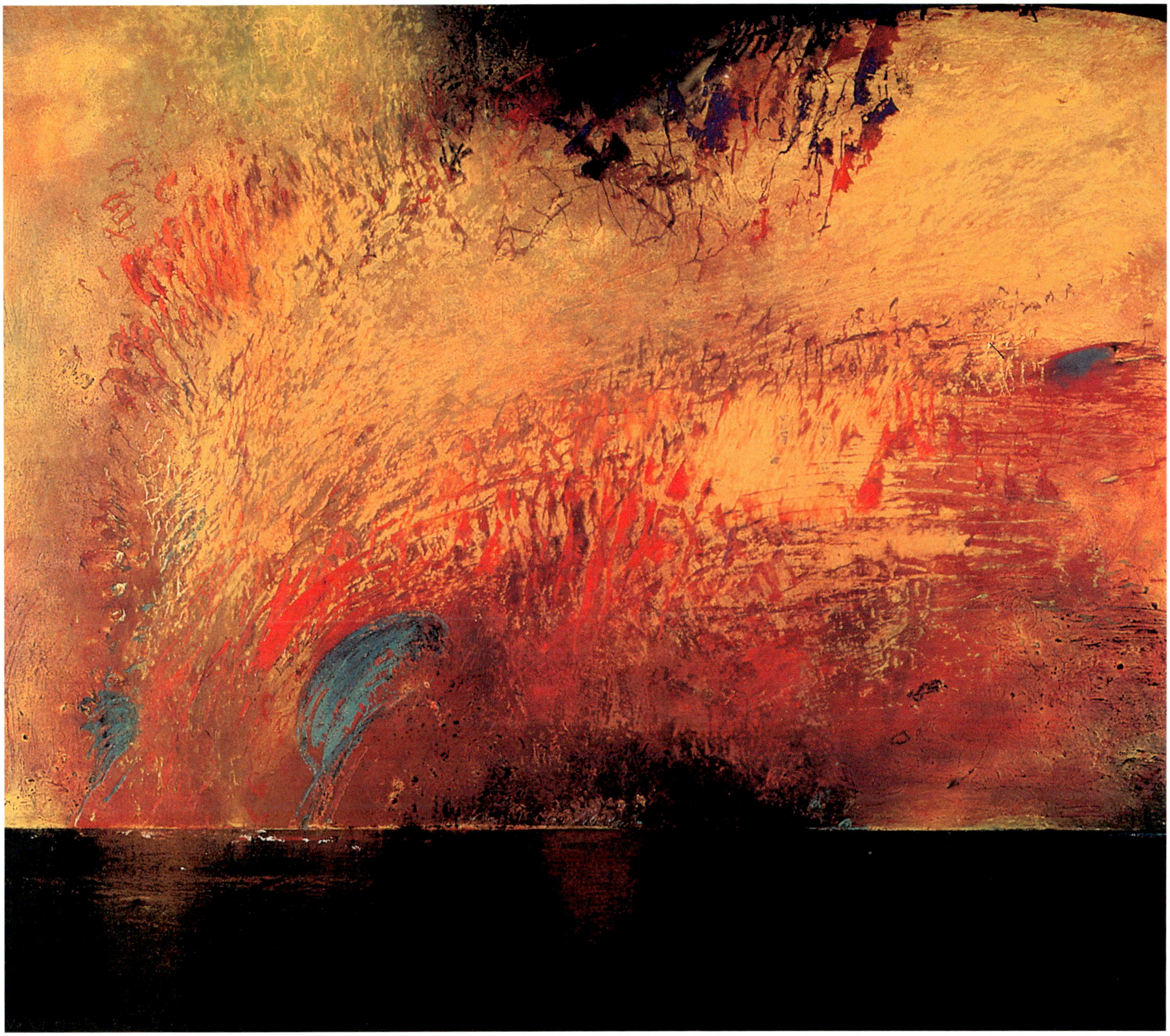

Plate 47

Valley of The Kings, Egypt 1994
Pastel on Paper
22 × 26 inches (56 × 66 cm)

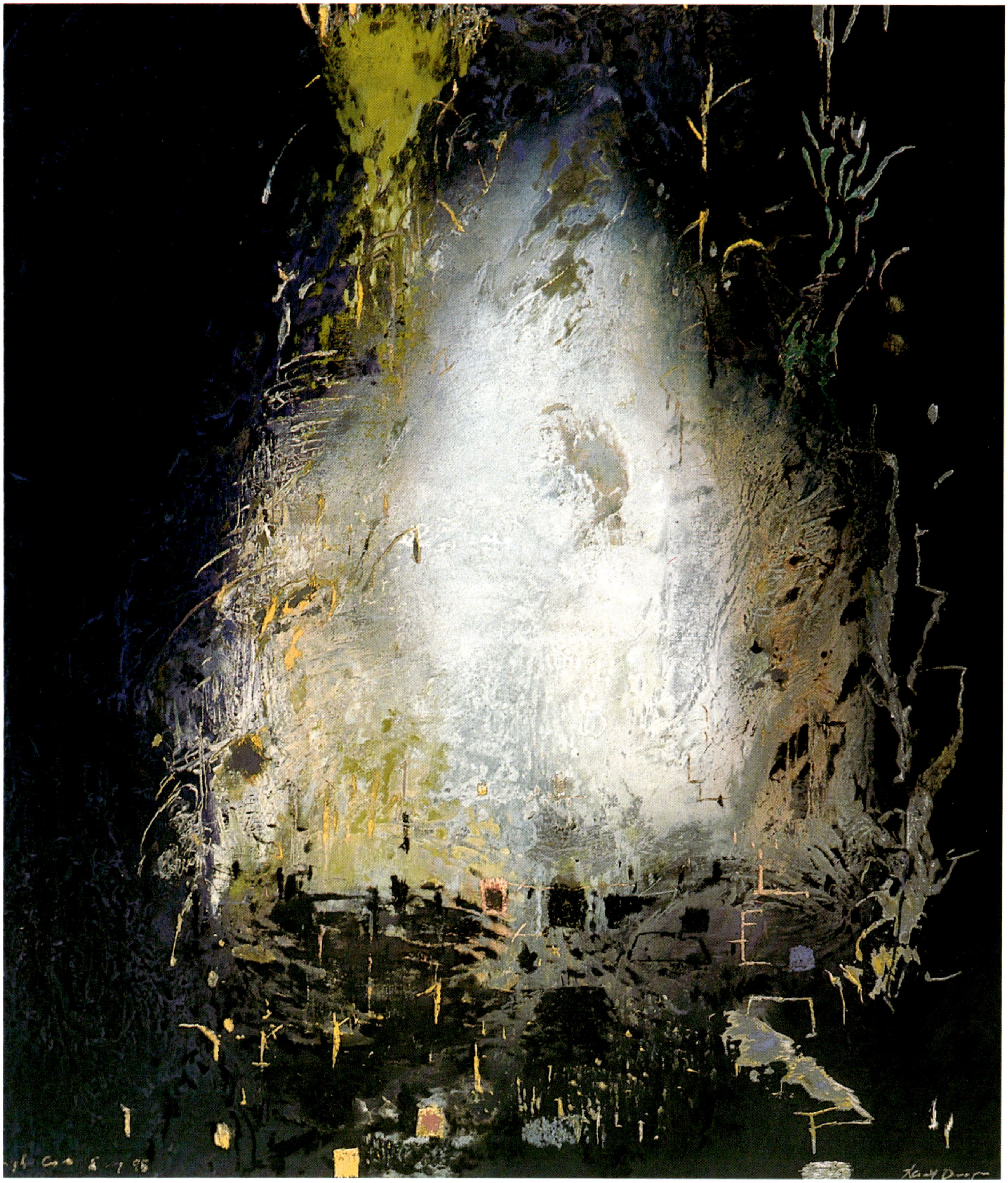

Plate 48

High Cave, Evening 1995

Pastel on Paper

20 × 18 inches (51 × 46 cm)

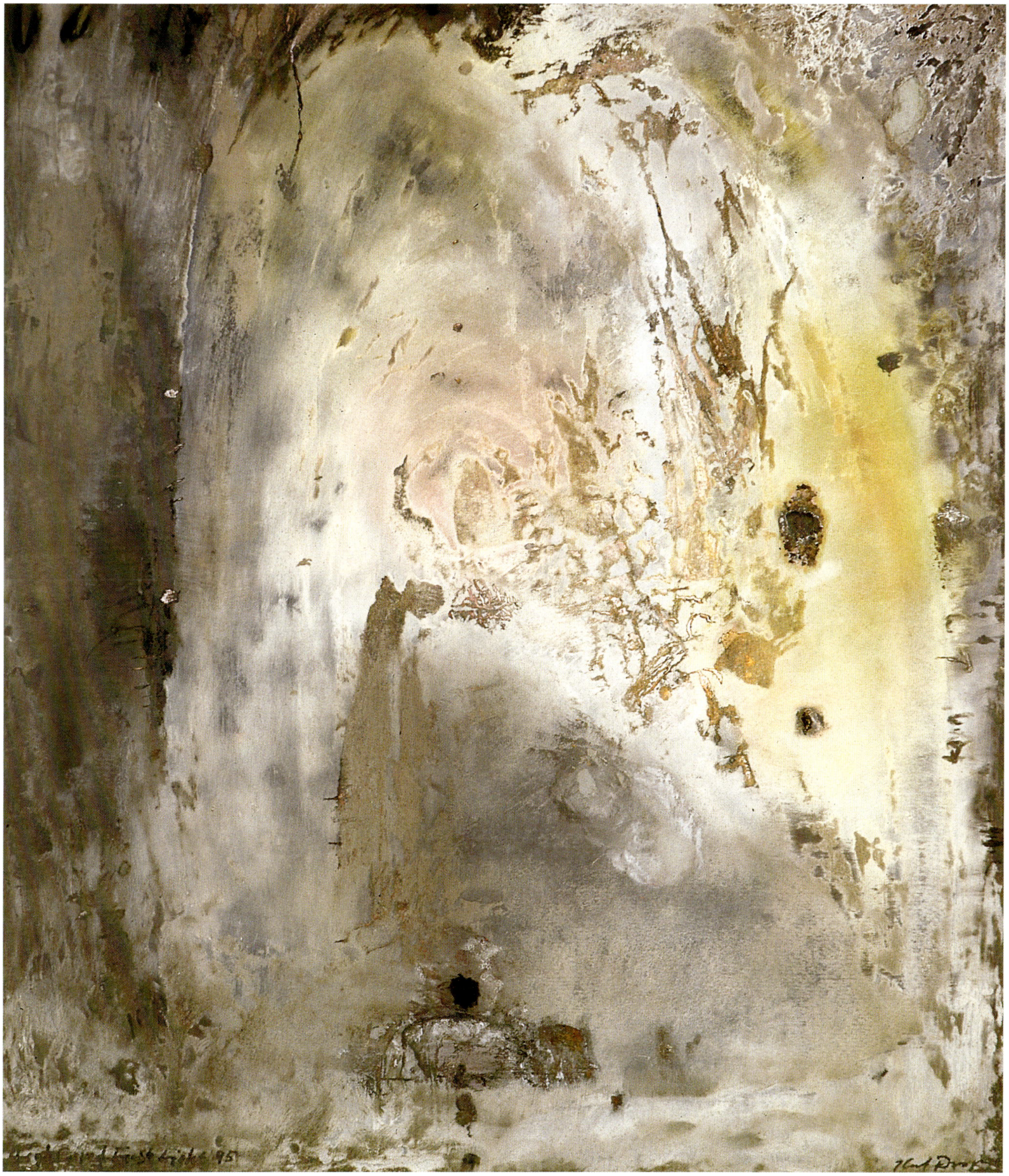

Plate 49

High Cave, First Light 1995
Pastel on Paper
20 × 18 inches (51 × 46 cm)

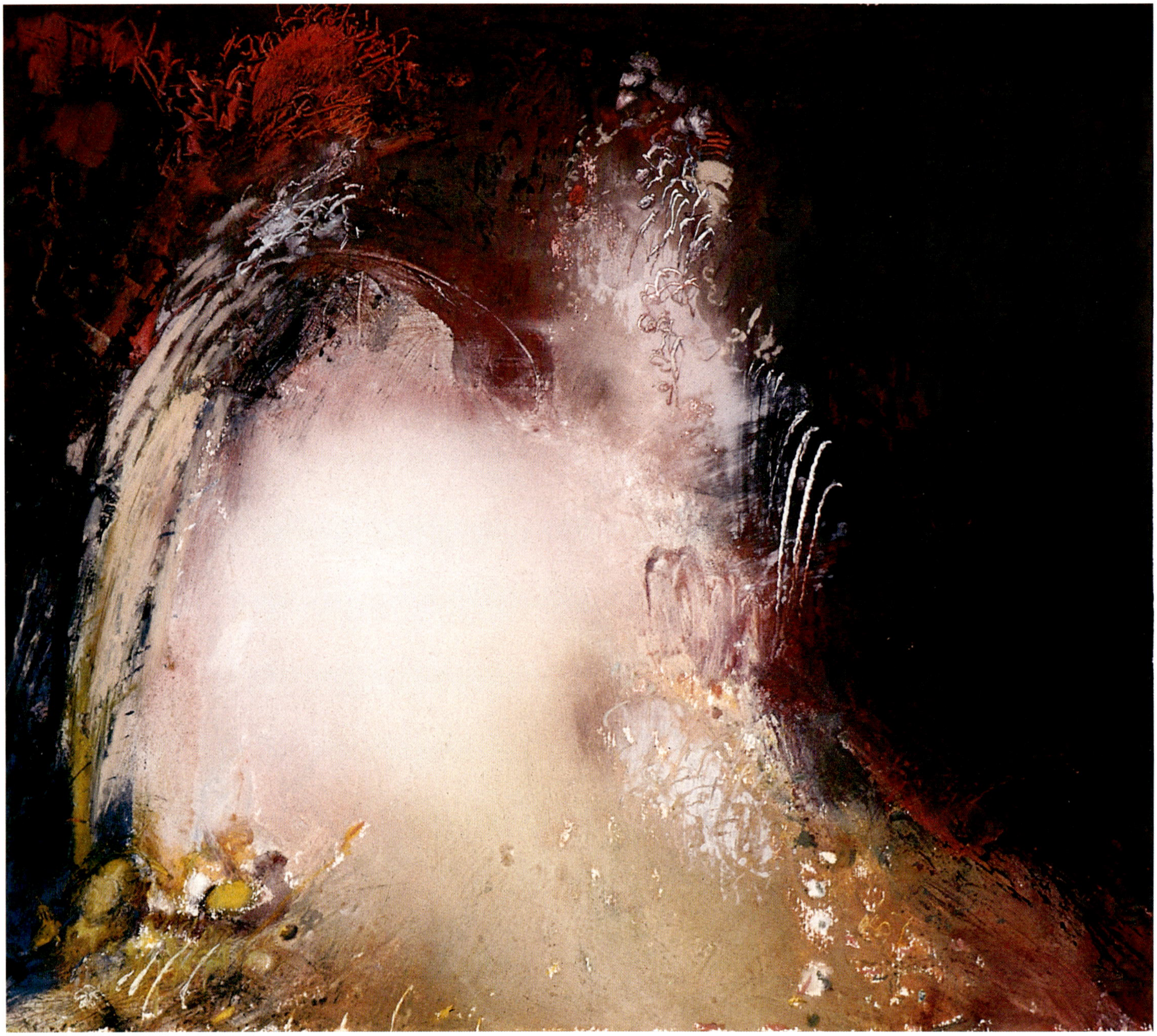

Plate 50
Rustrel 1995
Pastel on Paper
14 × 16 inches (36 × 41 cm)

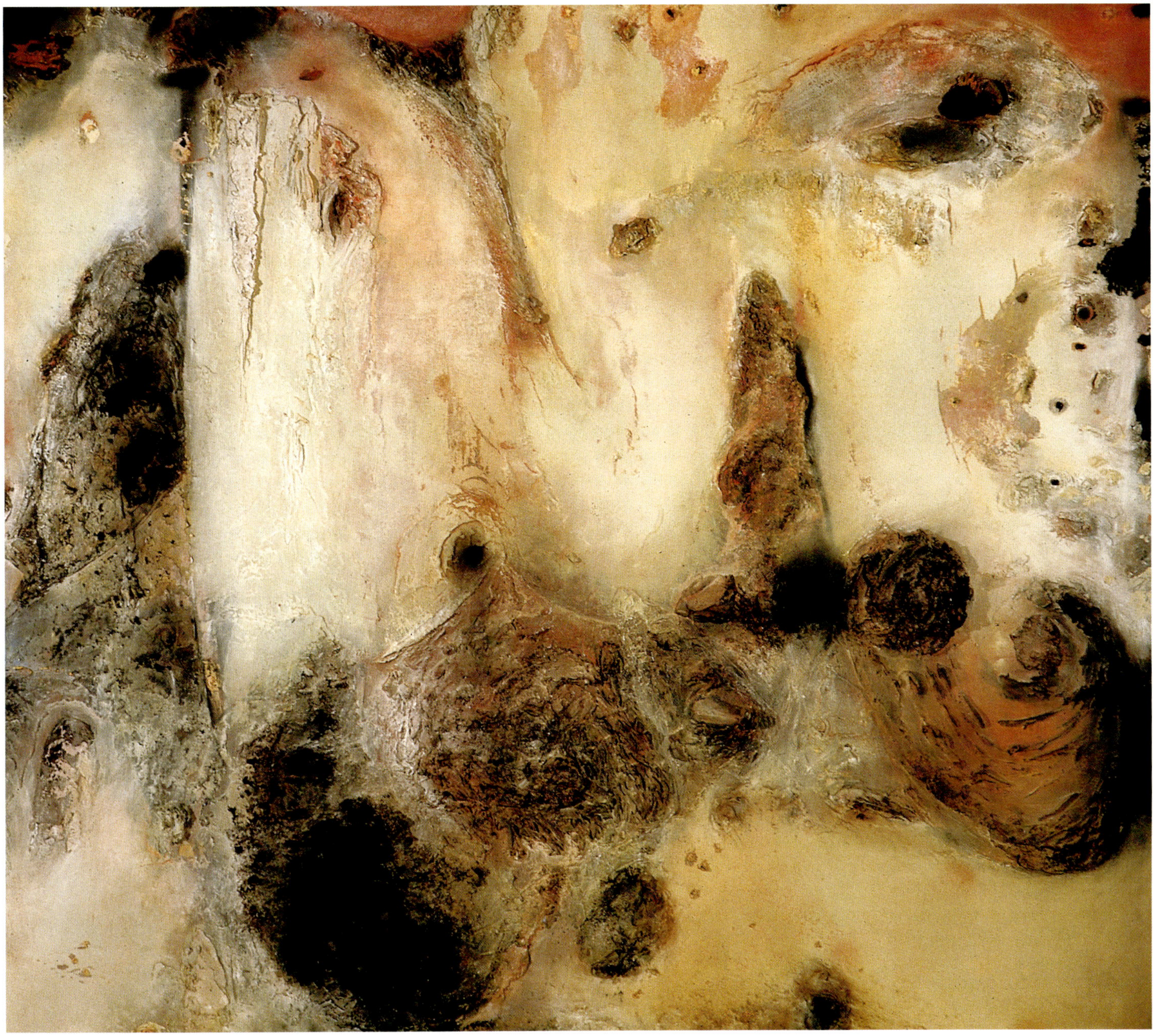

Plate 51

Rustrel, Noon 1995
Oil and Pigment on Wood
42 × 48 inches (105 × 122 cm)

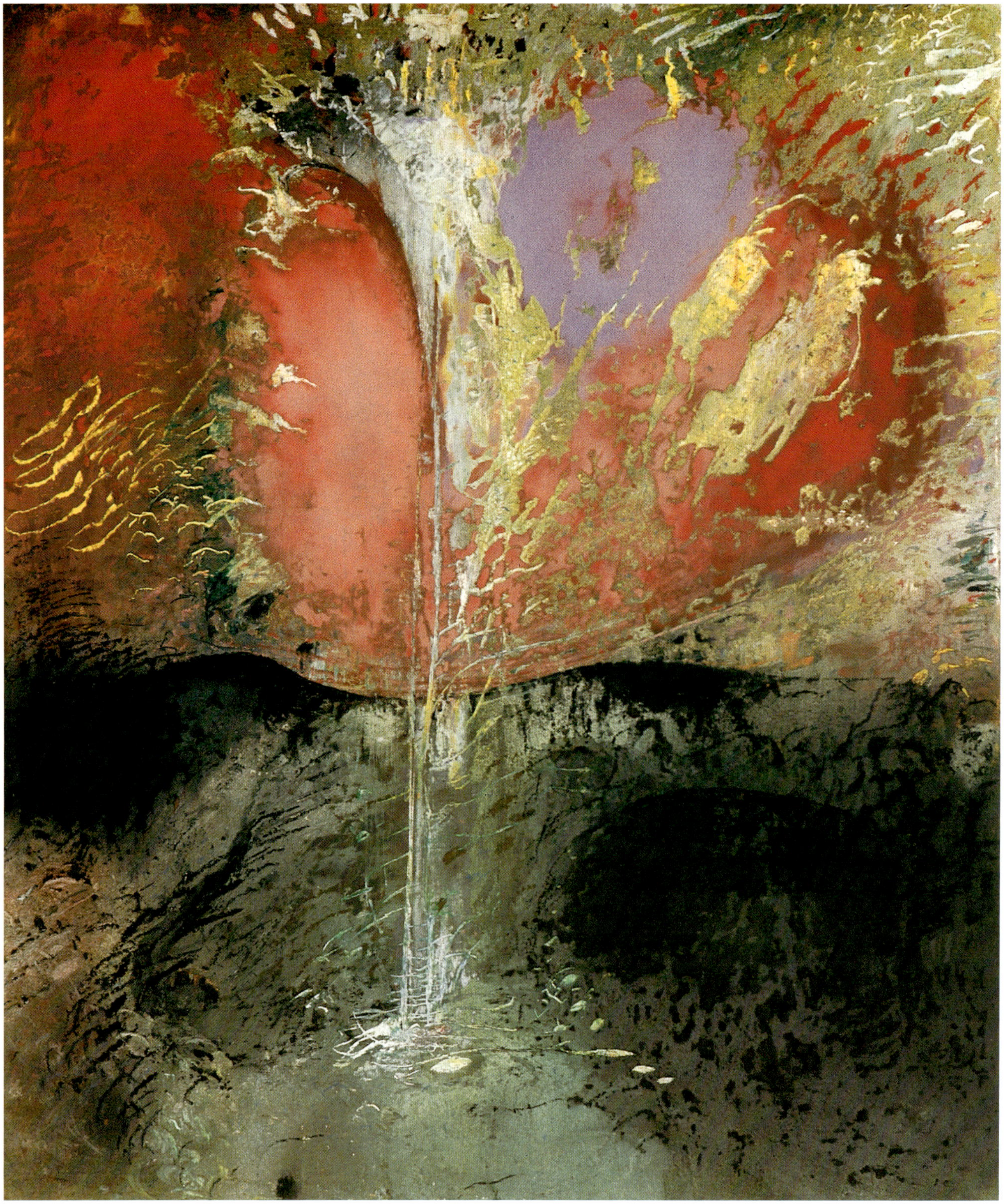

Plate 52

Waterfall, Rustrel, Provence 1995

Pastel on Paper

16 × 14 inches (41 × 36 cm)

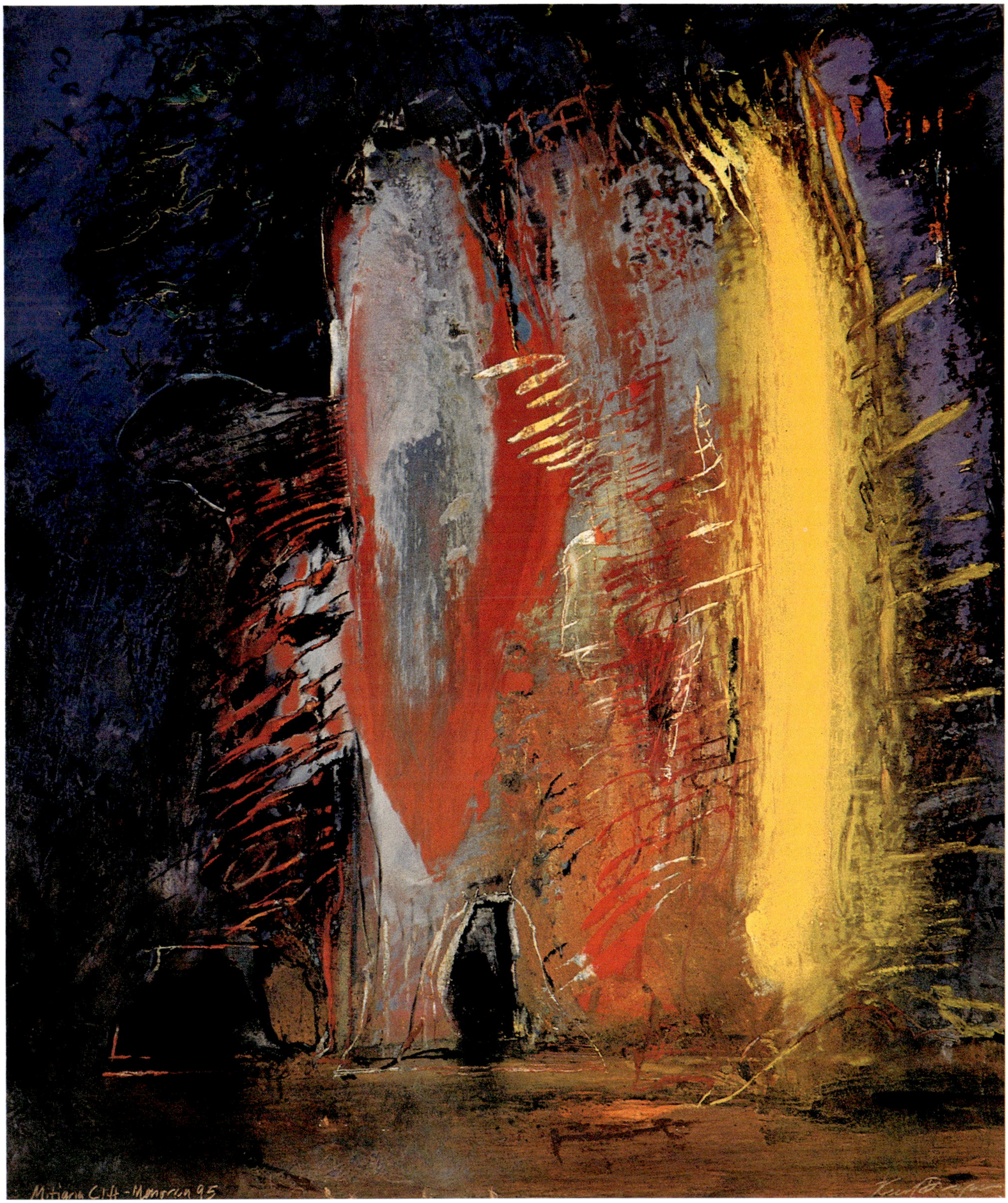

Plate 53

Mitjana Cliff, Menorca 1995
Pastel on Paper
16 × 14 inches (41 × 36 cm)

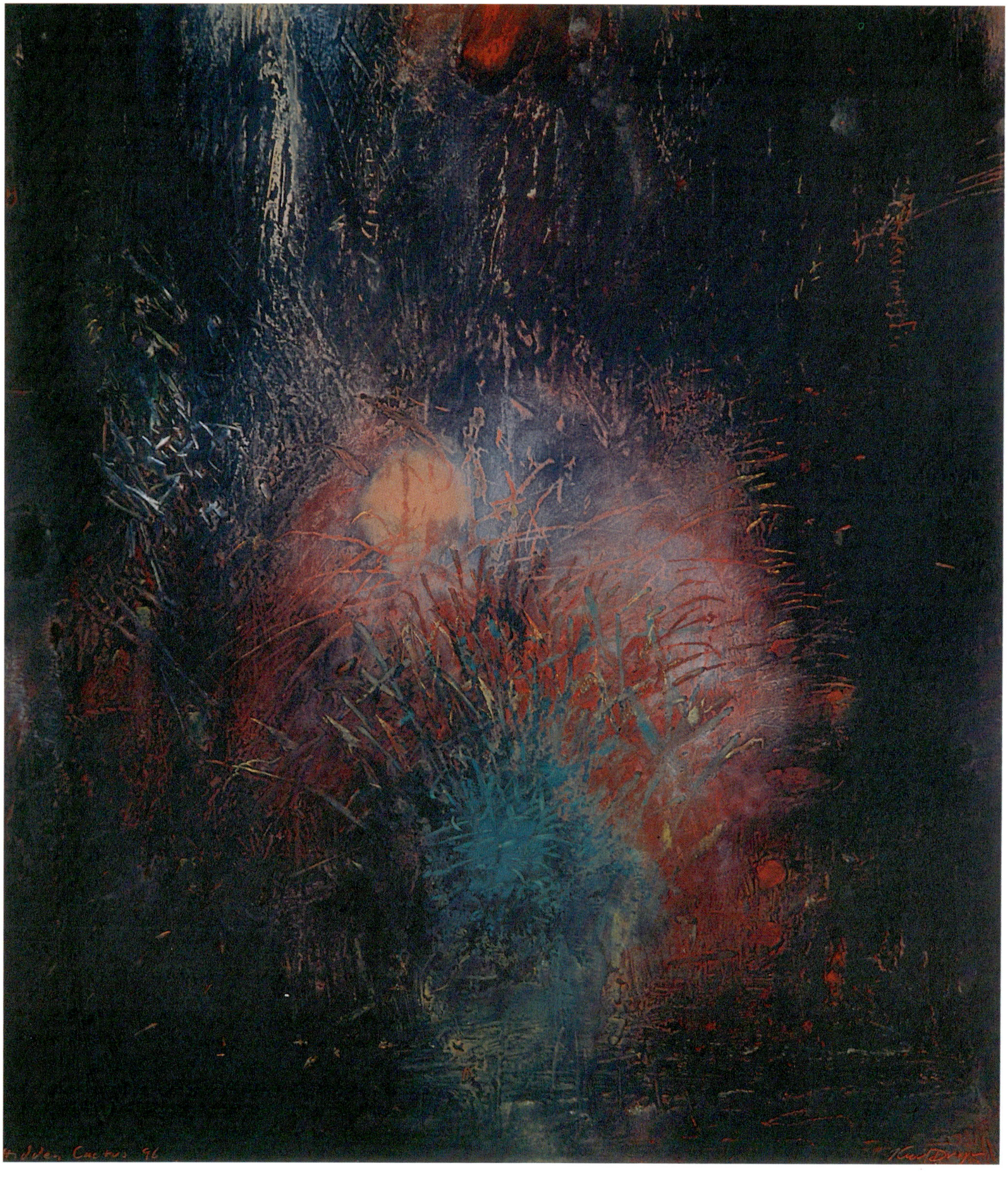

Plate 54

Hidden Cactus 1996

Pastel on Paper

20 × 18 inches (51 × 46 cm)

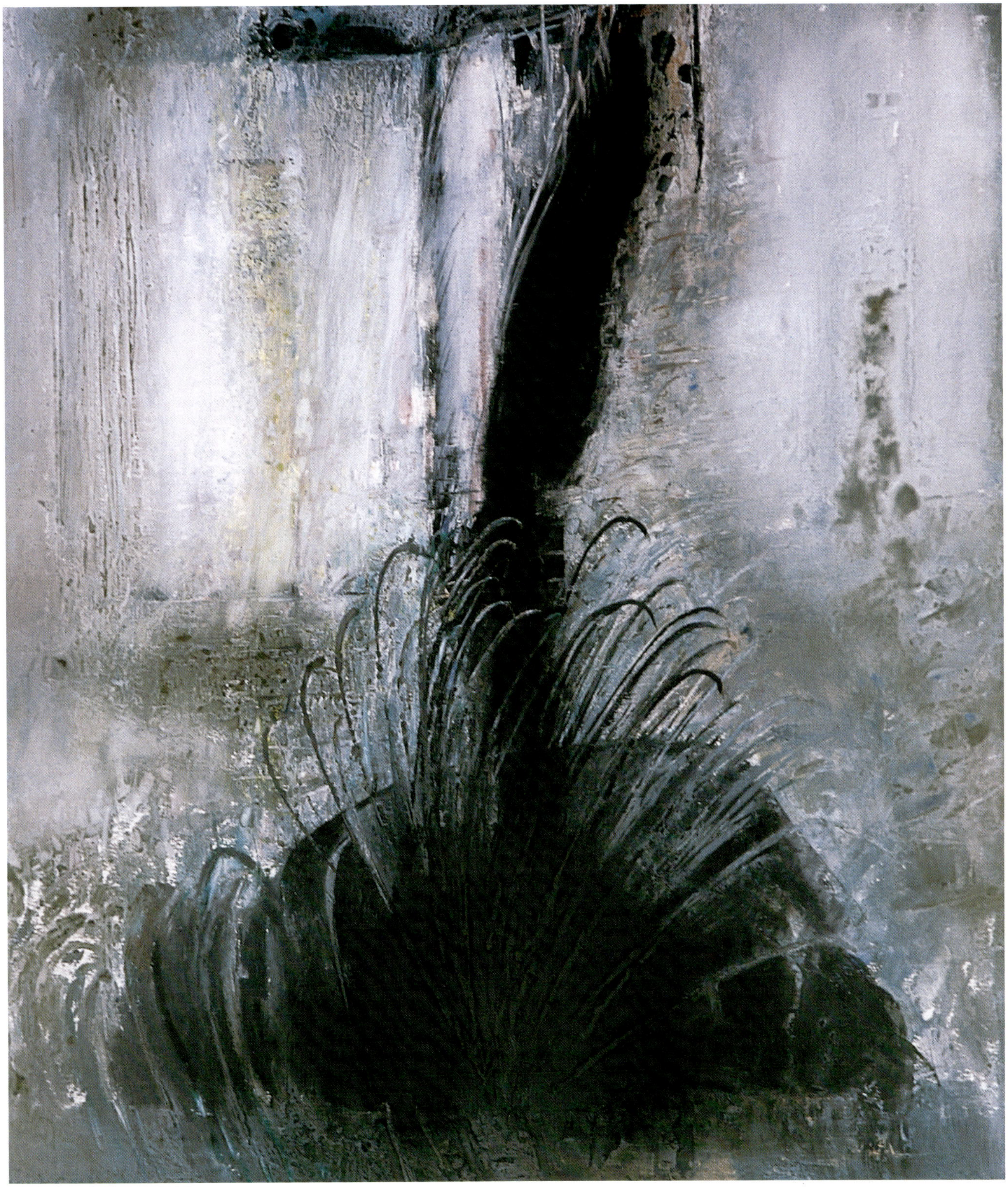

Plate 55

Secret Garden 1996
Pastel on Paper
20 × 18 inches (51 × 46 cm)

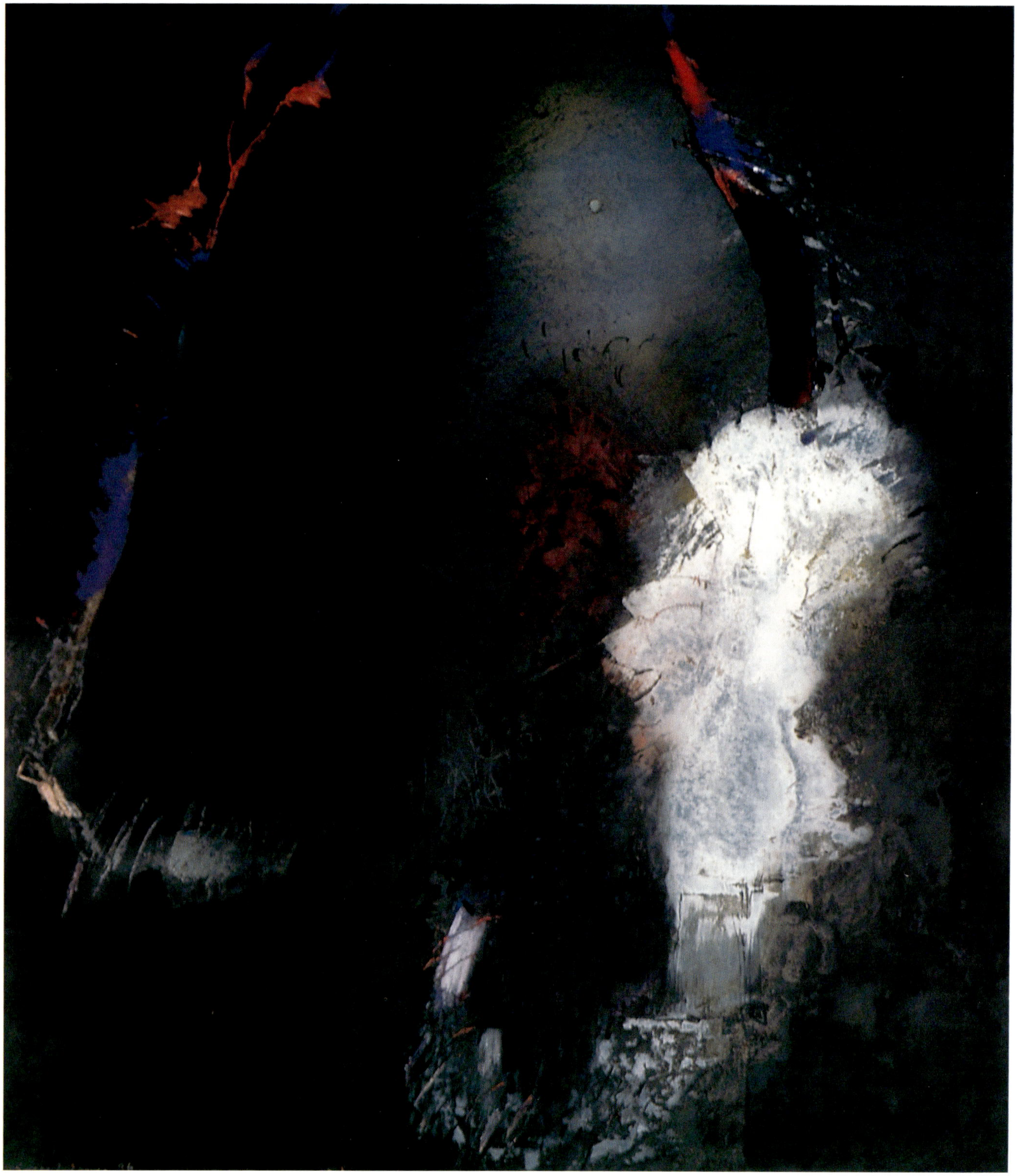

Plate 56

Sacred Stones 1996
Pastel on Paper
20 × 18 inches (51 × 46 cm)

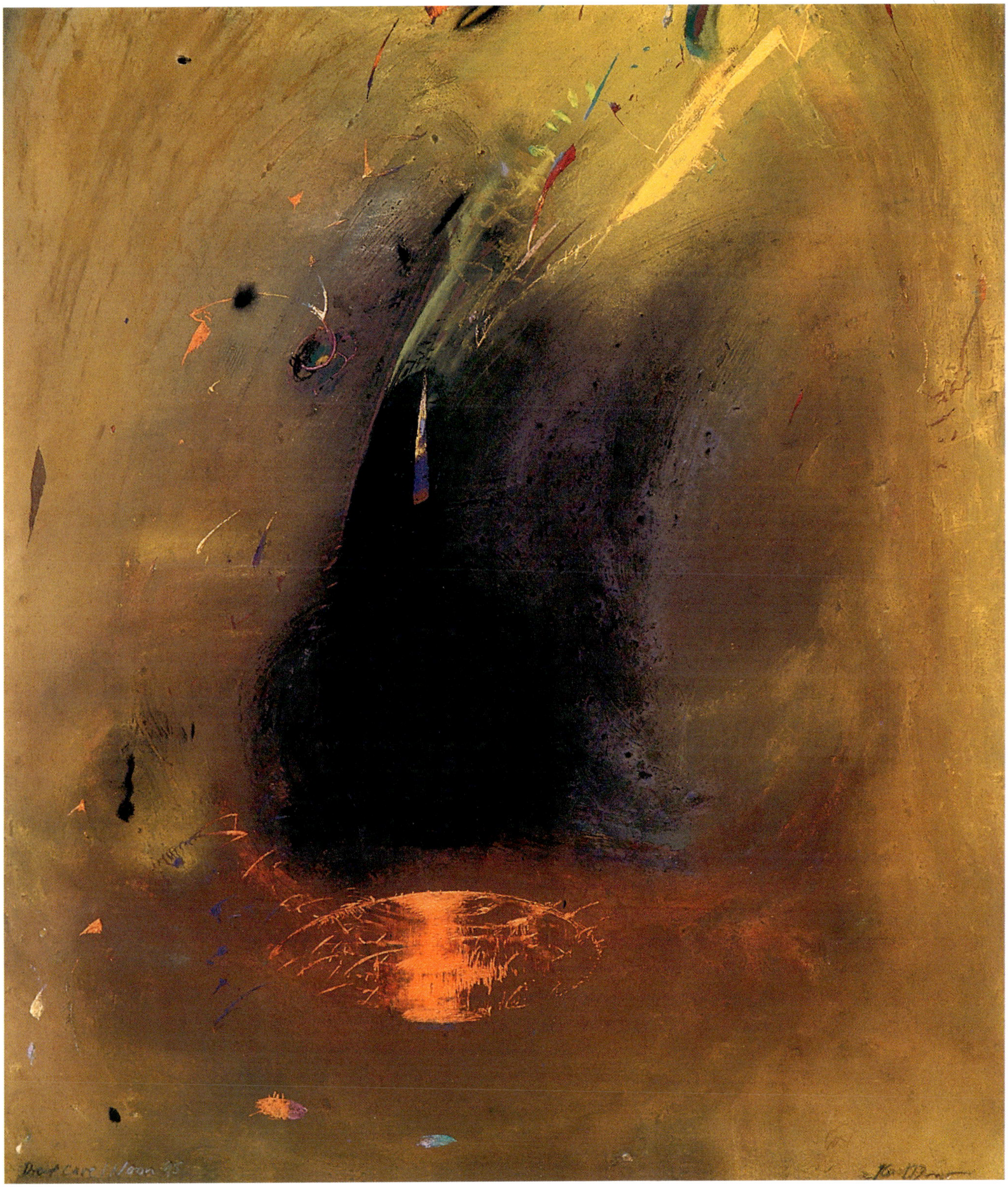

Plate 57

Deep Cave, Noon 1995
Pastel on Paper
20 × 18 inches (51 × 46 cm)

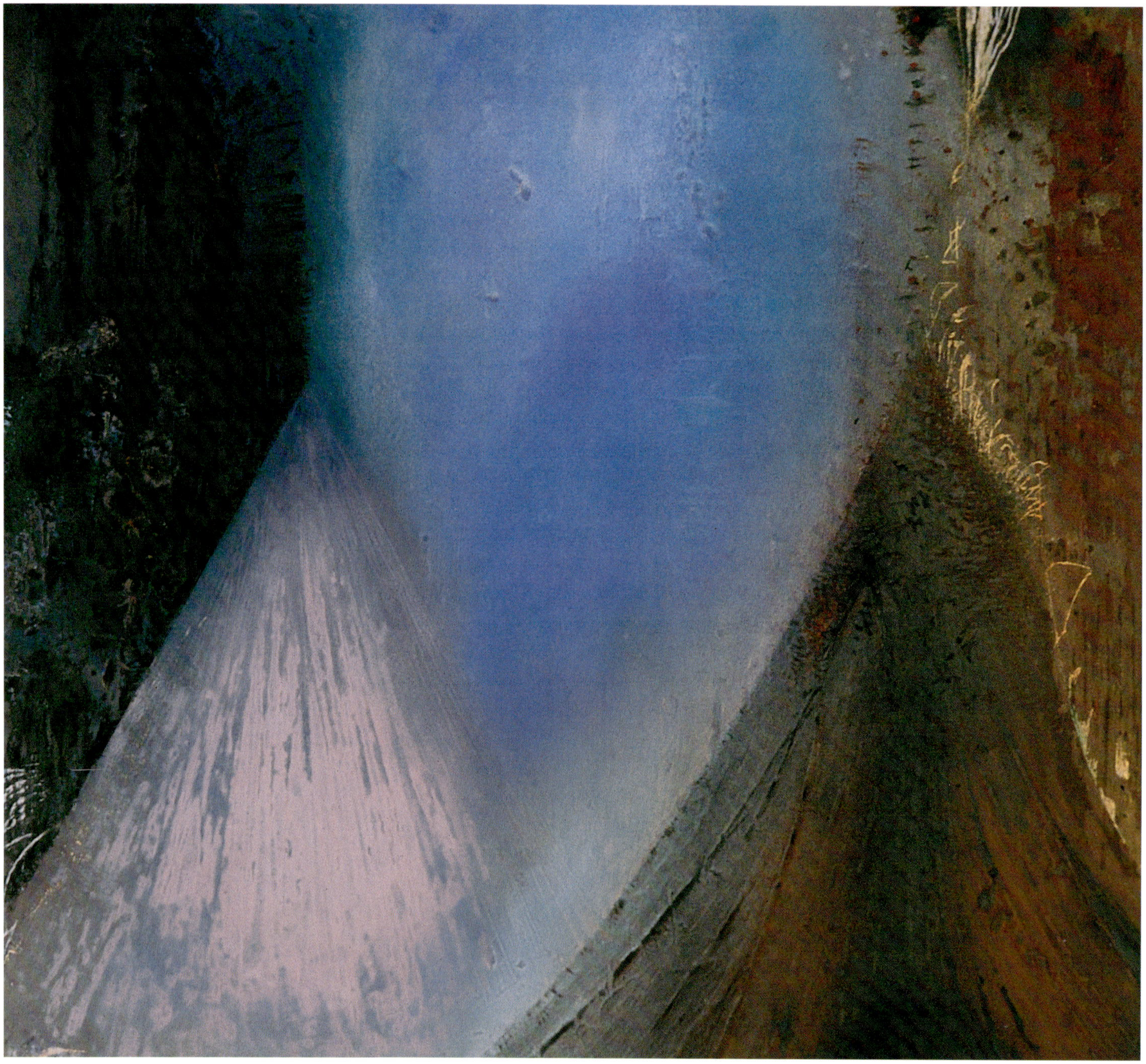

Plate 58

Aftermath 1996

Pastel on Paper

20 × 18 inches (51 × 46 cm)

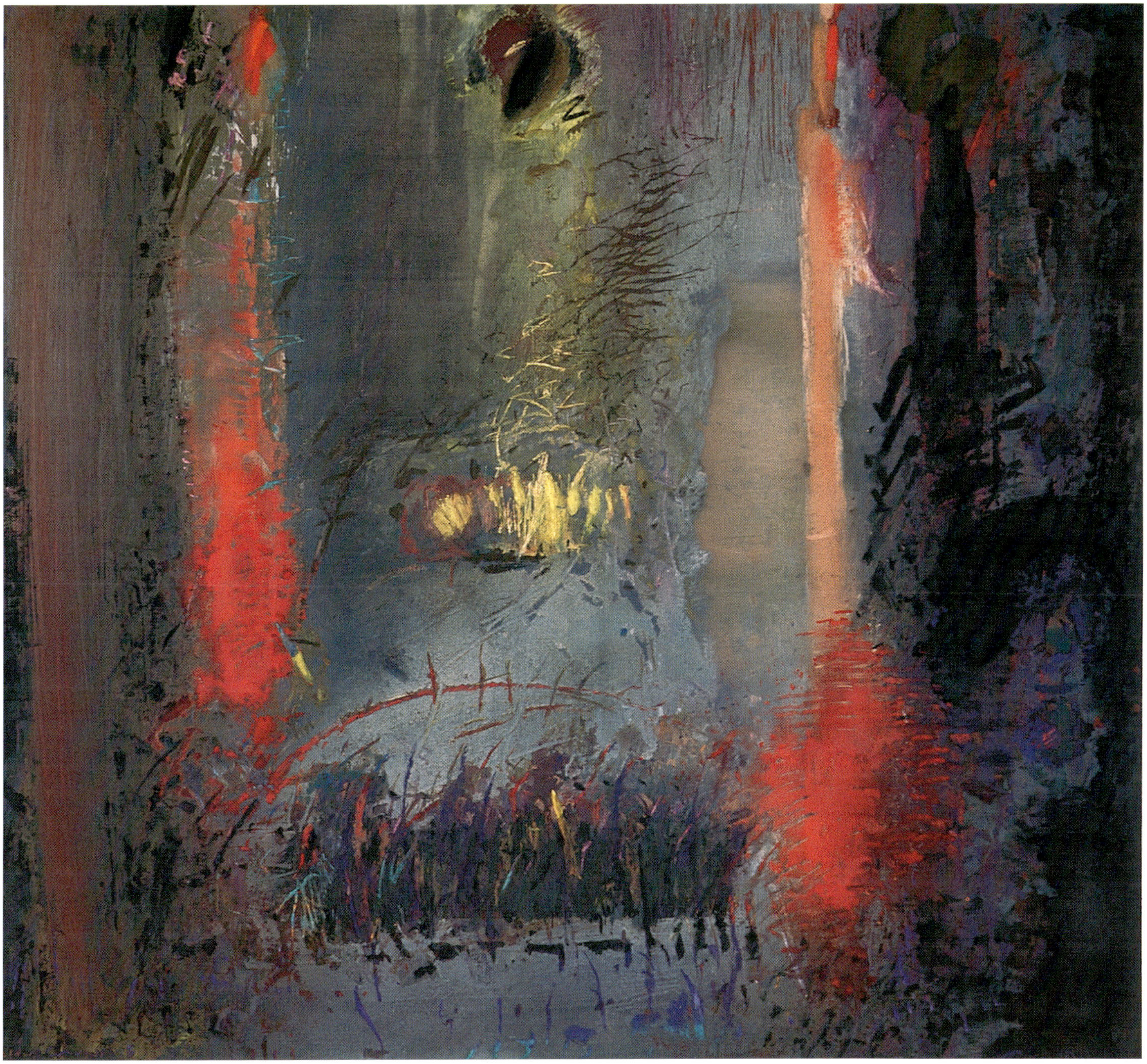

Plate 59

Below Ground 1996
Pastel on Paper
20 × 18 inches (51 × 46 cm)

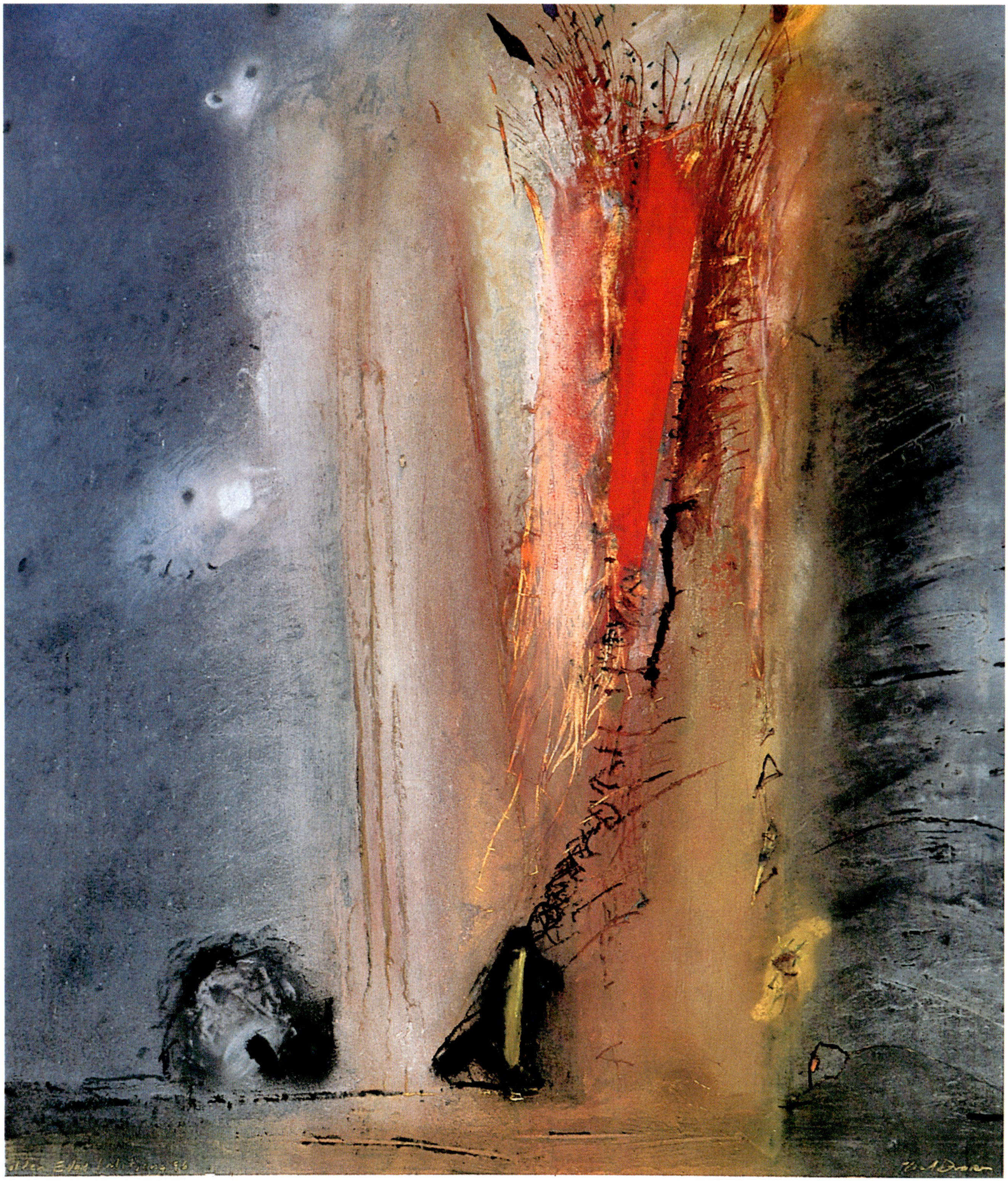

Plate 60

Golden Edge, Mitjana 1996

Pastel on Paper

20 × 18 cm (51 × 46 cm)

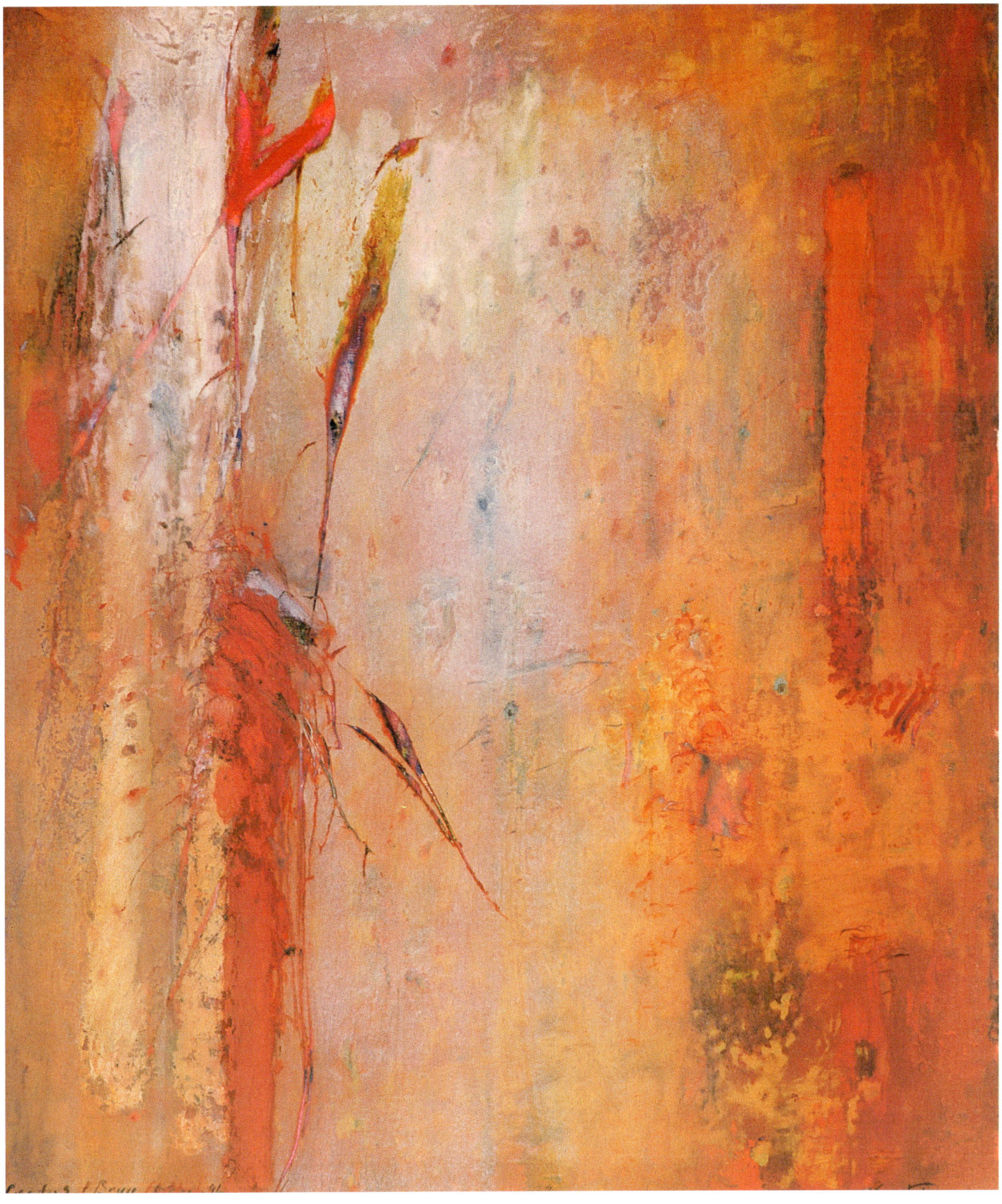

Plate 61

Cactus, Bryce, Utah 1996

Pastel on Paper

14 × 16 inches (36 × 41 cm)

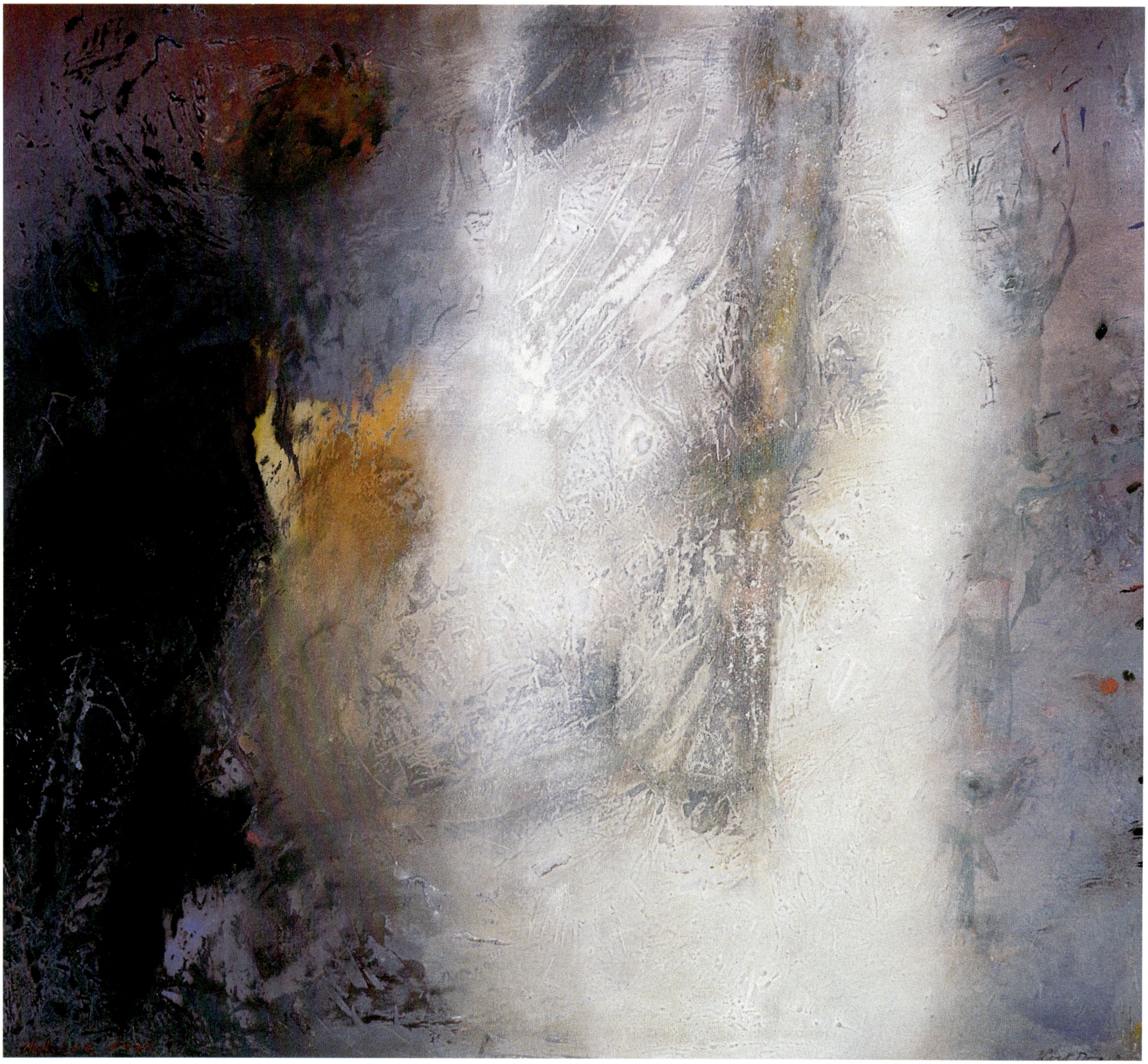

Plate 62

Mojave Dawn 1996
Pastel on Paper
18 × 20 inches (46 × 51 cm)

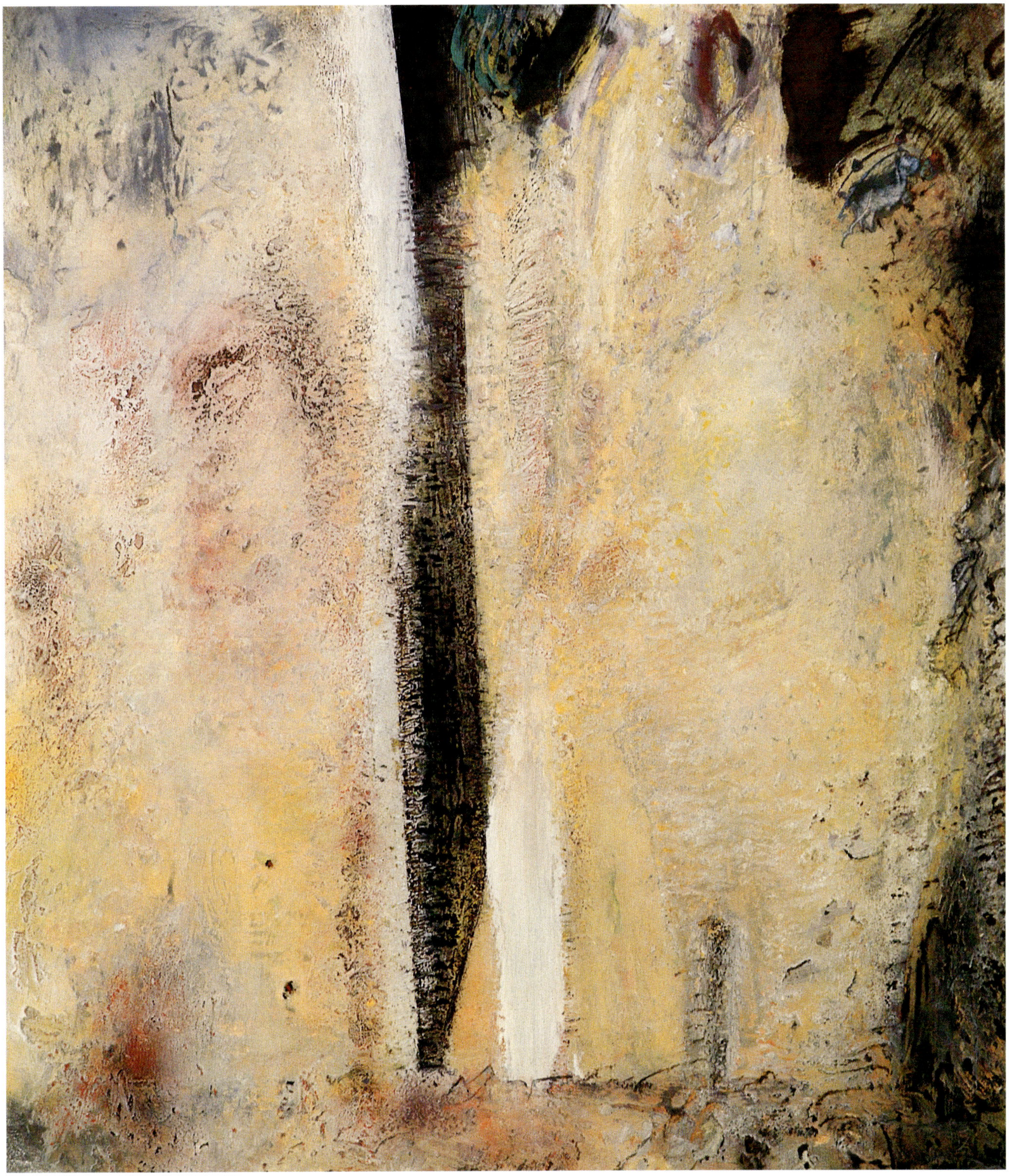

Plate 63

Weeping Moss Fall, Zion Canyon 1996
Pastel on Paper
20 × 18 inches (51 × 46 cm)

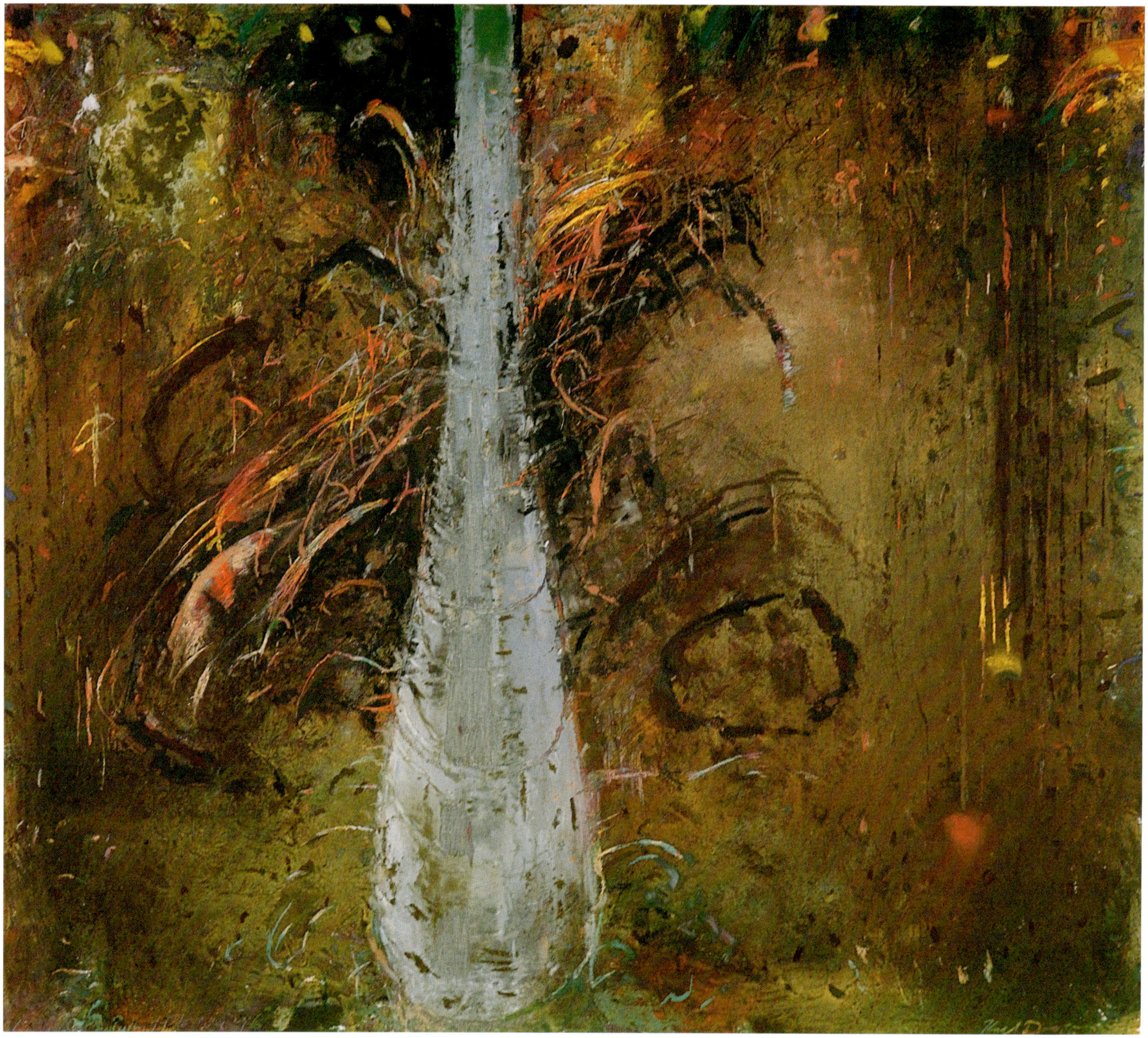

Plate 64

Palm, Florida 1996

Pastel on Paper

14 × 16 inches (36 × 41 cm)

Biographical Notes

1944 Born in Killamarsh, near Sheffield, Yorkshire.

1952 In hospital in Rivelin Valley, Sheffield with TB of the spine.

1956 Attended Killamarsh Secondary School. Encouraged to take art as a career by Jean Arblaster a recent graduate from Goldsmith's College.

1958 Attended Chesterfield Art School on Saturday mornings.

1959 Started full time at Chesterfield Art School.

1962 Attended Kingston School of Art in painting school but also worked in sculpture department. Met Bryan Kneale, Alfred Dunn, and Prunella Clough. John Carter is a fellow student.

1963 Met Heather Liévin Beste.

1964–5 Postgraduate year at Kingston concentrating on sculpture.

1964 Worked as an assistant to Bryan Kneale at his studio in Fulham Road. Met Henry Inlander, Elizabeth Frink, Hubert Dalwood and George Fullard. Also met Harry Miller of Redfern Gallery and started an association with the gallery that lasted until 1978.

1965 Young Contemporaries Prize for Sculpture. Married Heather Lievin Beste. Travelled in France, Switzerland, and Italy. Met Bryan Robertson at The Whitechapel Art Gallery.

1965–68 Attended sculpture department at The Royal College of Art under Professor Bernard Meadows. Tutors included Bryan Kneale, Ralph Brown, Robert Clatworthy, Peter Atkins, Jack Smith, and Hubert Dalwood. Contemporaries included Nigel Hall, John Panting, John Maine, Carl Plackman, Martin Naylor and Richard Wentworth. During this period made large painted constructions in wood relating to ambiguity and illusion. Drawings in pencil of impossible sculptural events and the first drawings in pastel.

1965 Exhibited Redfern Gallery Summer Exhibition, London.

Travelled to Europe for the first time.

1966 Son, Adam, born.

1968 Taught at Hornsey College of Art. Separated from wife and started living with Nadiya Jinnah. Studio in Borough Market, Southwark, London.

1969 First one man exhibition at The Redfern Gallery, London. Made the first large "Overhang" wall sculpture. Work purchased by The Arts Council and by Leicestershire Education Authority. Visited India and Pakistan and saw Ellora and Ajanta caves and the archaeological site of Moenjodaro.

1970 Travelled in Europe.

1971 Mark Rothko Memorial Award. Visited New York, Boston, Washington, Chicago, San Francisco and Los Angeles. Met Jasper Johns, Helen Frankenthaler, Lee Krasner-Pollock, Richard Diebenkorn, Larry Bell and Don Potts. Met the architect Phillip Johnson and visited his "Glass House" in Connecticut.

Exhibited in "British Sculptor's Drawings", a touring exhibition in South America and in "Eight Individuals" an Arts Council exhibition curated by Bryan Robertson.

1972 One of the youngest artists in "British Sculptors 1972" exhibition at The Royal Academy. Married Nadiya Jinnah. Visited East Africa twice.

1974 Large outdoor sculpture for the John Dalton Building, Manchester.

1975 Made a series of small box sculptures. Taught at Bristol School of Art where he met Paul Feiler, and at The Central School of Art, London.

1976 Albert Draper, father, died aged 79.

Started teaching at Goldsmiths College. Studio now at Kingsland Road, London EC2.

1977 Exhibited in The Silver Jubilee Exhibition of British Sculpture art Battersea Park, London. Taught at Camberwell School of art with Paul de Monchaux.

1978 Redfern Gallery exhibition included first large pastels on paper.

Elected to The Faculty of The British School in Rome. Started drawing almost exclusively in colour using pastel; mark making as opposed to line, with densities of coloured marks to create form and a more activated "space". Colour, both with the sculpture and the flat images, relating to energy and the emotive charge given to particular elements in a work.

Redfern Gallery exhibition of smaller scale work using metal and wood constructions with highly coloured and textured surfaces. Work even more related to landscape and objects existing within it.

Cut down teaching commitment and left London to live in Norfolk.

1979 Nadiya Jinnah, the artist's wife, accepted an invitation to stay with a cousin in New York. She has lived in New York ever since, she and the artist have remained close friends.

Taught at Goldsmiths College and Camberwell School of Art.

Began living with Jean Macalpine.

1980 Exhibited in the touring exhibitions, "The British Art Show" and "The Human Factor". Built a large sculpture for Bradford University. Spent time at The British School in Rome.

1981 Retrospective at The Warwick Arts Trust curated by Bryan Robertson. Included in "British Sculptors" in the Twentieth Century exhibition at The Whitechapel Gallery, London. Exhibited and travelled in Germany with Paul Feiler.

1983 Exhibited in "The Sculpture Show" at The Hayward Gallery, London. Three of the sculptures exhibited were very landscape based, highly coloured and projected from the wall above the spectator's head, reminiscent of the overhang series of the 1970s. First exhibition in Japan.

1984 Visited New York and stayed at Nadiya Jinnah's studio where he met John Albers, an artist making large coloured wall constructions. Adam Draper also spent time in New York before going to University to study law. It was the first time since Adam Draper was a child that father and son had spent a consistent amount of time together.

1985 Met Elizabeth Oustinoff in New York.

1986 Bought a small studio on the island of Menorca and has since spent several months each year working on paper in the Menorcan landscape.

1987 Took his 85 year old mother for her first journey abroad to Menorca. Exhibited in "The Hunter Collection of Twentieth Century British Masters" at The Courthould Institute, London.

1988 Working in North Yorkshire, Cumbria and The Lake District and made first visit to Dorset.

1989 Acquired a studio near the sea on Chesil Beach and rented a cottage in Fortuneswell, Dorset. Introduced by Paul Feiler to William Desmond of The Austin Desmond Gallery, London. Living in the country made possible by close association with The Austin Desmond Gallery and with the assistance of Adam Draper who organised everything in London for both Draper and Jean Macalpine. Continued to visit the North of England and Menorca.

During a working period in the North of England started to combine working methods he had developed with sculpture and produce paintings with resin, oil and pigment on wooden panels.

1991 Elected member of The Royal Academy of Arts, London. William Desmond died.

1992 Exhibited paintings in "The Poetic Trace: Aspects of British Abstraction" at Adelson Galleries, New York. Exhibited sculpture in "British Sculpture in the Twentieth Century" at Millfield Somerset. The inclusion of the artist in both these exhibitions underlines Draper's commitment to both media.

Dorothy, mother, died aged 89.

Visited Egypt.

1993 First exhibition with Hart Gallery.

After one man exhibition at Adelson Galleries in New York travelled in the South Western United States.

1994 Moved to Menorca. Draper and Macalpine drove through France with the Hart family to Provence. Visited the Verdon Gorge, the ochre quarries of Roussillon and Rustrel and the monastic site of Carluc abbey. Continued by train to Barcelona and then by ferry to Menorca. Established studio in farm building near San Clemente.

1995 Made two further visits to Provence, staying in Barcelona *en route*. Made first sculpture for four years; a low wall relief made of wood, steel and resins which evolved from feelings and perceptions of the night sea.

1996 Accompanied John Hart to Miami Art Fair.

Visited London for the wedding of Adam Draper to Grazia Giuliani. Travelled on from London with Macalpine to New York and thence to Phoenix for their second visit to the South West with Nadiya Jinnah and Robert Olsen. Visited Sedona, Grand Canyon, Bryce Canyon, Zion Canyon, Death Valley and across the Mojave Desert to Los Angeles.

Continues to live and work in Menorca.

K.D. & J.H.

Solo Exhibitions

1969	Redfern Gallery, London
1978	Redfern Gallery, London Cartwright Hall, Museum and Art Gallery, Bradford, Yorkshire
1981	Warwick Arts Trust, London E.G.K. Galleries, Stuttgart, Germany Alpirsbach Gallerie, Alpirsbach, Germany
1982	The Minories, Colchester Chapter Art Gallery, Cardiff, Wales
1984	Gallerie Nouvelles Images, Den Haag, Holland
1990	Hampstead Theatre Gallery, London
1991	Grape Lane Gallery, York Austin Desmond Gallery, London Glenn Green Gallery, Santa Fe, New Mexico, USA
1993	Adelson Gallery, New York, USA Friends Room, Royal Academy, London Hart Gallery, Nottingham
1994	Hart Gallery, London
1995	Bridport Arts Centre, Bridport, Dorset Hart Gallery, London Peter Bartlow Gallery, Chicago, USA Hart Gallery, Nottingham
1996	Hart Gallery, London

Group Exhibitions

1964 London Group, London

1965 Young Contemporaries
Summer Exhibition, Redfern Gallery, London

1968 Summer Exhibition, Redfern Gallery, London

1971 Seven Redfern Artists, Redfern Gallery, London
British Sculptors Drawings, Bonino Gallery, Buenos Aires (and touring South America)
Eight Individuals, Graves Gallery, Sheffield (and Arts Council tour)
Jacobs Ladder Inc., Washington DC, USA

1972 British Sculptors '72, Royal Academy, London
British Sculptors '72, Related Works, Redfern Gallery, London

1976 Arts Council, Recent Purchases, Hayward Gallery, London

1977 Tolly Cobbold Eastern Arts Exhibition, Fitzwilliam Museum Cambridge (and tour)
Royal Academy Summer Exhibition
Silver Jubilee Exhibition of Contemporary British Sculpture, Battersea Park, London
Yorkshire Sculptors, Yorkshire Sculpture Park, Bretton Hall, Yorkshire

1978 *Fragile Stones Make Art,* National Museum of Wales, Cardiff
Royal Academy Summer Exhibition, London
Works on Paper, Artist's Market, London

1979 Tolly Cobbold Eastern Arts Exhibition, Fitzwilliam Museum, Cambridge (and tour)
British Sculptor's Drawings. The Minories, Colchester
Contemporary Works on Paper, Gainsborough House, Sudbury

1980 *The Human Factor,* Arts Council Touring Exhibition
The British Art Show, Mappin Art Gallery, Sheffield (and tour)

1981 *British Sculpture in the Twentieth Century,* Whitechapel Art Gallery, London

1982 *Coloured Constructions,* Ikon Gallery, Birmingham

1983 The Sculpture Show, Hayward Gallery, London
Group Exhibition, Studio Odd, Hiroshima, Japan
Small is Beautiful, Angela Flowers Gallery, London

1984 *Questions About Sculpture,* Arts Council touring Exhibition
Group Exhibition, Friedus Ordover Gallery, New York, USA

1985 Contemporary Art Society Market, London

1986 *Hidden Landscape,* Juda Rowan Gallery, London
Contemporary Art Society Market, London

1987 Contemporary International Art Exposition, Chicago, USA
Art for the City, Lloyds of London
Contemporary Art Society Market, London
Royal Academy Summer Exhibition, London
Hunter Collection of Twentieth Century Modern Masters, Courtauld Gallery, London

1988 Contemporary International Art Exposition, Chicago USA
Group Exhibition, Louise Hallett Gallery, London
Warwick Arts Trust Collection, Warwick Arts Trust, London
Art in the Market Place, Bury St Edmunds, Suffolk
Contemporary Art Society Market, London
Landscape, Queen Elizabeth Hall, London

1989 Contemporary International Art Exposition, Chicago, USA
Contemporary Art Society Market, London
Artist in Residence, Chesil Gallery, Portland, Dorset

1990 International Gallery Invitational Art Fair, Chicago, USA
Contemporary International Art Exposition, Chicago USA
Art '90, Islington, London
ICAF, Olympia, London
Group Exhibition, Glenn Green Gallery, Santa Fe, New Mexico, USA
Royal Academy Summer Exhibition, London
Bath Art Fair, Bath
Group Exhibition, Louise Hallett Gallery, London
Contemporary Art Fair, Sydney, Australia
Contemporary Art Society Market, London

1991 Contemporary Art Fair, Miami, USA
Art '91, Islington, London
ICAF Olympia, London
Stonewall, ICA Galleries, London
Royal Academy Summer Exhibition, London

Contemporary Art Society Market, London
Wessex Artists, Parnham House, Dorset
Group Exhibition, On Line Gallery, Southampton

1992 *Aspects of British Abstraction, The Poetic Trace,* Adelson Galleries, New York, USA
British Sculpture in the Twentieth Century, Millfield, Somerset
Landscape, On Line Gallery, Southampton
Sense of Place, Cleveland Bridge Gallery, Bath
Art ' 92, Islington, London
Contemporary Art Society Market, London
Royal Academy Summer Show, London

1993 Hart Gallery, Nottingham
Royal Academy Summer Exhibition, London
Art '93, Islington, London
Chicago International Art Exposition, USA
Painting the Earth, John Jones Gallery, London
Contemporary Art Society Market, London
Small is Beautiful, Flowers East, London

1994 Hart Gallery, London
Art '94, London
Contemporary Art Society Market, London
Kenneth Draper, Jean Macalpine, John Hubbard, Bridport Arts Centre, Dorset
Royal Academy Summer Exhibition, London
Works on Paper, Adelson Galleries, New York, USA
Chesil Gallery, Portland, Dorset
Twentieth Century Art Fair, Royal College of Art, London
Space Redefined, Shad Thames Galleries, Butlers Wharf, London
Small is Beautiful, Flowers East, London
Landscape, New Academy Gallery, London

1995 Art '95, London
Royal Academy Summer Exhibition, London
Geneva Art Fair, Geneva, Switzerland
Manchester Fine Arts Fair, Manchester
Twentieth Century British Art Fair, Royal College of Art, London
Group Exhibition, Adelson Galleries, New York, USA

1996 Art Miami 96, USA
Art '96, London
Royal Academy Summer Exhibition
Twentieth Century British Art Fair, London

Public and Corporate Collections

Arts Council of Great Britain

Arts Council of Wales

Ashmolean Museum, Oxford

Arthur Anderson, London

Contemporary Art Society, London

Cartwright Hall Museum and Art Gallery, Bradford

Courtauld Institute, London

De Beer's Collection, London

Fitzwilliam Museum and Art Gallery, Cambridge

Harris Museum and Art Gallery, Preston, Lancashire

ICI, London

International Bank of Japan, London

Leicestershire Education Authority

Lloyd's of London

Mappin Art Gallery, Sheffield

Mischon de Reya, London

McCrory Corporation, New York, USA

National Museum of Wales, Cardiff

National Westminster Bank

Pearl Insurance, London

Unilever Plc, London

Royal Life Group

TSB Bank, London

Usher Gallery, Lincoln

Selected Bibliography

Barton, Walter, exhibition review, Gallerie Nouvelles Image, Holland, Het Financieele Dagblad, 9 April 1984

Crichton, Fenella, *"British Sculpture in the Twentieth Century"*, catalogue, Whitechapel Art Gallery, London, 1981

Diamond, Michael, *"Yorkshire Sculptors"*, catalogue, Yorkshire Sculpture Park, 1977

Drysdale, Helen, *"The Sculpture Show"*, Artscribe, August 1983

Ellis, Nancy, *"Fleeting Moments"*, Focus on Santa Fe, April 1991

Gill, John, *"Landscape"*, catalogue, Queen Elizabeth Hall, South Bank Exhibition, 1988

Gooding, Mel, *"The Poetic Trace"*, catalogue essay, Adelson Galleries, New York, March 1992

Hart, John, *"An Abstract Artist Working in the Landscape"*, catalogue essay, Peter Bartlow Gallery, Chicago, May 1995

Hitchmough, Wendy, *"Questions about Sculpture"*, Arts Council, May 1984

Januscek, Waldemar, "Review of The British Art Show", *The Guardian,* January 1981

Lambirth, Andrew, *"The Essential Ingredient", Royal Academy Magazine,* November 1991

McEwen, John, Reivew of Redfern Gallery exhibition, *The Spectator,* 11 March 1978

Martin, Barry and Robertson, Bryan and Packer, William, catalogue of Silver Jubilee Exhibition of Contemporary British Sculpture, July 1977

Middleton, Christopher, review of Contemporary Art Society Market, *Evening Standard,* November 1993

Moss, Colin, exhibition review, The Minories Art Gallery, Colchester, *Ipswich Evening Star,* 4 March 1982

Oustinoff, Elizabeth, *"British Abstract Painting"*, The Wall Street Transcript, New York, 22 January 1996

Packer, William, catalogue, The British Art Show, 1980

Petherbridge, Deanna, *"Coloured Constructions"*, review of Ikon Gallery, Birmingham, exhibition

Phillips, Tony, *"Artist in Search of the Essence of Place", Yorkshire Post,* March 1991

Rippon, Peter, catalogue essay, Cartwright Hall Museum and Art Gallery, Bradford, 1978

Robertson, Bryan, *"Kenneth Draper; Sculpture and Drawings 1962–81"*, catalogue, Warwick Arts Trust, April 1981

Robertson, Bryan, *"British Sculptors"*, exhibition catalogue, Royal Academy, London, January 1972

Robertson, Bryan, *"Eight Individuals"*, exhibition catalogue, Graves Art Gallery, Sheffield, August 1971

Roth, Colin, *"Reading the Landscape", Sheffield Telegraph,* 6 August 1993

Roth, Colin, *"Transient Landscape"*, exhibition catalogue, Royal Academy, London, June 1993

Spalding, Frances, *"Kenneth Draper"*, Contemporary Art, Spring 1993

Spurling, John, review of Warwick Arts Trust exhibition, 1 May 1981

Taylor, Russell, review of Warwick Arts Trust, *The Times,* 28 April 1981

Vaizey, Marina, *"Fragile Stones Make Art", Sunday Times,* 15 August 1975

Wadley, Nicholas, *"The Sculpture Show"*, catalogue, Hayward Gallery, London, August 1983